An Introduction Architectural Th

CW00546329

1968 to the Present

Harry Francis Mallgrave
and David Goodman

WILEY-BLACKWELL

A John Wiley & Sons, Ltd., Publication

This edition first published 2011
© 2011 Harry Francis Mallgrave and David Goodman

Wiley-Blackwell is an imprint of John Wiley & Sons, formed by the merger of Wiley's
global Scientific, Technical and Medical business with Blackwell Publishing

Registered Office
John Wiley & Sons Ltd, The Atrium, Southern Gate, Chichester, West Sussex, PO19 8SQ,
United Kingdom

Editorial Offices
350 Main Street, Malden, MA 02148-5020, USA
9600 Garsington Road, Oxford, OX4 2DQ, UK
The Atrium, Southern Gate, Chichester, West Sussex, PO19 8SQ, UK

For details of our global editorial offices, for customer services, and for information about how to
apply for permission to reuse the copyright material in this book please see our website at www.
wiley.com/wiley-blackwell

The right of Harry Francis Mallgrave and David Goodman to be identified as the authors
of this work been asserted in accordance with the UK Copyright, Designs and Patents Act 1988

Library of Congress Cataloging-in-Publication Data
Mallgrave, Harry Francis, 1947–
An Introduction to Architectural Theory : 1968 to the Present / Harry Francis Mallgrave and
David Goodman.
   p. cm
Summary: "A sharp and lively text that covers issues in depth but not to the point that they
become inaccessible to beginning students, An Introduction to Architectural Theory is the first
narrative history of this period, charting the veritable revolution in architectural thinking that has
taken place, as well as the implications of this intellectual upheaval. The first comprehensive and
critical history of architectural theory over the last forty years surveys the intellectual history of
architecture since 1968, including criticisms of high modernism, the rise of postmodern and
poststructural theory, critical regionalism and tectonics. Offers a comprehensive overview of the
significant changes that architectural thinking has undergone in the past fifteen years. Includes an
analysis of where architecture stands and where it will likely move in the coming years."– Provided
by publisher.
   Includes bibliographical references and index.
   ISBN 978-1-4051-8063-4 (hardback) – ISBN 978-1-4051-8062-7 (paperback)
   1. Architecture–Philosophy.   2. Architecture–Historiography.   I. Goodman, David,
1974– II. Title.
   NA2500.M277 2012
   720.1–dc22
                                          2010043539

A catalogue record for this book is available from the British Library

This book is published in the following electronic formats: ePDFs 9781444395976;
ePub 9781444395983

Set in 10/12.5pt Galliard by SPi Publisher Services, Pondicherry, India
Printed in Malaysia by Ho Printing (M) Sdn Bhd

01 2011

Contents

Illustrations

Prelude
The 1960s

From the close of World War II until sometime in the middle of the 1960s two grand ideals ruled the architectural profession. One was a political faith in the vision of modernity – the meliorist belief that by affecting social change and imposing a universal environmental order architects could improve the human lot and repair a globe wrought by physical and moral devastation. The second was the belief that the most efficient way to achieve this amelioration was through technology and its application. Stating these ideals in less prosaic terms, one might say that the techno-logical vision of a unified modernity had for two decades enchanted the mistress of architecture. Little did she suspect how swiftly his lure of excite-ment would pale.

In retrospect, we can of course find several signs of the impending separa-tion along the way. As far back as 1947, Lewis Mumford raised the possibil-ity of a regional modernism, only to be rudely censored by the self-anointed potentates of the Museum of Modern Art.[1] In the same year, Aldo van Eyck, at a Congrès International d'Architecture Moderne (CIAM) in Bridgewater, challenged the overly rationalist underpinnings of modern design, yet he found few backers.[2] In 1953, at another CIAM conference in Aix-en-Provence, teams of architects based in Algeria and Morocco pre-sented housing schemes far removed from approved CIAM models, while another team from London dared to challenge a few of the urban premises of the Athens Charter.[3] And in 1959, Ernesto Rogers, the influential editor of the journal *Casabella-continuità*, loaded a double-barreled salvo against the status quo. In one chamber was the shell of an "Italian Retreat" from modernism, based on the recent fascination of a few architects with the "Neoliberty" forms at the start of the twentieth century. In the second

An Introduction to Architectural Theory: 1968 to the Present, First Edition.
Harry Francis Mallgrave and David Goodman.
© 2011 Harry Francis Mallgrave and David Goodman. Published 2011 by Blackwell Publishing Ltd.

Figure P.1   BBPR, Torre Velasca, Milan (1950–1958). Image courtesy of Davide Secci.

chamber was the lethal pellet of historicism – that is, the desire to have a more tolerant modernism that would, on occasions, courteously entertain historical references. Oddly, the firing pin that had propelled the cartridge was Rogers's own design (his firm BBPR's) for the Torre Velasca (1950–1958), a modern concrete tower in downtown Milan whose cantilevered upper stories had for some critics evoked the "atmosphere" of Italian medieval towns. This time the response from official quarters was swift, as Rogers, at the CIAM'59 conference in Otterlo, was pounced upon by several critics who objected to his historical allusionism. And a few weeks earlier a glaring Reyner Banham had countered *Casabella*'s "Neoliberty" infatuation with an admonishing if not upbraiding metaphor:

> To want to put on those old clothes is to be, in Marinetti's words describing Ruskin, like a man who has attained full physical maturity, yet wants to sleep in his cot again, to be suckled again by his decrepit nurse, in order to regain the nonchalance of his childhood. Even by the purely local standards of Milan and Turin, then, Neoliberty is infantile regression.[4]

Technology and Ecology

By the close of the 1950s, Banham had, in fact, become a battalion commander within the technology forces, which in the next decade would enjoy their greatest triumphs. A man of literary brilliance, prolificacy, and acumen, he had spent the last half of the 1950s writing a dissertation on Italian Futurism under the tutelage of the eminent German refugee and historian Nikolaus Pevsner. He did so while participating in the animated discussions of London's New Brutalist movement and hobnobbing in particular with the iconoclastic wing of the Independent Group. The latter was an arts forum within London's Institute of Contemporary Arts, and its participants included Richard Hamilton, Lawrence Alloway, and John McHale. They were united in their hippish enthusiasms for American jazz, pop culture, Hollywood films, science fiction, and Detroit automobiles: testifying to the rising anima of a beat generation on the verge of reaching out for something bigger.

Banham's published version of his dissertation, *Theory and Design in the First Machine Age* (1960), was a milestone in architectural theory – less for its scholarship and more for its introductory and concluding chapters on "Functionalism and Technology." Banham's principal point was that the "First Machine Age," which had been inspired by such things as automobiles and ocean liners, had now been superseded (but not reversed) by a much more transfixing "Second Machine Age." Defining this descending era were the newfangled gizmos of televisions, radios, electric shavers, hair dryers, tape recorders, mixers, grinders, washing machines, refrigerators, vacuum cleaners, and polishers – those items that were empowering the "housewife" of today with more horsepower than an industrial worker commanded at the start of the century. If the automobile in the 1920s was simply a status symbol for cultural elites, the television ("the symbolic machine of the Second Machine Age") made democratic that crucial communicational objective of "dispensing mass entertainment."[5] All the new Machine Age lacked was a proper theory.

Through a series of lectures and writings over the next few years, Banham set out to repair this deficiency, and for him what was needed, from an increasingly radicalized perspective, was a more thoroughgoing embrace of technology and its conceptualization. Such a strategy was nevertheless fraught with dangers, at least for the increasingly complacent architectural profession:

> The architect who proposes to run with technology knows now that he will be in fast company, and that, in order to keep up, he may have to emulate the Futurists and discard his whole cultural load, including the professional

garments by which he is recognized as an architect. If, on the other hand, he decides not to do this, he may find that a technological culture has decided to go on without him.[6]

Banham's decision two years later, on the pages of London's leading architectural journal, *Architectural Review*, to put architecture "On Trial" for its vacillation must also be considered within the context of the contemporary faith in megastructural solutions for any and all urban problems.[7] Britain was already building several monolithic cities, but the younger generation had more grandiose aspirations. In the late 1950s the Hungarian-Israeli architect Yona Friedman, in founding the Groupe d'Etudes d'Architecture (GEAM), had broached the idea of "spatial city" by proposing a global effort to build 1000 new cities of three million inhabitants each. Friedman was working with a circle of artists and thinkers – among them Eckhard Schulze-Fielitz, Paul Maymont, Constant (Nieuwenhuys), and Frei Otto – and he proffered his "mobile architecture" as a response to the "perpetual transformation" of a restless society. Residents would now have the freedom to plug their "dwelling cells" anywhere into a multistory space-frame lifted above the abandoned landscape. Even food production would be cultivated in elevated urban greenhouses.[8]

In the same years, the Japanese Metabolists were producing their own technological extravaganzas in response to the population issues of urban crowding.[9] London, meanwhile, was being entertained by the comic-book fantasies of Archigram, another group of futurists smitten with the technological bug. Perhaps the decisive year for their efforts was 1964, when Peter Cook's "Plug-In City" and Ron Herron's "Walking City" made their spectacular debuts.[10]

The intellectual guru behind this grandiose euphoria was R. Buckminster Fuller, or "Bucky" was he was generally known to his worldwide admirers. Since the late 1940s Fuller had been stalking the lecture halls of architectural schools across all continents with his moral gospel of nonlinear thinking and "ephemeralization," by which a building should be judged not by the usual aesthetic beliefs but rather by its weight or degree of ecological integrity. If the American Institute of Architects had been willing to overlook the eccentricities of his "Dymaxion" house (the century's first definitive essay on sustainable thinking) as far back as 1928, by the early 1960s Fuller could no longer be ignored. His mailbox was packed with offers for visiting professorships and speaking engagements, and laurels were only just beginning to descend. Such publicity, of course, would culminate with the geodesic dome he built for Expo '67 in Montreal, but those who focus on this aspect of his thought overlook his more important contributions to theory.

As early as 1955 Fuller had been in contact with London's Independent Group and the artist John McHale, to whom (in a letter) he had criticized the "International Style" modernists for their superficial concern with the aesthetics of the bathroom rather than with the technology of the plumbing behind the walls. Banham was so moved by the criticism that he published a portion of the letter in the concluding chapter of *Theory and Design in the First Machine Age*.[11] McHale was also duly impressed, so much so that in 1962 he gave up his artistic practice to move to the United States and collaborate with Fuller. In that year he published the first architectural monograph on Fuller's work, and in the following year he worked with his mentor in compiling the first volume of the *Inventory of World Resources: Human Trends and Needs*.[12] By the end of the decade McHale himself would be recognized as a leading futurist.

Fuller, however, was already branching out in other directions. In 1963 he consulted with the Advanced Structures Research Team at NASA, which was planning the first manned flights to the moon. In his usual way, Fuller turned the problem on its head by referring the issue of an interspatial ecosystem back to Earth, where "space technology's autonomous living package and the automobile industry's engagement in livingry devices clearly indicate that the coming decade will see the mass production of autonomous living mechanics for use on earth."[13] In simpler terms, the Earth, too, was a spaceship, and the lessons of this research must be redirected to the world's housing problems because the "old building arts" (read "architecture") had essentially failed to keep up with advancing technologies and were, in any case, accommodating the housing needs of only a small portion of the world's population.

Such a theme was also echoed in 1963 in the "Delos Declaration," a pledge signed by Fuller and 33 other intellectuals on the sacred island of Delos – the mythical and legally uninhabitable birthplace of Apollo – after an eight-day cruise of the Greek islands. The cruise, patterned on the trip from Marseilles to Athens that had produced the Athens Charter, had been the brainchild of the architect and urban planner Constantinos Doxiadis, who gathered experts in various fields in an attempt to come up with a science (ekistics) to solve the problem of random global growth.[14]

Thus the idea of "world planning" becomes the keynote theme of Fuller's efforts in the second half of the 1960s, just as the notion that we command an interspatial planet with limited resources began to capture the public's attention.[15] Kenneth Boulding made this point cogently in a short paper that he prepared for the Committee on Space Sciences in 1965. Entitled "Earth as a Space Ship," he lambasted the fledgling ecological movement ("Ecology as a science has hardly moved beyond the level of bird-watching") for failing to see the implications of unrestrained population growth and pollution on the ecosystem.[16] What the world needed was to shift from fossil fuels to energies harnessed from the oceans and the sun, as well as to study the Earth's system of checks and balances. As he concluded: "We do not understand, for instance, the machinery of ice ages, the real nature of geological stability or disturbance, the incidence of volcanism and earthquakes, and we understand fantastically little about that enormously complex heat engine known as the atmosphere."[17]

Fuller responded in 1965 by launching the World Design Science Decade, a project that he originally intended to become the centerpiece of Expo '67. Better known as "World Game," the object was to hook up computers (another technological innovation) with college students from around the world in order to catalogue global resources and devise the most efficient ways of employing them. The project, originally centered at Southern Illinois University, came into fruition in the summer of 1969, and shortly thereafter hundreds of students were participating on campuses internationally, many in makeshift geodesic domes. In the same year, Ian McHarg published his classic work, *Design with Nature*. Fuller also contributed a bevy of books directed to environmental themes: *Utopia or Oblivion* (1969), *Operating Manual for Spaceship Earth* (1969), *I Seem to be a Verb* (1970), *Approaching the Benign Environment* (1970), *Intuition* (1972), and *Earth, Inc.* (1973). This torrent of writings culminated in the second half of the 1970s with the appearance of his two volumes on *Synergetics*, which brought into full view the prodigious scope of his accomplishments as a geometer. Architectural students in the 1960s had a particular fondness for Fuller's Daedalian ideas, especially because Bucky was, in turn, lauding the architect as the last of the comprehensive thinkers, indeed as humanity's last great hope.

Social Underpinnings of Modernism

If we turn to the sociological component of this technological fervor, we find a recurring caveat to this reformative vision – modernism's general lack of popularity with the public. None of this was particularly new, however. The stark forms of early modernists were not especially well received in Germany during the 1920s, and even less so in Britain in the following decade, when they arrived in the portfolios of German architects seeking asylum. The English critic J. M. Richards recognized this fact in 1940 when he opened his book *An Introduction to Modern Architecture* by acknowledging the public's dislike of the new style. He believed, however, that the public would come around when they became aware of modernism's aesthetic and constructional underpinnings.[18] Nevertheless, the problem persisted, so much so that in 1947 Richards once again brought the matter to the attention of CIAM, which, after some polite discussion, tabled the issue.

The situation was similar in North America, even though the corporate world in particular was quick to embrace the economic advantages of the new steel-and-glass technologies – tall buildings with curtain walls. In the United States opposition to the largely European face of international modernism actually had two roots. One was the alternative modernism that had been evolving in North America since the 1890s, first with the schools of Louis Sullivan and Frank Lloyd Wright and second with the various regional interpretations of modernism in the South and along the West Coast. Another source of discontent can be found in the "modern" urban design strategies of the postwar years. Few today remember that many of the urban renewal beliefs that are generally attributed to Lyndon Johnson's "Great Society" programs of the 1960s were first implemented during the Kennedy and Eisenhower administrations. And it was the bulldozing of the urban fabrics of so many American cities during these years – together with the social barriers of freeways often imposed by political machines – that contributed to the rapid urban decline of the 1960s. The high-rise "projects" that architects so glibly accepted would, within a decade, become the failed urban ghettos displaying all of the attendant problems of racial segregation, poverty, welfare, and crime.

In fact it was only in the 1960s that architects and critics began to recognize the serious limitations of such strategies or question the rationale of their existence. Jane Jacobs' *The Death and Life of Great American Cities* (1961), with its devastating attack on the "Radiant Garden City Beautiful," led the way and ushered in what might be called an appellate review of urban theory. She was, in fact, preceded in this regard on occasions by Lewis Mumford, but also by Kevin Lynch's *The Image of the City* (1960), which – through his cognitive analysis of a city's "Imageability" – challenged modernism's visual leveling of the urban environment. Herbert Gans, in the *Urban Villagers* (1962), vividly described the vibrant social life of one of Boston's Italian-immigrant communities – on the eve of its eradication by "urban renewal" efforts. Martin Anderson's *The Federal Bulldozer* (1964), with its sobering statistical analysis, coolly took apart the social and economic fallacies of such policies. And by the mid-1960s, social scientists such as Edward T. Hall, Robert Sommer, and Oscar Newman were exposing the social and physical failings of declining urban centers from anthropological, psychological, and architectural perspectives. Few of these studies, however, had any effect on the political decisions-makers in Washington, or elsewhere for that matter.

An interesting early study in this regard was the small book *Community and Privacy* (1963), coauthored by Serge Chermayeff and Christopher Alexander. The Russian-born Chermayeff had arrived at Harvard University by way of Britain and Chicago's Institute of Design, and his principal focus was on the sociology of housing. The book's stated intention was to lay the foundation for "the development of a Science of Environmental Design," an architectural discipline that would draw upon and integrate analytical research from other sciences.[19] It is also one of the first ecological studies of the postwar years, as the authors place much emphasis on countering the urban flight to the suburbs and addressing the stress of modern life. Yet it suffered from one fatal flaw – the blank-slate belief that human "taste" was generally malleable, and that all it would take to alter human behavior was a little governmental persuasion.

Nevertheless, part two of the book became the springboard for the evolving work of Christopher Alexander. The Austrian had immigrated to England with his family during the war years and eventually studied mathematics and architecture at Cambridge University. In the late 1950s he began doctoral studies at Harvard, and in *Community and Privacy* he supplemented the work of Chermayeff by setting out 33 design variables for prototypical urban housing, which he organized (with the aid of IBM's 704 computers) into sequences of groupings. This parametric design strategy, made necessary he felt by the "insoluble levels of complexity today," was also the basis for his doctoral dissertation, "The Synthesis of Form; Some Notes on a Theory," which he completed 1962.[20] It appeared in print two years later under the title *Notes on the Synthesis of Form*.

This book, with its analytic and synthetic model for designers, represents another face of the 1960s: the desire to find a sophisticated design methodology to accommodate the many social variables that should be taken into account. His approach was to locate possible design parameters, synthesize them into subsets and tree diagrams, and work through all potential "misfits," or unsatisfactory interactions between form and content. He also distinguished between "self-conscious" and "unselfconscious" design, by which he challenged what Western architects believed to be good design (for Alexander the perfect correspondence between form and content) with examples from indigenous or third-world cultures. Here, he argued, existing building traditions and local materials tended to filter out cultural biases. The book and the dissertation conclude with an appendix containing 141 design parameters for the design of an "Indian Village."

Alexander's inductive model, as he himself later noted, had one problem, which was that the programmatic phase of his design process was largely subjective. But there was also another issue. At the Team 10 meeting in 1962 Alexander had presented his work on the Indian village and engaged in a heated discussion with Aldo van Eyck, who likewise was interested in an architecture grounded in humanist ideals.[21] The incident led Alexander to reflect on his own tree-like diagrams, and in an essay of 1965, "A City is Not a Tree," he amended his earlier mode of diagramming in favor of a semi-lattice structure, whereby branches can overlay with one another in multiple ways.[22] Examples of tree-like thinking, for Alexander, were many of the new cities that had been started or built in recent years – Columbia and Greenbelt in Maryland, British new towns, Chandigarh, and Brasília. All had failed, he argued, because of their functional separation of parts and hierarchical structures. His contrary (anti-modern) example of a semi-lattice or "natural" city was Cambridge, England, where the individual colleges, instead of forming a defined campus separate from the town's activities, are interspersed within the surrounding coffee houses, pubs, shops, and student lodgings. Such richness or ambiguity, he suggests, is the nature of human life.

Alexander's paper represented an interesting turning-point in his theoretical development. His work, up until this time, had largely fallen under the positivistic rubric of design methodology, but with his founding of the Center for Environmental Structure at Berkeley in 1967, he shifted his efforts to creating "patterns" for architectural design. Gone were the mathematical symbols and lattice diagrams, which were replaced with the more flexible notion of a descriptive "pattern" – an "if/then" solution to a particular problem predicated on a context and backed up by research. These patterns could be applied to the individual buildings, to small parts of buildings, or to cities as a whole.

The system made its debut in 1968 with *A Pattern Language Which Generates Multi-Service Centers*, but perhaps a more influential spur to his development was his involvement with a United Nations housing project for Lima, Peru, for which the architect, Peter Land, was serving as Project Manager. Land was a graduate of London's Architectural Association and later joined the faculty at Yale University. In 1966 he convinced the Peruvian government and the United Nations to sponsor, among other projects, a major international competition for a demonstration housing project, *Proyecto Experimental de Vivienda* (PREVI), that would seek prototypical solutions for third-world housing. In opposition to the "superblock" schemes so evident in the 1960s, Land's plan of 1970 called for a high-density, compact development of low-rise housing that separated pedestrians from automobiles and featured an internal pedestrian spine

Figure P.2   Image depicting a "Cell Gateway," from Christopher Alexander, Sanford Hirshen, Sara Ishikawa, Christie Coffin, and Shlomo Angel, *Houses Generated by Patterns* (1969). Image courtesy of the Center for Environmental Structure.

around which were gathered community facilities, gardens, and individual neighborhoods totaling 450 units. Clustered housing arrangements included interior patios, through-ventilation, and expandable systems featuring inexpensive, earthquake-resistant construction. Twenty-four architectural firms contributed to the project – 12 Peruvian teams and 12 international firms, including the office of Alexander.[23]

Alexander and his associates responded not just with plans but with another book of 67 patterns, *Houses Generated by Patterns* (1969), largely devised from field research conducted in Peru. The patterns, which Alexander hoped "may begin to define a new indigenous architecture for Peru," incorporated such features as clustering, inwardly focused housing "cells," parking (tiny lots), and the emphasis on pedestrian routes. His patterns were particularly interesting in their sensitivity to Peruvian cultural habits, such as the need for an evening dance hall, walk-through schools, strict intimacy gradients, and transitional entrances within the layout of individual houses. They were less successful in a constructional sense, as well as in their overall intention to reestablish "vernacular" traditions. They nevertheless became the basis for his highly influential studies of the following decade, which we will consider later.

1968

All of this activity, however well intentioned, was interrupted by the cataclysmic events of the late 1960s. In the United States the assassination of John F. Kennedy in 1963 had caused the first crack in America's Cold War facade, and within a year his successor, Lyndon B. Johnson, would make the calamitous decision to escalate the Vietnam conflict and supply the necessary infantrymen through a much expanded military draft. At the same time, the Civil Rights Movement, led by Martin Luther King Jr, was taking shape in the American South. Political protest was at first peaceful, but after a few legislative victories in local and national voter registration, the violence in Selma and the rioting in Watts would, by 1965, shatter the calm. And with each summer encounter, the conflagrations in the Black ghettos across the country grew more violent and widespread. These riots took place alongside the ubiquitous antiwar marches, which increasingly galvanized a broad coalition of disenchanted youths. This ideological spectrum of these "baby-boom" protesters ranged from Marxists to pacifists, feminists, academics, celebrities, and of course the hippies. Overnight an entire generation, urged on by the anti-establishment lyrics of a newly electrified music, united in a counter-cultural rebellion that was immortalized by Marshall McLuhan and Quentin Fiore's phrase, "You can't *go* home again."[24]

European students were no less volatile, but the malaise seems to have been driven more by internal factors. The young in Europe, in general, were also far more serious in their politics, with their nearly unanimous socialist fervor being differentiated only by varying strategies of militancy. By the mid-1960s the perennially unstable governments of Italy, for instance, had descended into a condition of sustained anarchy and guerrilla warfare as the system came under attack from a revolutionary coalition composed of students and trade unions in the north to discontented peasants in the south. This fact, too, had its architectural implications, because Marxist theory – spanning the cultural divide between the anti-industrialism of William Morris to the technocratic anxiety of Herbert Marcuse – was generally suspicious of, if not openly hostile to, technological progress.

Also playing into the European chaos were the street theatrics of the 1960s. One of the more vocal of these groups was the Dada-inspired Situationist International, a leftist coalition formed in 1957. After various permutations, the tactics of Guy Debord came to define the group in the late 1960s, the principles of which he had outlined in his book *The Society of the Spectacle* (1967). It was in many ways an updating of Max Horkheimer and Theodor W. Adorno's earlier thesis regarding the "culture industry," in which Debord outlined the stratagem of 221 short theses (many of them willfully plagiarized and dissimulated from others), from which he attacked advanced capitalism, the mass media, consumer culture (commodity fetishism), religion, and family – in short, anything remotely connected with "bourgeois" life. In the end he argued that Western culture had become hopelessly addicted to the "spectacular images" viewed nightly on the evening news, and there was little hope of remedying the situation. The Situationists chose to counter this debilitating habit by acting out anarchic "situations" on the street; in fact they prided themselves on being "specialists in play."

1968 became the quintessential year of the spectacle, both in Europe and elsewhere. For the United States it opened portentously with an American surveillance ship being captured off the North Korean coast, and one week later the Vietcong launched their Tet offensive in South Vietnam, in which 60 000 soldiers crossed into the south and penetrated all the way to Saigon. The fierce opposition to this bloodbath would lead Lyndon Johnson, by the end of March, to back out of his run for a second term in office, throwing the American presidential race wide open. Meanwhile, the year opened in central Europe with the Slovak Alexander Dubček ousting the first secretary of the Communist Party, Antonín Novotný. It marked a jubilant revolt of the Czech and Slovakian people from 20 years of Soviet rule, leading to the "Prague Spring," in which the population, long cut off from the rest of Europe by the Iron Curtain, celebrated their newfound freedom of expression.

This ebullience proved a little too much for French students, who in March would take over the Nanterre campus of the University of Paris and demand major university reforms. April witnessed the tragic assassination of Martin Luther King Jr, which inflamed already high tensions. The arrest of demonstrators at the Sorbonne in early May touched off the guerilla tactics, strikes, barricades, and rioting that cordoned off much of Paris for nearly two months. Italian students were simultaneously occupying most of the major universities, all the while joining with workers in shutting down large sectors of Italy's economic production. In June, Robert Kennedy was gunned down in a hotel kitchen in Los Angeles, and the summer not only witnessed the usual race riots and antiwar demonstrations but also the live television coverage of the "police riot" at the Democratic Party's convention in Chicago. And as angry students and intellectuals in Europe were glibly hoisting banners depicting Fidel Castro and Che Guevara, the Soviet premier Leonid Brezhnev, in early August, responded to the Czechoslovakian people's "socialism with a human face" with tanks and 500 000 Warsaw Pact troops. A shackled Dubček was dragged to Moscow for "consultation" and returned to Prague television cameras a few weeks later to renounce his crimes – tearfully, of course. The paradoxes inherent in the political and military spectacles of 1968 were, for many observers, seemingly underwhelming.

Neither did the once high aspirations of modern architects elude the sound and fury of this year. As we suggested earlier, champions of modernity and progress, with all of their benign hopes for creating a better world, had, up until this time, presented a nearly unified vision of the future. This noble professional persona, along with its utopian impulses, lay fractured in ways that no one as yet fully understood. Not only was this mantra of common purpose and technological progress soon to be rejected by the younger members of the profession, but – even more unsettling – the mistress of architecture would indeed leave the household. She could no longer *go* home.

Part One
1970s

1

Pars Destruens
1968–1973

If the social and political events of 1968 made manifest the outlines of an architectural crisis of confidence, it certainly did not offer much in the way of details or explanation. In fact, if one simply looks at the professional journals and published texts of around this time, one might be hard pressed to find any evidence of a rupture with past practices. For instance, Vittorio Gregotti concluded his *New Directions in Italian Architecture* in 1968 with a chapter on the student revolts within Italian schools of architecture, but none of his illustrations suggested a pending break with the modernist tradition. In Europe the most significant project on the boards in 1968 was the complex planned for the Munich Olympics of 1972, a design of Günther Behnisch in collaboration with Frei Otto. Similarly, Robert Stern ended his *New Directions in American Architecture* of 1969 with Paul Rudolph's project for Stafford Harbor, Virginia – fully within the mainstream of high modernism. In the same year, Louis Kahn, with buildings going up in Exeter, New Haven, Fort Worth, and India, was representing the Philadelphia School, while one of the busiest offices in the United States, Kevin Roche, John Dinkeloo and Associates, was overseeing the construction of Memorial Coliseum and the Knights of Columbus complex in New Haven. If there was one omen suggesting the demise of modernism in 1969 it was the passing of Walter Gropius and Mies van der Rohe – the last two "masters" of the gilded pantheon.

But journals and books do not always tell the story, particularly in that the principal divide that came out of 1968 was a generational one. Moreover, it was a divide that would oppose the ideological platform of high modernism, not with a unifying counter-strategy but rather with a fragmentation of theory, tentative starts and stops in how, indeed, one

An Introduction to Architectural Theory: 1968 to the Present, First Edition.
Harry Francis Mallgrave and David Goodman.
© 2011 Harry Francis Mallgrave and David Goodman. Published 2011 by Blackwell Publishing Ltd.

could proceed. There was also a sharp political and cultural divide that separated North American and European theory in the years surrounding 1968, which can be illustrated by reviewing the contrary positions of Robert Venturi and Aldo Rossi. Both published important books in 1966 in which they voiced their quiet dissatisfaction with the status quo. Both continued to develop their ideas over the next few years, and both, subsequently, would lead identifiable schools of thought that – by the middle of the 1970s – could be characterized as distinct branches on the sprouting tree of "postmodernism." Nevertheless, the two schools were radically at odds in their theoretical underpinnings.

Venturi and Scott Brown

Robert Venturi was the first to establish his credentials as an apostate. He received his architecture degree from Princeton in 1950 and, after stays in the offices of Oscar Stonorov, Louis Kahn, and Eero Saarinen, he won the Rome Prize in 1954 and embarked on an extended residence in that city. He entered private practice in Philadelphia in 1957 and within a few years had carried out a number of small commissions, among them the design of his mother's house in Chestnut Hill (1959–1964), the North Penn Visiting Nurses Association (1961–1963), and the Guild House (1961–1966). Equally important for his development was his connection with the University of Pennsylvania, where in the early 1960s he taught one of the first courses on theory within an American architectural program. From his notes for this class he composed a preliminary manuscript for a book in 1963, and three years later, after revisions, it was published by the Museum of Modern Art under the title *Complexity and Contradiction in Architecture*.

The book, which aspired to be a "gentle manifesto," is more complex than a first reading might suggest. To start with, it is a composite humanist tract drawing upon the recent work of Louis Kahn and Alvar Aalto, the anthropological perspective of Aldo van Eyck, the semiotic interests of Tomás Maldonado, the sociology of Herbert Gans, as well as Venturi's own fascination with both mannerism and the relatively recent phenomenon of pop art. It opens with a plea for a mannerist phase of modernism, which he articulates through a set of formal or compositional maneuvers drawn in part from literary theory. These are strategies for injecting complexity and contradiction into design, which he explains in chapters with such titles as the "Double-Functioning Element," "Contradiction Adapted," and "Contradiction Juxtaposed."

Another novelty of the book is its heavy reliance on historical examples, many of which are mannerist and baroque buildings from Italy and the United Kingdom. They serve to buffer his case for visual complexity and ambiguity, and this use of history to support a contemporary case for design was unusual at this time. Still another aspect of the short book is its frank, polemical tone. In an often cited example, he subverts such high-minded modernist clichés as Mies van der Rohe's reported adage, "Less is more," by playfully responding "Less is a bore." Then again, his examples, repeatedly drawn from architects like Kahn and Aalto, testify to the fact that his rejection of "the puritanically moral language of orthodox Modern architecture" was by no means unconditional or even considerable at this date. Moreover, Venturi presents his (often perceptual) arguments for a mannerist phase of modernism with a certain literary aplomb.

But the book on occasions also betrays what would become Venturi's evolving thought. In scattered places in the later chapters, the theme of formal ambiguity is conjoined with sub-themes that are lurking, as it were, within the text. One is his fondness for "rhetorical" or "honky-tonk" elements drawn from popular culture. Venturi justifies their incorporation into a new and more inclusive architecture first on the basis of their (pop-art inspired) realism and second as a gesture of social protest against a political system currently engaged in an unpopular war.[1] Another sub-theme to emerge is Venturi's incipient populism. For instance, in arguing against Peter Blake's comparison of the chaos of "Main Street" with the orderliness of Thomas Jefferson's campus at the University of Virginia, Venturi insists that not only are such comparisons meaningless but they also raise the question of "is not Main Street almost all right?"[2] It is a scarcely subtle challenge to modernist sensibilities with regard to the postwar emphasis on large-scale planning and compositional order, and Venturi's concluding sentence of the book reveals that he was already on the verge of adopting a more radical position with respect to the issue: "And it is per-haps from the everyday landscape, vulgar and disdained, that we can draw the complex and contradictory order that is valid and vital for our architec-ture as an urbanistic whole."[3]

It is around this time – in 1965 or 1966 – that the formidable influence of Denise Scott Brown also becomes evident. This Zambian-born archi-tect, together with her husband, Robert Scott Brown, had come to the University of Pennsylvania in the late 1950s to study under Kahn. Robert died in a tragic accident in 1959, but Denise advanced her interest in urban studies by taking courses with David Crane, Herbert Gans, and Paul Davidoff, among others. Prior to coming to Philadelphia, she had attended the Architectural Association in London and thus had a front-row seat for the "New Brutalist" phenomenon of the mid-1950s. It was in part this critical perspective (a gritty antipathy toward high modernism) that she brought to Penn, and after joining the faculty she collaborated with Venturi in the course of theory between 1962 and 1964.

The following year Scott Brown took a visiting position at the University of California at Berkeley, where she co-taught a course with the somewhat controversial urban sociologist Melvin Webber. In a now classic essay of 1964 he had taken to task the axiom that cities should be organized around a central downtown hub or regional center. He pointed to the transformation taking place in communication patterns – the fact that many businesses interact not locally but nationally or globally – and argued that in the future it will be these electronic patterns (not such traditional features as urban spaces) that will become "the essence of the city and of city life."[4]

Scott Brown, together with Gordon Cullen, responded in 1965 with several articles under the title "The Meaningful City," which analyzed the city under the four themes of perception, messages, meaning, and the modern image. What united these analyses was the idea of a "symbol," which was at heart a criticism of the city as envisioned by postwar planners. In the view of Scott Brown, planners were failing to understand urban forms and the symbolic way in which most inhabitants read them: "We do not lack for symbols, but our efforts to use them are unsubtle and heavy handed. In the planning offices of most cities even this much is not achieved, and the situation goes by default."[5] This focus on urban communication was the new perspective that Scott Brown offered Venturi – when the two architects married in the summer of 1967. From this juncture their writings and ideas became a collaborative effort.

Venturi's populism and Scott Brown's urban focus first became evident in a joint studio the two taught at Yale in 1967, which considered the redesign of a subway station in New York City. In the following year, as much of the world was descending into chaos, the two architects offered their Yale students a studio on "The Strip" in Las Vegas. The results were first published in two essays that appeared in 1968, and together they formed the cornerstones of their book *Learning from Las Vegas* (1972).

In the first essay the two chided modern architects for their elitist and purist displeasure with existing conditions, and especially the commercial vernacular of the city. In their view, the professional establishment was pretentiously abandoning the tradition of iconology and thereby standing aloof from the "architecture of persuasion." Comparing their recent trip to Las Vegas to the revelation architects traditionally experience when visiting the historic squares of Italy, Venturi and Scott Brown made their point in an overtly controversial way:

Figure 1.1   *Learning from Las Vegas,* by Robert Venturi, Denise Scott Brown, and Steven Izenour, published by The MIT Press, © MIT 1972.

> For young Americans in the 1940s, familiar only with the auto-scaled, grid-iron city, and the antiurban theories of the previous architectural generation, the traditional urban spaces, the pedestrian scale, and the mixtures yet continuities of styles of the Italian piazzas were a significant revelation. They rediscovered the piazza. Two decades later architects are perhaps ready for similar lessons about large open space, big scale, and high speed. Las Vegas is to the Strip what Rome is to the Piazza.[6]

In their second essay of 1968, Scott Brown and Venturi drew their famous distinction between the "sign which *is* the building" (the duck) and the "sign which *fronts* the building" (later to be named the decorated shed). They candidly expressed their preference for the latter, if only because it "is an easier, cheaper, more direct and basically more honest approach to the question of decoration; it permits us to get on with the task of making conventional buildings conventionally and to deal with their symbolic needs with a lighter, defter touch."[7] The implications of this preference for their own practice would, of course, be immense, but so too would their well-defined break with modernism's technological vision. Actually, they emphatically made this last point in the final pages of *Learning from Las Vegas* by countering Mies van der Rohe's "symbolically exposed but substantially encased steel frame" with John Ruskin's "once-horrifying statement" that architecture is but "the decoration of construction."[8]

Such sentiments would not go unchallenged, but interestingly the push-back came not from established modernists but from younger architects of the same generation with competing views. In 1970 the Argentine painter Tomás Maldonado, who some years earlier had pioneered courses on communication at the Hochschule für Gestaltung at Ulm, responded sharply to such ideas by insisting that the neon signs of Las Vegas repre-sented neither a populist act nor a condition of visual richness but rather "chit-chat," a "depth of communicative poverty" that simply pandered "to the needs of casino and motel owners, and to the needs of real estate speculators."[9]

An even more pointed rebuttal appeared in 1971 in a special bilingual issue of Italy's leading journal, *Casabella*, a number that was orchestrated by Peter Eisenman. Scott Brown was appropriately allowed to set the stage with an essay entitled "Learning from Pop," in which she expanded the lesson plan of Las Vegas by noting that architects should also study "Los Angeles, Levittown, the swinging singles on the Westheimer Strip, golf resorts, boating communities, Co-op City, the residential back-grounds to soap operas, TV commercials and mass mag ads, billboards, and Route 66."[10] Another part of the new curriculum is the beloved sub-urban home and its owner's quaint touches of respectability: sweeping lawns, decorative plantings, driveway gateways, columns, and coach lamps beside the front door (her Yale studio of 1970 was entitled "Learning from Levittown"). Architects should come here to learn, she continues, in part because of the massive failure of urban renewal programs in America, in part because of the liberal culture of elitism that rules the profession. Scott Brown counters with a defiant populist stance:

> The forms of the pop landscape are as relevant to us now, as were the forms of antique Rome to the Beaux-Arts, Cubism, and Machine Architecture to the early Moderns, and the industrial midlands and the Dogon to Team 10, which is to say extremely relevant, and more so than the latest bathysphere launch pad, or systems hospital (or even, *pace* Banham, the Santa Monica pier).[11]

Scott Brown's relatively brief polemic was rejoined by much lengthier remarks by Kenneth Frampton, which picked up where Maldonado's earlier criticisms had ended. With opening citations by Hermann Broch, the Vesnin brothers, Hannah Arendt, and Herbert Marcuse – as well as some particularly gruesome photographs of an automobile accident by Andy Warhol – Frampton counters her main contention with great seriousness:

> Do designers really need elaborate sociological ratification *à la* Gans, to tell them that what they want is what they already have? No doubt Levittown could be brought to yield an equally affirmative consensus in regard to current American repressive policies, both domestic and foreign. Should designers like politicians wait upon the dictates of a silent majority, and if so, how are they to interpret them? Is it really the task of under-employed design talent to suggest to the constrained masses of Levittown – or elsewhere – that they might prefer the extravagant confines of the West Coast nouveau-riche; a by now superfluous function which has already been performed more than adequately for years by Madison Avenue? In this respect there is now surely little left of our much vaunted pluralism that has not already been overlaid with the engineered fantasies of mass taste.[12]

Frampton further rejects the values of a society that gauges its standard of living by its automobiles, television sets, and airplanes, and it is ultimately the critical theory of the Frankfurt School that he embraces as well as the ideas of Clement Greenberg – where the role of the artistic avant-garde is precisely to resist capitalist culture and its seemingly inevitable production of kitsch.

Rossi and Tafuri

Rossi's thought during these same years displays a similar antipathy toward modernist ideals, but from a very contrary perspective. The Milan native received his architectural training at that city's Polytechnic University in the 1950s, and, while still a student, he was invited by Ernesto Rogers to write for *Casabella-continuità*. Altogether, Rossi penned 31 articles, which included book reviews and essays on both historical and topical issues, such as the Neoliberty phenomenon. In the early 1960s he began his academic career, and in 1965 he joined the faculty at his alma mater in Milan. His architectural output in the first half of the decade was minimal, with his most important projects being the Loosian-inspired Villa ai Ronchi (1960) and the monumental fountain for the city-square at Segrate (1965). The latter, with its generous cylindrical support and extruded triangular pediment, announced his fascination with primary forms, very much in the reductive tradition of the Marc-Antoine Laugier.

Rossi's turning point, on the theoretical front at least, was his book of 1966, *L'architettura della città* (architecture in the city). The study has several important (mostly Marxist) antecedents, among them studies by

Giuseppe Samonà, Leonardo Benevolo, and Carlo Aymonino.[13] As with Venturi's contemporary effort, Rossi's book injects a breath of freshness into the otherwise languid discourse of the mid-1960s. Based on the work of a number of French geographers, it is a scholarly study as well as a sustained argument against many of the tenets of modern planners. Rossi's mission, as he later describes it, is nothing less than a search for the "fixed laws of a timeless typology."[14]

The specific focus of Rossi's book is the European city, the city defined by its architectonic elements or cultural physiognomy. Such an emphasis leads to an exposition of critical terms endowing each city with its lived "consciousness" – notions such as artifacts, permanences, monuments, memory, and locus. Collectively, they are the primary elements of a city that allow it to persist over time and are the source of ritual and the city's collective memory. The notion of typology is also central to Rossi's argument. In this regard he follows the lead of the neoclassicist Antoine-Chrysostome Quatremère de Quincy, who had defined "type" as "not so much the image of a thing to be copied or perfectly imitated as the idea of an element that must itself serve as a rule for the model."[15] For Rossi the need to return to these timeless urban types becomes his leading argument – both as an alternative to practices of design inspired by the Athens Charter and to his critique of "naive functionalism." Advocates of the latter view, Rossi argues, divest architectural form of its autonomous value by reducing design to a programmatic scheme of organization and circulation, a practice that Rossi likens (invoking Max Weber) to a commercialization of urban design. The idea of a traditional type, by contrast, allows historical considerations back into architecture, for it is that which (in its recovery of such things as cultural monuments) is both vital and closest to architecture's "essence." And even though Rossi does not explicitly make a case for recalling pre-industrial or eighteenth-century urban design strategies and forms, the suggestion is at least implied and will be developed by others.

In the same year in which *L'architettura della città* appeared, Rossi was teaming with Giorgio Grassi to produce the competition design for San Rocco Housing in Monza, the first of his larger typological schemes. Grassi also followed upon Rossi's effort in 1967 with his book *La costruzione logica dell'architettura* (The logical construction of architecture). It too aspired to be a "genealogy of rationalism," that is, "a scientific study of architecture and the classification of its elements" on a "rational and transmittable basis."[16] Grassi took his idea of a typological manual back to the seventeenth- and eighteenth-century handbooks of Pierre Le Muet, Charles-Etienne Briseux, and Roland Fréart de Chambray, but his formal explorations lay closer to the housing and urban typologies of Heinrich Tessenow, Ludwig Hilberseimer, and Alexander Klein – early modernists whose work was little known at this time. These efforts by Rossi and Grassi were undertaken with the aim of imposing on architecture a "stabilization" of its formal types. Thus, by 1967 a basis had been laid for a new direction for Italian theory, and what remained was simply to give this foundation – from a critical perspective – a precise political calibration. The year 1968 provided the perfect occasion and the medium was Manfredo Tafuri, who, at the start of the year, had moved to Venice to take the chair at the Istituto Universitario di Architettura di Venezia (the IAUV), the city's architectural school.[17] Within a few years he would forge a Milan–Venice axis with Rossi.

Tafuri arrived in Venice amid a highly charged political atmosphere. In the winter and spring of 1968 the architecture school was being occupied by students, who were denying the faculty (including Tafuri) entry to the school. Massimo Cacciari, Francesco Dal Co, and Cesare De Michelis had recently formed the critical journal *Angelus Novus*, which was exploring the writings of the Frankfurt School as well as the socialist architecture of the 1920s. Cacciari and Dal Co were also involved with *Contropiano*, a Marxist journal that was challenging the institutional structure of the Italian Communist Party (PCI) from a position on the left. The staff of *Contropiano* included the well known activists Alberto Asor Rosa, Mario Tronti, and Antonio Negri – the last two of whom were at that moment engaged in a furious debate over tactics.[18]

Tafuri brought with him his first critical study of contemporary architecture. In its understated but transparent political tone, *Teorie e storia dell' architettura* (Theories and history of architecture) today seems to situate itself between the revolutionary theories of Georg Lukács and the analytic detachment of Walter Benjamin. Indeed, one of the book's intentions was to draw a parallel between the political situation of the 1920s and contemporary thought. The leitmotif for Tafuri is the term "operative criticism," a concept that refers to those critics who read history as an explanation of more recent trends – that is, those who cull and misread the past through the use of convenient ideological judgments serving the present. The word "ideology" is also laden with political import. The Marxist term signifies the false "class consciousness" of the bourgeoisie (religious, cultural, aesthetic) that prevents the proletariat from attaining true consciousness of its revolutionary potential. Tafuri's contention, in essence, is that the books of many modern histories had been cooked, because, in short, the architects of the 1920s had failed in their revolutionary ambitions.

Tafuri supports this contention with his notion of instrumentality: how criticism has since become a tool for ideological or false theorizing.

In surveying recent architecture theory, from Peter Collins to Aymonino, he finds the persistent desire of many to impose more scientific methods of analysis through the application of such strategies as structuralism, semiology, and typological research. And whereas he admits such methods do actually hold out some promise, Tafuri is quick to dismiss the tacit bond between capitalism and the semantic gamesmanship of many modern-day writers (Venturi) who embrace historical notions like "ambiguity" in order to justify their own design preferences.[19] Ultimately, Tafuri wants to affirm history's autonomy or theoretical separation from contemporary practice, and calls for this to be done not only out of intellectual embarrassment over the distortions through which so many historians have interpreted the past but also out of a sense of impotency in the face of capitalism's advanced development. Today the historian's role is not to explain away the crisis by resorting to the past, but actually to intensify or increase the current malaise. The historian must address the anguish of the present but of necessity with a note of intellectual despair. In later reminiscing on this period of the late 1960s, Tafuri invoked the paradigm of Francis Bacon's *pars destruens* – the "negative part" of the inductive process that seeks to liberate the mind from errors.[20]

As Tafuri settled into Venice, his political views advanced. In 1969 he penned for *Contropiano* an essay entitled "Toward a Critique of Architectural Ideology," the first of four critical essays that he wrote for this journal. Here he brings the problem of architecture's false consciousness into sharper political focus, because – in his "psychoanalysis" of the previous two centuries – he rejects the slightest possibility of modernist optimism or utopian salvation. The analysis begins with the eighteenth-century theorists Laugier and Giovanni Battista Piranesi, both of whom, Tafuri insists, set the current crisis in motion: the latter with his celebration of the "fragment" that displaced the baroque insistence on the whole. In Tafuri's fast-paced chronology, the utopian projects of the nineteenth century also failed miserably, as this century exhibited only "the unrestrained exhibition of a false conscience that strives for final ethical redemption by displaying its own inauthenticity."[21] The twentieth century fared no better, and even the "heroic" resistance of the avant-garde movements of the 1920s receives little praise in Tafuri's analysis. This is because whether the strategy was De Stijl's programmatic control of artistic production or the Dadaists' "violent insertion of the irrational," the endgame was always the same. In a prescient remark that highlighted changing architectural perceptions, he argued that all efforts to resist the capitalist order were usurped or drafted into the service of secular capitalism, that is, "large industrial capital – makes architecture's underlying ideology its own."[22]

What this travesty bodes for architecture in 1969 is obviously nothing good. If Tafuri in his dialectic does not go so far as to reiterate Hegel's insistence on the death of architecture, the zeitgeist of finality nevertheless still haunts the present, even for those political activists temporally buoyed by the illusion that they are enjoying a brief "moment in the class struggle." Kurt W. Forster perhaps best encapsulates the severity of Tafuri's indictment by noting "the fundamental impossibility of any meaningful cultural action within the historical confinement of the present."[23] This is the case, Tafuri argues, as much for the "polyvalent images" of Venturi as it is for the "silence of geometries" of Rossi. Architecture, barring the unlikely revolution, is now stripped of its revolutionary appeal.

In 1973 Tafuri expanded this essay into his popular book *Progetto e utopia*, translated into English as *Architecture and Utopia*. He now fortifies his Rorschäch method of analysis with the sociological theories of Weber, Benjamin, and Karl Mannheim, as well as the "negative thought" of his friend Massimo Cacciari. In this new and depressing light, Dada's "desacralization of values," or Benjamin's "end of the aura," can no longer be seen as irrational processes because their "destruction of values offered a wholly new type of rationality, which was capable of coming face to face with the negative, in order to the make the negative itself the release valve of an unlimited potential for development."[24] The two design strategies that he sees currently unfolding – semiology and compositional formalism – both fall under "capital's complete domination" and are doomed in a revolutionary sense. If semiology's search for symbolism is simply an acknowledgment that architecture has already lost its meaning, the formalist approach of architects like the "New York Five" is similarly fated to be consumed by the market forces of commercialization. The architect and critic have but one role to play, which is "to do away with impotent and ineffectual myths, which so often serve as illusions that permit the survival of anachronistic 'hopes of design.' "[25] Architecture, even more ruthlessly that Venturi had suggested, is thereby shorn of any and all meliorist intentions.

The Milan Triennale

From such a starkly nihilist perspective, it is clear that Venturi and Scott Brown's populist embrace of Las Vegas could not be interpreted by Tafuri as anything other than a capitulation to capitalist forces, but within a few years Tafuri's censure of Rossi would become tempered. In 1969 Aymonino invited Rossi to design his first major building, the Gallaratese, a housing complex outside Milan. Rossi responded with a type of "corridor

Figure 1.2   Aldo Rossi, Gallaratese, Milan, Italy. Image courtesy of Alessandro Frigerio.

housing" displaying extreme prismatic rigor: two buildings supported on narrow fins running sequentially 182 meters in length, narrowly gapped, and fitted with squared window openings. Whereas Tafuri at first seems to have been taken back by Rossi's De Chiricoesque inspiration – "frozen in spaces abandoned by time" – he later nearly praised "the sacred precision of his geometric block" for remaining "above ideology and above all utopian proposals for a 'new lifestyle.' "[26] Rossi's selfless sacrifice, better yet, abandonment, was, of course, exceeded by the architect's otherworldly yet much applauded primitive typology for the expansion of the San Cataldo Cemetery in Modena, the first designs for which appeared in 1971. Here the primeval silence of the forms seems entirely appropriate for people who, in the words of Rafael Moneo, "no longer need protection from the cold."[27]

Rossi, in fact, was able to offer an explanation for such designs when he was named architectural curator of 15th Triennale of Milan, which took place in 1973. The exhibition was an architectural extravaganza that made the reputations of many young designers, and in retrospect the most important event was the exhibition catalogue itself, *Architettura razionale*

(Rational architecture), which would now serve as a manifesto for a new movement. Rossi opened the polemic by championing typology and rationalism not as some vague response to the complex problems of today, but rather as "a more concrete way of working."[28] Another section of the catalogue featured excerpts from the writings of Ernesto Rogers, J. J. P. Oud, Adolf Loos, J. A. Ginzburg, Giorgio Grassi, and Hans Schmidt – all to buffer the case for a latter-day typology taking its inspiration in part from the spirit of the 1920s. The heart of the catalog, however, was Massimo Scolari's essay, "Avanguardia e nuova architettura (Avant-garde and new architecture), which sought to position historically the new rationalist movement, now to be known as *La Tendenza* (the trend).

Scolari traced this new "critical attitude" to the urban debates of the 1960s in Italy as well as to the circle of architects involved with *Casabella-continuità* and the Milan Polytechnic, which included Rossi, Ernesto Rogers, and Vittorio Gregotti. If Rossi's book of 1966 becomes the defining moment for *La Tendenza*, the political events of 1968 brought the issues into sharper focus. Tafuri's anti-utopian insistence on architectural autonomy, for example, allows him to be seen as "one of the most passionate 'planners' of the *Tendenza*."[29] Similarly, Rossi's typological "process of essentialization" defines the pivotal point at which both the neo-avant-garde's denial of disciplinary discourse and architecture's "bourgeois" contamination are overcome by a *"global refounding of architecture."*[30] This is true because Rossi's "rigid world with few objects," like the historiography of Tafuri, no longer allows the possibility of advanced technological thinking, and indeed the architect now must be selective in turning to any recent modernist sources. Through such an ideological backdoor enter such seemingly inexplicable works as East Germany's "New City" at Halle and East Berlin's Karl-Marx-Allee – planning types now approved for contemporary appropriation, presumably for reasons of their political coloration alone. More generally, *La Tendenza* becomes defined by its strict ties to historical types (not specific forms), its focus on the city, its urban morphology, its monumentality, and indeed by the way it values prototypical or Platonic form.[31]

If the neoclassical architect Etienne-Louis Boullée would have concurred whole-heartedly with such sentiments, not all critics in the early 1970s were willing to go so far down the path of rationalist austerity. The historian Joseph Rykwert, someone who had long-standing ties to Italian architectural circles, provided one of the few stinging retorts to Rossi's and Scolari's contentions: "So that's it, then. Architecture may stay alive as long as she stays dumb. Dumb and beautiful maybe, but dumb. Those of us who refuse this condition are sternly set aside."[32]

The IAUS and the New York Five

Still another sign of the discontent manifesting itself during these polemically active years can be found in the efforts of Colin Rowe and Peter Eisenman. Rowe had initially studied architecture, but after a wartime accident he enrolled at the Warburg Institute in London 1946, where he turned his focus to history under Rudolf Wittkower. While still a student, he wrote his influential essay, "The Mathematics of the Ideal Villa" (1947), which compared the composition of Palladio's Villa Malcontenta with Le Corbusier's Villa Stein at Garches.[33] The essay helped to popularize the style of Le Corbusier in a country that would soon become obsessed with him as both an architect and a person. Yet Rowe, like many of his peers, was also looking toward America and in 1952 he traveled to Yale to take courses with Henry-Russell Hitchcock. Thereafter he traveled extensively within the United States and by chance, in 1953, he was offered a teaching position at the University of Texas at Austin.

The timing and location was propitious. The school's new director, Harwell Harris, had been lured to Texas from his practice in Los Angeles with the mandate to build a first-rate program.[34] The old and new faculty – among them Bernard Hoesli, John Hejduk, Robert Slutzky, Lee Hirsche, John Shaw, Lee Hodgden, and Werner Seligmann – would, because of their innovative curriculum and unique emphasis on visual and formal complexity, become known as the "Texas Rangers."[35] The Rangers, however, began to go separate ways in 1956, when Harris left Texas for North Carolina State University. Rowe taught briefly at Cornell University before returning to England and Cambridge University, where he became a lecturer between 1958 and 1962. In the last year he accepted a professorship at Cornell, where he created an urban design program that remains his legacy.

It was at Cambridge that Eisenman met his mentor. The Newark native had attended Cornell University in the early 1950s and, after working in a few offices, had enrolled at Columbia University in 1959. The following year he received a fellowship to study Gothic architecture at Cambridge. Rowe and Eisenman befriended one another and it was Rowe who guided Eisenman on summer architectural tours of the Continent in 1961 and 1962, during which time Eisenman was introduced to the first group of Italian "Rationalists" from the late 1920s and early 1930s, in particular to the work of Giuseppe Terragni. This latter became one focus of Eisenman's doctoral dissertation, "The Formal Basis of Modern Architecture," which was accepted by Trinity College in 1963.[36]

Figure 1.3   Giuseppe Terragni, Casa del Fascio, Como, Italy. Image courtesy of Frans Drewniak.

Although the dissertation was a very early work of Eisenman, it neverthe-less set the tone for many of his deliberations over the next two decades. He completed it just after Christopher Alexander had finished his dissertation and it shares a similar positivistic spirit, although it derives from the theories of Rowe. The latter's idea of "transparency," which he had earlier fashioned with Robert Slutzky, had effectively suppressed the semantic dimension of architecture in favor of a more abstract and conceptual analysis of visual form.[37] Eisenman, in turn, sets out to devise a theory deriving entirely from the analytical properties of form itself. These properties include such things as volume (where space resides), mass, surface, and movement. Notions such as "syntax" and "grammar" also play heavily into his discussion, and it marks the start of his long-standing aversion to everything related to sym-bolism. Terragni's Casa del Fascio features prominently in his analysis, as the cube's abstract laying of planes becomes central to his conceptual dia-gramming of hidden axes, recessed planes, and vectors. In effect, Eisenman was searching for a purely rational reading of form.

Upon returning to the United States, Eisenman joined the faculty at Princeton University and, together with Michael Graves, founded the

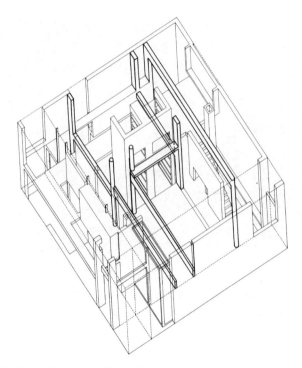

Figure 1.4   Peter Eisenman, House I, Princeton, New Jersey (1967). Courtesy of Eisenman Architects.

Conference of Architects for the Study of the Environment (CASE) in 1964, a group that initially included Henry Millon, Stanford Anderson, and Richard Meier (a cousin of Eisenman).[38] Others who later were involved with the group included Kenneth Frampton, Jacquelin Robertson, Mario Gandelsonas, Tom Vreeland, Anthony Vidler, John Hejduk, and Charles Gwathmey. Robert Venturi and Vincent Scully were invited to the first CASE meeting in 1964, although they left the event when their differences with others became apparent. The success of CASE varied over the years, but one important event orchestrated by Eisenman was the exhibition "Five Architects," which took place at the Museum of Modern Art in May 1969. Its significance, however, would not be known until a few years later.

Even before this date Eisenman had become less enamored with CASE, and in 1966 he approached Arthur Drexler, the director of architecture at the Museum of Modern Art, and proposed the creation of a new institute to study urban problems – a crisis visibly manifest in the urban conflagrations of this time. Drexler turned to the museum board, and two of its trustees provided start-up funds for the new organization. Thus, in October 1967, the

Institute of Architecture and Urban Studies (or IAUS) was legally born, with Eisenman serving as its director and Drexler as the chairman of the board. The IAUS was a multifaceted enterprise from the beginning. On one front (and only in the first years) it was a non-profit urban think-tank that solicited monies from private and governmental agencies for the study of the urban environment. In another and more consistent way, it served as a center for theoretical research and planning – a graduate school in effect, in which faculty from schools in the Northeast would hold visiting seminars or teach one or more days a week. The IAUS also hosted symposia and exhibitions, as well as founding a critical journal. All of this was taking shape in 1967, as Eisenman received his first architectural commission, and from this time forward, the two – his practice and theory – would become interchangeable.

The Barenholtz Pavilion in Princeton (1967), better known as House I, forged this interdependence.[39] Eisenman drafted remarks in 1969 to explain his design intentions, and the underlying theme was the germinating idea of "cardboard architecture," a term that had been used in a pejorative sense by Frank Lloyd Wright in 1931 to refer to the planar and detail-less architecture of Le Corbusier.[40] Eisenman, however, embraced the term and offered the intention "to shift the focus from our existing conception of form in an aesthetic and functional context to a consideration of form as a marking or notational system."[41] Rosalind Krauss later characterized this intention by noting that Eisenman "wanted to unload the physical envelope of all function (this column 'means' support) and all semantic associations (brick 'means' warmth, stability, etc.). In their place he entertained the notion of the 'model' as a way of generating form, of exploring ideas, quite apart from the necessities of real structure or the properties of real material."[42]

Hence, cardboard architecture for Eisenman came to refer to the logical, generative operations related to form, operations in themselves devoid of meaning except on an abstract level. In House I, for instance, he employed three strategies to give prominence to these "deep structures" (now appropriating a term from Noam Chomsky).[43] One was the attempt to delimit conventional meanings through the use of whites or neutral colors and flat textures. Another was to mask the structure, in this case by making some columns and beams non-load-bearing. At the same time, these false structural signs were to call attention to the underlying conceptual structure of the design, sometimes by revealing ambiguities, sometimes by their very absence. Thus, if Le Corbusier in his Villa Savoye had employed certain forms symbolically to recall the details of ocean liners, Eisenman sought out a syntactic organization of forms (a grammar, if you will) in which all semantic references or symbolic allusions are rigorously precluded.

Several essays Eisenman wrote in the early 1970s developed these ideas in greater depth. In one article written for *Casabella* in 1970, Eisenman drew upon his dissertation to argue that just as Le Corbusier (with his metaphors to modernity) had shifted design sensibilities from pragmatic (functions and structural) to semantic (symbolic and iconic) concerns, so Terragni's Fascist headquarters in Como had moved architecture into a syntactic realm, specifically by the organization of its facade "as a series of vertical planes articulated in such a way as to define a single frontal plane, the spatial order seen as recessional from this frontal reference."[44] In another essay from this period, Eisenman offers his strategy of "conceptual art" specifically as a conceptualized response to Venturi's embrace of "pop art."[45] All of these efforts owed much to Rowe and Slutzky's notion of phenomenal transparency.

Eisenman was also the instigating force behind the exhibition catalogue *Five Architects: Eisenman, Graves, Gwathmey, Hejduk, Meier*, which appeared in a small run in 1972.[46] Of course, the exhibition "Five Architects" had taken place in 1969, and it was conceived principally as an event for the architects to display their work and elicit critical remarks from other CASE members. All were young architects, professionally speaking, although Richard Meier had been in practice since 1963. Michael Graves and Charles Gwathmey had received their first commissions in the late 1960s, and the former "Texas Ranger" Hejduk participated with his drawings for House 10, the Bernstein House, and One-Half House. The book contained several important essays, among them pieces by Frampton, Rowe, and Eisenman.

Frampton's essay, "Frontality vs. Rotation," helped to establish his place within American critical theory. He had been trained at the Architectural Association in the early 1950s, or in the heyday of New Brutalism. And although he studied for a while under Peter Smithson, his initial sympathies were closer to the ideas of Richard Hamilton, John Miller, Alan Colquhoun, and Reyner Banham. In the first half of the 1960s he had worked in the office of Douglas Stephen and Partners and served as the technical editor of the journal *Architectural Design*. In 1965, at the instigation of Eisenman, Frampton joined the faculty at Princeton University, where he also befriended Maldonado. It was the latter's political orientation (inspired by the Soviet realism of Hannes Meyer) that fitted best with Frampton's own radicalization in the late 1960s, during which time he assimilated the ideas of Adorno, Marcuse, and Arendt. These authors reveal that, in his theoretical outlook at least, Frampton was never in line with the formalist concerns of Eisenman, even though the latter (sometime around 1965 or 1966) encouraged him to become "the Sigfried Giedion of the group."[47]

In his essay for the book, which was an expansion upon his earlier remarks, Frampton undertook a quite conventional analysis of the group's designs by considering the overriding strategy as the imposition of grids, entries, frontality, diagonal axes, and the every-present "theme of erosion." He recognized Wrightian compositional motifs in Hejduk's House 10 and Terragni's influence in Eisenman's House I, yet he was less forthcoming in elaborating upon "certain syntactical references to Le Corbusier" found in the work of the other three architects. Instead, he preferred to relate Meier's Smith House and Graves's Hanselmann House, for instance, to Marcel Breuer's design for the Gropius House of 1938 and even to American shingle-style homes of the late 1880s.[48] One almost senses his political unease at the fact that he was witnessing a full-blown "neo-modern" revival shorn of any political ideology.

Yet Rowe, who had since drifted from the circle of Eisenman, seized precisely this issue in the most pointed terms:

> For we are here in the presence of what, in terms of the orthodox theory of modern architecture, is heresy. We are in the presence of anachronism, nostalgia, and probably, frivolity. If modern architecture looked like this c.1930 then it should not look like this today; and, if the real political issue of the present is not the provision of the rich with cake but of the starving with bread, then not only formally but also programmatically these buildings are irrelevant.[49]

Gathering steam, Rowe proceeds to unravel the ideological trappings of modern theory around 1930: its location at the "matrix of eschatological and utopian fantasy," its formulation as an objective response to "a compilation of recognizable empirical facts," and most importantly, the architect as the passive midwife to history, operating as it were under this "Positivist conception of fact" and "Hegelian conception of manifest destiny." Rowe also characterizes high modern theory as a "constellation of escapist myths" and concedes that its central "socialist mission" has since "dissolved in the sentimentalities and bureaucracies of the welfare state."[50] What this aporia says about the reincarnation of early modernist forms in 1972, Rowe concludes, is simply revival: a faddish replication of forms from modernism's heroic era, yet now stripped of any pretense of a new and better world.

Such analysis, however candid, would in no way impede the growing fame of the New York Five as a recognizable entity, or the growth of the IAUS. The latter's journal, *Oppositions*, made its debut in September 1973, and the three founding editors – Eisenman, Frampton, and Mario

Gandelsonas – were quick to establish a varied and high level of discourse.[51] The journal's inaugural editorial defined its goal to be one of "critical assessment and re-assessment," addressing itself toward "the evolution of new models for a theory of architecture."[52] The earlier issues display an alliance along a critical front with Rossi and Tafuri – no doubt in part due to the New York Five's participation in the Milan exhibition in 1973. Some of Rossi's designs were introduced to the North American audience in one early issue, while Tafuri's influential essay, "L'Architecture dans le Boudoir," became his first text translated into English.[53] Here Tafuri characterized the reductive experiments of Rossi and Eisenman as an "architecture of cruelty" – that is, an approach to design that, in its retreat from the functional and social concerns of the real world, could be equated with the libertine sadism of Marquis de Sade. Among others connected with the Milan–Venice axis to contribute articles were Francesco Dal Co, Giorgio Ciucci, Massimo Scolari, and Georges Teyssot. The journal, throughout its notational run of 26 issues (until 1984), therefore composed a wide-ranging tapestry of historical, theoretical, and critical issues, and its chief merit lay in the fact that it was the first American journal of critical substance.

2

The Crisis of Meaning

If Venturi's populism, Italian Rationalism, and the initiatives of the IAUS provided three legs of the platform of postmodern thought, it remains to consider the fourth support upon which much of the theory of the next two decades would be built. It was the widespread perception that modernism had failed because of limited vocabulary – that is, its failure to connect or communicate with people.

In several instances we have already used such terms as "syntactic" and "semantics," words that became increasingly bandied about in the late 1960s. And although both relate to the modern linguistic sciences of semiotics and semiology (which will be used interchangeably here), architectural concern with the meaning of form had been an age-old problem. The earliest texts of both Judaism and Christianity, for instance, describe at length the symbolism applied to such works as the Temple of Jerusalem, while Vitruvius's well known account of the origin of the three Orders – the Doric male, Ionic female, and Corinthian daughter – provides an important insight into the anthropomorphic basis of form in classical times. And Renaissance architects were also explicit in wanting to provide architectural design with an underlying humanist cosmology. By the eighteenth century, as the French Architectural Academy consolidated the tenets of Western theory, the meaning of form had become a well-defined trope within the formal discourse of architecture. What distinguishes these efforts from those of the 1970s is the latter's intention to channel such thinking into a more rigorous model.

Semiology and semiotics – generally speaking, the study of signs – take their start in two distinct foundations. In 1916, in a posthumous publication, there appeared Ferdinand de Saussure's *Course of General Linguistics*,

An Introduction to Architectural Theory: 1968 to the Present, First Edition.
Harry Francis Mallgrave and David Goodman.
© 2011 Harry Francis Mallgrave and David Goodman. Published 2011 by Blackwell Publishing Ltd.

in which the Swiss theorist distinguished the more invariable rules of "language" (*langue*) from the more individual aspects of "speech" (*parole*), both operating through conventional signs and meanings. He called his new science semiology. Also around the turn of the twentieth century, the American philosopher Charles Sanders Peirce proposed a logical study of language that he termed semiotics, a proposition upon which Charles W. Morris elaborated in a more substantial way in his *Foundations of the Theory of Signs* (1938). Against Saussure's dualistic structure, Morris proposed a tripartite model for linguistic analysis by dividing the field into the realms of syntactics, semantics, and pragmatics. He defined syntactics as the "relations of signs to one another in abstraction from the relations of signs to objects or to interpreters" – therefore referring to the rules of syntax or grammar of any sign or linguistic system. Semantics, by contrast, "deals with the relation of signs to their *designata* and so to the objects which they may or do denote." Therefore, semantics deals with the relation of signs to their meanings, which will later emerge as an important area of architectural interest because it considers specifically the meaning of forms. Pragmatics, the third area, considers "the relation of signs to their interpreters."[1]

Morris made one further distinction that would later resonate within architectural circles by dividing semantic signs into the three groups of indices, icons, and symbols. Whereas indexical signs point to or indicate their meaning (a one-way street sign, for example), icons exhibit properties of the content to which they refer (a concession stand in the shape of the item that it sells). Symbols, by contrast, are arbitrary or culturally established signs, such as the use of Doric columns on a bank to denote the strength and security of the financial institution.

What also makes the model of Morris important to architecture was his connection with the "New Bauhaus" in Chicago. This school was founded in 1937 by the Chicago Association of Arts and Industries, and László Moholy-Nagy, a recent refugee to the United States, was named its first director. Although the association pulled out of the venture after one year, Moholy-Nagy reconstituted the school first as the School of Design and later (as it is today known) as the Institute of Design. During the 1940s he, and his successor Serge Chermayeff, put together an impressive faculty that included Gyorgy Kepes, George Fred Keck, Ralph Rapson, and briefly, Buckminster Fuller and Konrad Wachsmann. Morris, who was a professor of philosophy at the University of Chicago, was brought into the school specifically to teach a course on "Intellectual Integration," which was intended to unify theories of art, science, and technology under his theory of signs, based on the premise that every human activity can be analyzed as "a certain type of sign structure."[2] Morris had also been active since the mid-1930s with the movement known as "Unified Science," which – through the efforts of Otto Neurath, Niels Bohr, John Dewey, Bertrand Russell, and Rudolf Carnap – was seeking a theoretical foundation for all knowledge.

Morris taught his course in the early 1940s with little fanfare, but his efforts were recognized a decade later by another Bauhaus second-coming: the Hochschule für Gestaltung, which was founded in 1953 in Ulm, Germany.[3] Several former masters and students of the Bauhaus, among them Johannes Itten, Josef Albers, and Walter Peterhans, were hired by the new school, but the school's first director, Max Bill, struggled with the issue of how closely the new curriculum should follow the original Bauhaus curriculum. Bill resigned his directorship in 1956 during a faculty revolt led by Otl Aicher and Tomás Maldonado, both of whom were aware of the Unified Science movement; and in the following year Maldonado introduced a seminar on semiotics that also incorporated topics in cybernetics, information theory, systems theory, and ergonomics. Maldonado, like Horkheimer and Adorno before him, was intrigued by the persuasive power of the telecommunication industries and advertisers, and he argued that meaning in design "must be studied to its most subtle implications." This objective in turn suggested that designers should also be trained to know the work of "linguists, psychologists, social psychologists and sociologists; and also, of course, the representatives of modern semiotics."[4] Maldonado, as we have seen, moved on to Princeton University in the 1960s.

Semiotics and Architecture

Maldonado made his argument in five essays that appeared in the London journal *Uppercase* in 1962.[5] But even before this date, two architects who had also taught at the Hochschule für Gestaltung – Joseph Rykwert and Christian Norberg-Schulz – were advancing their own interest in meaning. Rykwert, in a fascinating essay of 1960 entitled "Meaning and Building," was, in fact, critical of the Ulm experiment. He was an opponent of the rationalist predilections of high modernists, especially the "preoccupation of designers and architects with rational criteria" for design. Instead, he called for designers to attend to architecture's emotional power – not haphazardly, but rather by drawing upon the research of sociologists, anthropologists, and psychologists, as well as our mythopoetic legacy. Presaging some of the ideas of Venturi and Scott Brown by

several years, he urged architects to study such media as American adver-
tising, and to do so not to copy the lessons but to learn how someone
defines their particular place in the world – be it some "little piece of cas-
tellation or the fretwork on the gable" found on one's home. Semiotics,
he argued, could provide such a framework, but only in a broader sense:
"Through a semantic study of environment we can discover the means of
discoursing in our buildings. Only that way will we be able to appeal to the
common man again."[6] This becomes the theoretical basis from which
Rykwert will later – in 1973 – condemn the typological rationalism and
acute silence of Rossi's designs and the polemics of *Tendenza*.

Norberg-Schulz came to the matter from a different perspective, although
his position would shift diametrically within a few years. In his ambitious
study *Intentions in Architecture* (1963), the Norwegian architect sought
a comprehensive and "satisfactory *theory of architecture*" not just by bringing together the tripartite semiotic scheme of Morris with all "relevant
information from psychology, system theory, and information theory"
(as taught at Ulm), but also by more strenuously probing the boundaries
of meaningful architectural form. Architecture for Norberg-Schulz was "a
synthetic activity which has to adapt itself to the form of life as a whole,"
although he devised his own theory largely on positivistic or quasi-scientific
foundations.[7]

The Ulm experiment, as its curriculum became known, touched off a
flurry of semiotic investigations during the 1960s. Italian theory – in particular the writings of Sergio Bettini, Giovanni Klaus Koenig, Renato De
Fusco, and Umberto Eco – sought to find ways to apply semiotics to architectural theory.[8] In London the initiative was undertaken by two architects
in doctoral programs: the Canadian George Baird and the American Charles
Jencks. In 1966 the two devoted a whole issue of the journal *Arena* to the
issue of semiology – essays that would be expanded three years later in their
influential book *Meaning in Architecture*. At heart, however, there remained
the problem of whether to follow the semiotic model of Morris or the
semiological system of Saussure.

Baird and Jencks initially followed the latter's binary method, and with
some early success. For instance, in the former's essay " 'La Dimension
Amoureuse' in Architecture," Baird compared two recent projects of
Eero Saarinen and Cedric Price through the Saussurean duality of *langue*
(language, collective and unconscious) and *parole* (speech, individual,
conscious, and expressionistic). The details of Baird's analysis – both
Saarinen and Price, in opposite ways, concern themselves excessively
with the *langue* of design at the expense of rhetorical power of *parole* –
provide a measure of insight, but more important is Baird's observation

that architectural meanings share not a one-dimensional concordance with a symbol (as conventional linguistics sometimes suggests) but compose an especially rich field of meanings consisting of metaphor, metonymy, ambiguity, and varying degrees of rhetorical nuance.[9] Similarly, in his main essay from this period, Jencks stressed that meanings are dependent on specific contexts, conventions, or simple accidents, and, moreover (or because of this), they are also often unstable in their shelf life. In a viewpoint that presages poststructural arguments of the following decade he concludes that "the frontiers of meaning are always, momentarily, in a state of collapse and paradox."[10]

The book of Jencks and Baird was so successful in directing interest to this field, that three years later, in 1972, an international conference on architectural semiotics took place in Castedelldefels, Spain.[11] The organizers were Geoffrey Broadbent, Juan Pablo Bonta, and Tomás Llorens, and Peter Eisenman made the trek from New York. Many of the papers at Castedelldefels point to the high expectations now attached to the possibility of architectural semiotics. Broadbent, for example, drew upon Noam Chomsky's research on syntactics, but in a way entirely different from that simultaneously suggested by Eisenman. If the latter was following Chomsky's emphasis on syntactics, Broadbent, in mimicking the algorithmic process of Chomsky's methodology, proposed four "deep structures" for architecture with semantic overtones, from which he further deduced four generational rules or approaches to design: pragmatic (trial-and-error), typologic (types), analogical (analogies), and canonic or geometric design. He went on to consider how Charles Moore and William Turnbull had infused the Faculty Club at Santa Barbara with allusions to the Spanish colonial character of the area, while Ricardo Bofill had drawn upon aspects of the local Mediterranean vernacular in the design of Xanadu – with its strong colors, sweeping lines, and local roof tiles. Both strategies, Broadbent felt, injected modern architecture with a much-needed infusion of meaning and assisted it in becoming a cultural symbol.[12]

The papers of Bonta and Jencks at the conference in Castedelldefels were also significant. Bonta turned away from both the semiotic systems of Saussure and Morris in favor of one by Eric Buyssens and Luis J. Prieto, which focused on communication as a system of indicators and signals. This model allowed him to posit the two additional categories of intentional indicators and pseudo signals: the former indicators intentionally produced by the designer but not recognized by the interpreter, the latter signals unintentionally produced by the designer but read by the interpreter. The advantage of this approach, which Bonta later expanded into his book *Architecture and Its Interpretation* (1979), was that it underscored the omnipresence of meaning in architecture, whether it is intentional or not.[13]

Jencks once again argued on behalf of "rhetoric" – that is, for giving priority to the "symbolic sign" (representation) over and above the "indexical sign" (in his view favored by modernism) and the "iconic sign" (as found in Saarinen's TWA terminal). In this way, he believed, semiotics would not only become a tool for designers but also for critics to employ in considering the failings of modernism.[14] Alan Colquhoun, who also attended the conference, went even further in this regard by insisting that because of the methodological incongruities between language and aesthetics, semiotics should be used only as a critical tool.[15]

Meanwhile, other models of semiotics were also being proffered. At a conference held in Virginia in 1973, Mario Gandelsonas, who was joining Eisenman as one of the three editors at *Oppositions*, was also dubious about applying semiotics to architectural design, in part because he felt that architects had limited knowledge of semiotic concepts, in part because, politically, they had yet to make that vital distinction between ideology and theory.[16] He was, of course, employing ideology in the Marxist sense of false consciousness, whereby ideology preserves existing conditions, including the status quo of architectural practice. In the same year, Gandelsonas and his wife, Diana Agrest, made the same point in an expanded way in their essay published in the first issue of *Oppositions*. Here they argued that semiotics can offer the architect some assistance, but only when "it can also suggest theoretical strategies in our battle against a specific ideology, architectural ideology."[17] Agrest and Gandelsonas, very familiar with the most recent French criticisms of rationalist thought, were, in fact, already straddling the line of poststructural theory.

Also in 1973, Umberto Eco published an English translation of the architectural chapters of his book *La struttura assente* (1968). His version of semiotics, which combined elements of Morris with those of Saussure, viewed architecture as a system of communication whose forms were composed of denotation (function) and connotation (ideology), tentatively read through the lenses of technical, syntactic, and semantic codes. Yet Eco was at the same time interested in advancing semiotics into the realm of design. For one thing, he was interested in architecture's relationship with mass culture, or architecture as a profession seeking mass appeal through techniques of psychological persuasion and thus bound to the short-lived whims of fashion. He also considered (although he was not especially open to it) what he termed "avant-garde subversiveness," in which the architect, in an act of Adornoesque defiance, is charged with intentionally violating conventional codes. These maneuvers, he concluded, effectively conspire to leave any system rather open-ended in its prescriptions, and he instead pointed the architect to contemporary research in sociology, anthropology, and psychology.[18]

All of these efforts mark the first half of the 1970s as the apogee of semiotic interest among architects, but at the same time the lack of success in applying it in any compelling way to the nuances of design was pushing semiotics out of the methodological arena and into the realm of criticism. And in the last regard, semiotics was in many ways the perfect tool to criticize modernism for its willful sparseness of symbolic meaning. It indeed became an important tool for rejecting the tenets of modern theory in the second half of this decade.

Five on Five

It was within this context that the book *Five Architects* appeared in December 1972, and the first significant response to the publication took the form of five essays in the journal *Architectural Forum* simply entitled "Five on Five." The motivating force behind this response was Robert A. M. Stern, who had studied at Yale University under Vincent Scully and who was an advocate on behalf of Robert Venturi. In 1966 Stern had organized a successful exhibition for the Architectural League of New York entitled "40 under 40," which featured the work of younger architects such as Venturi.[19] Three years later Stern produced his first book, *New Directions in American Architecture*, which not only brought the work of Venturi and Charles Moore to the forefront of discussions but also elicited contentious responses from European reviewers because of an "Afterword" in which he aligned their efforts with the social upheaval taking place in the late 1960s.[20] Also in 1969, Stern formed a partnership with his Yale classmate John Hagmann and began his career as a designer, and in the following year he joined the faculty at Columbia University.

"Five on Five" is a critique of the work of the New York Five by the architects Stern, Moore, Jaquelin T. Robertson, Allan Greenberg, and Romaldo Giurgola.[21] In the opening essay Stern noted the near simultaneous appearance of *Five Architects* with Venturi and Scott Brown's *Learning from Las Vegas*, and this seeming coincidence, in his view, spelled out competing strategies that defined the two alternative camps: the "European/idealist" outlook of the Five against the "American/pragmatic" perspective of Venturi, the "exclusive" against the "inclusive" in their respective assimilation of the present and past. One was also good, the other much less so. If the inclusive *Learning from Las Vegas* was "helping us at least to break from the hot-house aesthetics of the 1920s" by bringing diverse influences into design, the "exclusive" tendencies of the Five, led by Colin Rowe ("the intellectual guru of the group"), were effectively returning architects to the limited aesthetics of Le Corbusier and the 1920s, and thereby depriving contemporary architects of their own chance to engage in revolution. Stern "most vehemently" objected to Eisenman's Chomskian effort to "divorce architectural experience from culture." He also censured Richard Meier for poor design at the Smith House, and for choosing shoddy exterior finishes at the Saltzman House. He found the work of Michael Graves to be burdened with too much "technique" and "inflation," a criticism that Stern also extended to the "slick" production of the book *Five Architects.*[22]

The responses of the other four architects pursued a similar line of criticism. Greenberg decried the Five for adhering to the European "official line" of modernism (as advanced by Nikolaus Pevsner, Sigfried Giedion, and, more recently, Banham), while Giurgola objected to the obsessive formalism of their work, which he felt was based on a "slippery dialectic, learned citation, aesthetic exclusivism and basic indifference."[23] Moore, with considerable irony, admitted to liking some of the forms of "the 'Cardboard Corbu' people," but found their various attempts to explain them lacking conviction.[24] Robertson, in the longest and most thoughtful of the essays, gave faint praise to the Five's "buildings *as* drawings," but also found them contextually unappealing in their elitist allegiance to the "museum world" of high art. In summary, the resurrection of the neo-Corbusian "style, unpopular from the outset, is not now in good health, and is only being maintained precariously in a special isolation wing through the donated intravenous feeding of the 'art world.' "[25]

The editors of *Architectural Forum* also weighed in and referred to the criticisms of the five respondents as merely a "confrontation between various philosophical camps" – if to some the criticisms seemed somewhat severe in tone, they were in fact little more than professional jousting.[26] This view is similar to that taken by Paul Goldberger, who reviewed the book and the five responding essays a few months later. He appreciated the "stimulating" outlines of the debate, although he found the fact that the discussion was restricted to two ivy-league circles in the Northeast (Cornell and Yale) "somewhat parochial." More insightfully, he also recognized that the design sympathies of the two camps were in truth greater than their essential differences. One attribute in common was their "indifference to megastructures, computer design, and other examples of super technology." Another was their elitism, or better still, their embrace of history. The inclusivist architects, in Goldberger's view, simply drew their symbols from a broader array of sources, whereas their supposed adversaries restricted their stylistic revival mostly, although not entirely, to the forms of Le Corbusier.[27]

Gray and White

Yet the provincial nature of this debate would not last for long, because in the spring of 1974 a conference was called at UCLA. Variously titled "Four Days in May" or "White and Gray Meet Silver," it was in fact the last of the CASE conferences (the group founded by Eisenman and Graves in 1965), this time hosted by Tom Vreeland, Cesar Pelli, Anthony Lumsden, Craig Hodgetts, and Eugene Kupper. Here labels were affixed to the competing camps, as the New York Five became the "Whites" and their adversaries, led by Venturi and Stern, became the "Grays." The hosting architects, all of whom had migrated to Los Angeles, were still hesitant to declare themselves the "Silvers," but it was by all accounts a lively affair. Scully served as the apologist for the Grays, while Rowe was summoned to defend the honor of the Whites, although not without "feeling like a Marxist when confronted with so many large single-family houses."[28] The up-and-coming Japanese journal *a + u: Architecture and Urbanism* devoted a special issue to the gathering – a clear sign that the new movement had media traction.[29]

In the following year, 1975, two events further stoked publicity. One was a draft version of Colin Rowe and Fred Koetter's later book "Collage City," which first appeared in the pages of *Architectural Review*. The second was a retrospective exhibition at the Museum of Modern Art entitled "The Architecture of the Ecole des Beaux-Arts."

Rowe's essay "Collage City" is perhaps the less influential of the two, yet it is significant in that he effectively resigned from the camp of the Whites to embrace the historical proclivities of the Grays. In a work that touches upon everything from Thomas More's ethical utopia to the dynamiting of Minouru Yamasaki's Pruit-Igoe housing project in Saint Louis, Rowe, in his criticisms of the failure of late modernism, spared none of its trappings. He scorned the technological fantasies of Archigram as well as the feigned nostalgia of Harlow, and the telltale sign of his Popperian faith in tradition is found in his appropriation of Isaiah Berlin's distinction between the hedgehog and fox. The former is someone who knows (and designs) one big thing; the latter is someone who knows (and designs) many small things. For the present era, Rowe prefers the fox. Therefore

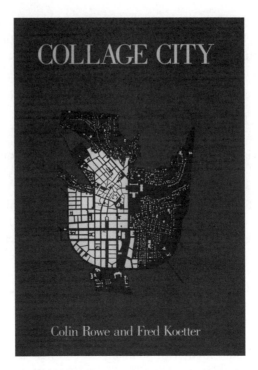

Figure 2.1   Cover of *Collage City*, by Colin Rowe and Fred Koetter, published by The MIT Press, © MIT 1979.

the complex at Versailles, with its geometrically determined forms, was the creation of a hedgehog, while the somewhat random collection of smaller buildings of Hadrian's Villa at Tivoli bore the mark of a fox. Palladio, Mies, Fuller, and Frank Lloyd Wright were all hedgehogs. Giulio Romano, Nicholas Hawksmoor, John Soane, and Edwin Lutyens were all foxes. Modernism's early fascination with "total design" was rejected in favor of Claude Levi-Strauss's notion of a *bricoleur*, that is, someone who works with existing elements in a modest way. This metaphor in fact circumscribed Rowe's entire urban theory, as he now admitted that "it is better to think of an aggregation of small, and even contradictory set pieces (almost like the products of different régimes) than to entertain fantasies about total and 'faultless' solutions which the condition of politics can only abort."[30] The urban planner should now approach the design of the city like someone making a collage, that is, by inserting or assembling pieces within a pre-existing context, though not without the avant-garde virtues of obliquity and irony. What is also interesting is that many of his preferred images were of Roman and Renaissance prototypes. Giambattista Nolli's eighteenth-century map of Rome was the new paradigm for this early version of postmodernism.

The exhibition "The Architecture of the Ecole des Beaux-Arts" inflicted an even deeper bruise on the professional status quo. The show, consisting of 240 drawings, was curated by Arthur Drexler and quickly proved to be an extravaganza in its own right. Not only were the eighteenth- and nineteenth-century drawings in themselves a stunning and somewhat nostalgic throwback to a nearly forgotten age, but the essays contained in the book that grew out of the exhibition – written by Richard Chaffee, Neil Levine, and David Van Zanten – constituted some of the first historical investigations of nineteenth-century French theory. Therefore, above all of its affectations, it was a rare display of scholarship.

Drexler, who had been with the Museum of Modern Art since 1951, first served as Philip Johnson's assistant before taking over the directorship of the Architecture and Design Department of the museum in 1954. As we have seen, he became the chair of the board of the IAUS in 1967, and on behalf of the museum he wrote short prefaces for both Robert Venturi's *Complexity and Contradiction in Architecture* and the catalogue *Five Architects*. His views regarding modernism, once compatible with those of Hitchcock and Johnson's *International Style*, had likewise evolved. In his Preface to the Beaux-Arts catalog, he characterized the "messianic fervor" of Bauhaus modernism as "naïve when it is not actually destructive," although he also admitted that the new freedom growing out of the "relaxation of dogma" had not presently found a suitable outlet or direction. In his view, the architecture of the Ecole des Beaux-Arts merits study, if only because these accomplished drawings might provoke "a more rigorous critique of philosophical assumptions underlying the architecture of our time."[31]

In his lengthier essay for the book *The Architecture of the Ecole des Beaux-Arts* (1977), Drexler modified his position by embracing the materiality (appearance of mass) as well as the delineatory aspects of nineteenth-century architecture, including its use of ornament. This was not simply a rejection of modernism's "pursuit of an absolute" and the austere forms of its "engineering style" in favor of an architecture that allows "drawing as scenography" but a far more sweeping retreat from the Fullerian touchstone of ephemeralization. In essence the "significant post-modern fantasy of architectural form makes mass and weight serve as symbolic assertions of the free spirit, contradicting the earlier rationalist commitment to a determinist architecture based on structural and economic necessities." Consequently, our "fantasy now is to escape from dematerialization, which we associate not with the world to come but with the disorientating technological world of the here and now. The new image of hope is earthbound."[32]

No less interesting were the critical reviews for the show and its publications. Writing for the British journal *Architectural Design*, Robin Middleton seemed almost giddy with delight in pointing out that Drexler, the "worthy successor to Philip Johnson, American mandarin of the modern movement" has flipped in his design sympathies. "He now loathes the architecture that the modern movement has spawned," he notes, "and is intent to make known his disillusion."[33] Ada Louise Huxtable, writing for the *New York Times*, also saw the exhibition within the broader context of a "counter revolution," one in which "the gospel according to Giedion and Gropius that preached functional and formal purity and rejection of the past – is being increasingly debated and denied." If the exhibition at the Museum of Modern Art had not produced the "expected shock waves," it was only because architecture's new "young Turks" had in fact already embraced the creed of "historical eclecticism."[34]

Variations on a Theme

Both Rowe's embrace of historicism and the Beaux-Arts exhibition created a problem for Peter Eisenman. In effect they scored for the Gray camp, and the exhibition had even taken place on turf that Eisenman at this time must have regarded as largely his own. Not surprisingly, his reply shortly followed. In January 1976, through the auspices of the IAUS, he called a special "Forum" at the museum to discuss the exhibition, in which the selected reviewers were generally negative. George Baird acknowledged the success of the museum's "intent to shock," but at the same time he feared that the exhibit might eventually lead to "a resurgent vulgar historicism" in the tradition of Minoru Yamasaki and Edward Durell Stone.[35] Ulrich Franzen professed amusement at the "sudden and divine revelation" that modern architecture was now declared dead, while Paul Rudolph labeled the "highly seductive and finally nostalgic prettified drawings" as suitable for "presentation only."[36] Denise Scott Brown was one of the few responders to dissent. In comments submitted in writing, she vilified the Museum of Modern Art – a "Johnny-come-lately to the Beaux-Arts scene" – for picking up a legitimate theme for an exhibition but for all the wrong reasons, chief of which was the Beaux-Arts tradition of elitism. She challenged the institution to step down from its pedestal and tackle such issues as "social relevance, openness to the pluralist aesthetic and understanding of the everyday environment."[37]

In the summer and fall of 1976, Gandelsonas and Eisenman also weighed in with editorials in *Oppositions*, both of which sought to reframe recent developments in different terms. In his editorial "Neo-Functionalism," Gandelsonas argued that there were two competing ideologies that had developed since the late 1960s: neo-rationalism and neo-realism. Whereas the former perspective, defined by the ideas of Rossi, Eisenman, and Hejduk, sought an autonomous language for architecture "that speaks about itself" and therefore transcends history and culture, neo-realism took its start in the thought of Venturi and embraces the multitude of historical and cultural forces. Yet these two ideologies, Gandelsonas dissented, were united in their "Manichean view of functionalism as a negative and regressive ideology," and in this sense both were only continuing or "developing fragments" of functionalism. In rejecting the symbolic limits of earlier functionalism (where form simply symbolized function), Gandelsonas put forth the alternative of a "neo-functionalism," essentially a new synthesis uniting the neo-realist and neo-rationalist critiques around the issue of meaning. In effect, the idea of neo-functionalism would seek to introduce "the problem of meaning within the process of design in a systematic and conscious way," presumably within the framework of semiotic theory.[38]

Eisenman took a new very different tack in the succeeding issue of the journal and broke new ground with his editorial "Post-Functionalism." Keenly sensitive to the recent atmospheric changes, he began by noting that the "critical establishment" has informed us that we have entered a new era of "post-modernism," for which he felt a sense of relief, "similar to that which accompanies the advice that one is no longer an adolescent." The two poles of this new era had been defined by the exhibition in Milan in 1973 and by the Beaux-Arts exhibition of the previous year. If the former sought to return architecture to an autonomous discipline, the latter, with its embrace of history, sought to chart the future course of architecture in the past. Both trends, however, were false metrics, for both logically still operated within the definitional relationship of form (or type) and function (or program). Hence, both remained within the epistemological confines of Renaissance humanism. Not only did the functionalists of the 1920s oversimplify the form-function relationship, but lately English revisionist functionalists, such as Reyner Banham and Cedric Price, had even posited a type of "neo-functionalism" with their spirited idealization of technology. Functionalism in every guise, for Eisenman, must therefore be seen as a "species of positivism."[39]

Eisenman responded with the supposition that indeed a critical shift in Western thought did take place sometime in the nineteenth century – the shift from humanism to modernism – although architecture had of yet not partaken in the implications of this shift. If other arts, such as music and literature, toyed with post-humanist concepts of abstraction, atonality, and atemporality, architecture had remained fixed in its form/function duality, based on the premise that man was still the *"originating agent"* in the creation of form. Eisenman aligned this new *"episteme"* (a reference to Michel Foucault) with "post-functionalism," a "modernist *dialectic*" that exploited the tendency to view form as a pre-existing geometry or, conversely, to read form "as a series of fragments – signs without meaning dependent upon, and without reference to, a more basic condition." The term "post-functionalism" therefore admitted to this "absence," the absence of the human being as the centering agent of the world. Architecturally, this was the "new consciousness" falling upon us.[40]

Eisenman's essay is important for two reasons. First, it signaled his break with both the Italian Rationalists and with the New York Five. Second, it revealed his new-found fascination with European poststructural theory, which at the time (in the United States at least) had few admirers. Nevertheless, events were moving too quickly and indeed were overshadowing the significance of his announcement. In April 1976 a group of West Coast architects – consisting of Thomas Vreeland, Anthony Lumsden, Frank Dimster, Paul Kennon, Eugene Kupper, and Cesar Pelli – put together an exhibition at UCLA under the banner of the "Silvers." John Hejduk, James Stirling, Charles Moore, and Charles Jencks all came to town. This event was followed one month later with another exhibition at Pelli's newly completed Pacific Design Center, which displayed the work of the "Los Angeles Twelve." Little united the work of the exhibitors, except perhaps a fondness for glass, detailed in such a way as to minimize mullion or surface disturbances. Charles Jencks, however, was especially enamored with Pelli's "Blue Whale," and he summarized the work of the Silvers as "unmistakably in the Stick-Tech tradition of Neutra, Eames, Soriano, Ellwood and Koenig" – all those architects Banham had referred to in his book, *Los Angeles: The Architecture of Four Ecologies*, as "The Style That Nearly Didn't Make it."[41]

Not wanting to be left out in the cold, the Midwest soon marched out its postmodern regiment known as "The Chicago Seven."[42] The impulse here was a German exhibition that was making its way to the shores of Lake Michigan entitled "100 Years of Architecture in Chicago." It honored the first Chicago school at the turn of the twentieth century and the Miesean tradition after 1938.[43] Protesting the narrowness of this historical selection (thereby omitting many Chicago modernists during the intervening years), Stuart E. Cohen and Stanley Tigerman prepared a counter-exhibition, "Chicago Architects," which first opened in 1976 at Cooper Union before running concurrently with the German show in

Figure 2.2 Stanley Tigerman, "The Titanic," © Stanley Tigerman, Tigerman McCurry Architects, 1979.

Chicago.[44] Tigerman, who was a graduate of Yale, was a friend of both Eisenman and Hejduk, and he was intent on opening up another front to the debate. And the alternative exhibition was followed by two additional exhibitions – "Seven Chicago Architects" and "Exquisite Corpse" – as well as a spirited colloquium that took place at the Graham Foundation in October 1977.[45] The panel included representatives of the Whites, Grays, Silvers, as well as Jencks, James Stirling, and Toshio Nakamura. Among other notable productions related to this burst of activity was Tigerman's famous paean to a sinking of the Miesian Crown Hall – *The Titanic (1978)* – and the tongue-in-cheek, twin-volume series of "Late Entries" to the Chicago Tribune Competition of 1922 submitted by architects from the 1970s.[46]

Finally, in the summer of 1976, Robert Stern once again took it upon himself to set in order the ever more confusing events with an article in the French journal *L'architecture d'aujourd'hui* – in large part by repeating what he had proclaimed earlier. He now defined the new phenomenon of "Post-Modern" architecture (the "close" of modern architecture is

conceded) essentially and exclusively as a friendly competition between
the White and Gray camps. Eisenman's melancholic notion of "Post-
Functionalism" is juxtaposed to Stern's own vision of "Post-Modernism,"
which he defines as "a kind of philosophical pragmatism or pluralism
which builds upon messages from "orthodox Modernism' as well as from
other defined historical trends." Modernism, for Stern, begins in the middle of the eighteenth century, and what is called the Modern Movement is
but the starkly "puritanical phase" of the style. Central in Stern's vision of
"Post-Modernism" is his argument that the public never accepted the
abstract language of this puritanical phase, hence it now warmly embraces
the recovery of the "the poetic tradition of design" that was just put on
display at the Beaux-Arts exhibition.[47]

From this position, Stern articulates the principal strategies of postmodernism, among them the use of ornament and explicit historical reference,
eclecticism, incomplete or compromised geometries, voluntary distortions, and buildings being allowed to change over time. Above all, Gray
buildings "have facades which tell stories," a narrational outlook that he
traces to the cultural and landscape theories of Vincent Scully, to Neil
Levine's semiotic reading of Beaux-Arts forms, and to George Hersey's
"studies on the associationism of mid-nineteenth-century English architecture." All of this, of course, is diametrically opposed to the "White"
architects, who limit themselves to the modernist forms of the 1920s.[48]

Two years later Stern again exalted the Grays as the "first post-modern
generation of architects," succeeding three phases of modernism. The
first generation of modernists flourished in the 1920s; the second, in the
1950s and 1960s; and the third generation are represented by the Whites,
now reduced to Richard Meier, Charles Gwathmey, and Peter Eisenman.
Stern was buoyed by the fact that Romaldo Giurgola and Michael Graves
had recently come over to the side of the Grays, and he succinctly summarized the Gray's design strategies by their use of contextualism, allusionism, and ornamentalism. Stern, as he had done nearly a decade earlier,
also tied the birth of postmodernism to the liberalism of the Kennedy
years, to the anguish of the Johnson presidency and the Vietnam War,
and to the "almost tragic dimension" of the Nixon years.[49] This rather
facile political rationalization of theory is relevant only because Stern was
well aware that he was also battling forces on another front. To many
European Marxists, American postmodernism, as it was becoming defined,
was nothing less than political surrender – a capitulation to the forces of
capitalist and commercial exploitation.

3

Early Postmodernism

The first actual use of the term "post-modernism" to define a stylistic period is unclear. Joseph Hudnut employed the term in an essay of 1945 when he wrote in defense of humanist design values and as a critique of the industrial houses of Walter Gropius.[1] The historian Nikolaus Pevsner again adopted the term in 1966, but in a pejorative sense of antimodernism.[2] The term was also bandied about in 1974 by "Robert Stern, Paul Goldberger, Arthur Drexler and other New Yorkers," according to Charles Jencks, but no paper trail seems to exist.[3] And in 1975, Joseph Rykwert referred to the "post-Modern Movement style of Paul Rudolph."[4] The tipping point, however, appears to have been the essay Charles Jencks published in the fall of 1975, "The Rise of Post Modern Architecture."[5] From this moment forward, the term rather quickly insinuates itself into architectural currency.

Since completing his doctoral work at London University in 1970, Jencks, a native of Baltimore, had remained attached to London circles. Between 1971 and 1974 he published no fewer than four books, perhaps the most important of which was his *Modern Movements in Architecture* (1973).[6] Its timing, nevertheless, was somewhat premature in that it appeared a year or two before the decisive nature of the changes affecting architecture became fully evident. In another study of 1972, coauthored with Nathan Silver, Jencks championed the cause of adhocism in design, which he saw – similarly to Colin Rowe – as the logical alternative to the bulldozer and the planning policies of a central governmental authority.[7] In still another essay written for *Architectural Design* in 1973, Jencks applauded "Ersatz in LA," in which he, with considerable irony, commended the semantic playfulness of Grauman's Chinese Theater in

An Introduction to Architectural Theory: 1968 to the Present, First Edition.
Harry Francis Mallgrave and David Goodman.
© 2011 Harry Francis Mallgrave and David Goodman. Published 2011 by Blackwell Publishing Ltd.

Hollywood, the Big Donut Drive In, and "Room 8," a plot in a pet cemetery prepared for a cat.[8] He was at this time also establishing a home in Los Angeles.

All of these themes are woven together in the essay "The Rise of Post Modern Architecture," a moniker he chose with some hesitation. As he explains his choice of words:

> The only way to kill off the monster is to find a substitute beast to take its place and decidedly 'Post Modern' won't do the job. We need a new way of thinking, a new paradigm based on broad theory, which enjoys a large consensus. No such theory or consensus exists at the moment and it is in the nature of the case that such things take a long time to develop – perhaps another 20 years.[9]

Jencks proceeded to consider the earlier criticisms of modernism by the Smithsons, Aldo van Eyck, and other members of Team 10, but he also asserted that their alternative architectural language had remained abstract and for the most part impersonal in its expression. Against the backdrop of these failed attempts at reform, Jencks upholds the strategies of social realism (the sociology of Jane Jacobs), advocacy planning, restoration and preservation, adhocism, Ersatz design, radical traditionalism, and political reorganization as the most promising long-term strategies. With words recalling the outlook of the nineteenth-century architect Thomas L. Donaldson, Jencks also names semiotics and radical eclecticism as the specific tools to carry out the dirty deed:

> Today's designers have not mastered different codes. The result is that architects remain under-employed and the pluralism of the city is stifled. If the architect were trained in four or five different styles, then he could control the ways his forms communicate with much greater effect. A radical eclecticism would be born, reflecting the actual variety of the city and its subcultures.[10]

The Language of Postmodernism

The 20 years that Jencks had foreseen as necessary to create a new style would soon conflate rather dramatically. For scarcely two years had elapsed when he – in 1977 – published his best-selling book, *The Language of Post-Modern Architecture*. The architect and critic, now drawing upon his semiotic studies, no longer had any doubts that the death of modernism had indeed taken place. Indeed, he was almost precise in giving the exact

minute of modernism's demise: "July 15, 1972, at 3:32 p.m. (or therea-
bouts) when the infamous Pruit-Igoe scheme, or rather several of its slab
blocks, were given the final *coup de grâce* by dynamite."[11] He was, of
course, referring the demolition of Yamasaki's crime-ridden and much
vandalized urban-renewal project in Saint Louis, which housing authorities mercifully dispatched with explosives after it had become the symbol
of the failed urban renewal strategies of the 1950s and 1960s.

Jencks's book was successful on many levels, as its numerous reprints
have since demonstrated. In its original form, it was a sleek and voguish
visual production, rather lavishly produced with a multitude of color
images (relatively rare at the time), discussions of historical and contemporary buildings, as well as architectural and pop-cultural allusions – ranging
from John Nash's Royal Pavilion at Brighton to a waterbed scene from the
James Bond film *Diamonds Are Forever*. The text runs parallel and somewhat
independent of the captioned images, allowing the "hurriedreader," to
whom Sigfried Giedion once referred, to ignore the main text for the most
part and read the book through the illustrations and captions.[12] And if, for
Jencks, Mies van der Rohe becomes the depreciated poster child of modernism's disdained "univalent architecture" (architectural signs based on
one or a very few meanings), the German architect does not stand alone
in his uncommunicative disgrace. Frank Lloyd Wright, Gordon Bunshaft,
I. M. Pei, Aldo Rossi, and Herman Hertzberger, among others, are also
issued citations for their semiotic muteness, whereas Eero Saarinen, Jørn
Utzon, and Le Corbusier escape with a warning ticket, if only because of
the "superabundance of metaphorical responses" evoked in their respective designs for the TWA Terminal, the Sydney Opera, and the chapel at
Ronchamp.[13] The few architects praised for their early postmodernist
essays include Ricardo Bofill (Walden Seven), Richard Rogers and Renzo
Piano (Pompidou Centre), Michael Graves (early houses), and Cesar Pelli
(the Blue Whale). The kitsch of Beverly Hills and the lure of the silver
screen holds a particular fascination for Jencks. For the psychedelic semi-
otician now informs the reader, among other facts, that Jane Fonda, in the
movie *Barbarella*, was "always shown surrounded with viscous, shiny plastic and soft, hairy fur."[14] Never before had architectural theory been presented in such tactile terms.

It is only when the hurried reader arrives at the final chapter that one
learns what the author really means by polyvalent (or "radical schizo-
phrenic") architecture. It is the historical eclecticism of Robert Stern,
Robert Venturi, Charles Moore, William Turnbull, Minoru Takeyama, and
Ralph Erskine, among others. Jencks therefore comes down on the side of
the Grays, whose semiotic language is responsive to multiple codes – that

is, "towards the traditional slow-changing codes and particular ethnic meanings of a neighbourhood, and towards the fast-changing codes of architectural fashion and professionalism."[15] Jencks generally prefers the latter, and
postmodernism, in his view, generally marches to a lighter rhythm.

   One theme that reappears throughout the book is the issue of metaphor. The limitation of early modernism, for instance, was its adoption of
the "factory metaphor" or "machine metaphor" with all of the industrial
hardness that such an analogy suggests. The TWA terminal and Sydney
Opera gain their popularity from their evident suggestions of birds, sails,
and turtles, but this interpretation of metaphor at the same time restricts
it to the somewhat superficial level of buildings-as-objects – a broader
limitation inherent in semiotic efforts to conceptualize the architectural
experience. Jencks himself, in the last pages of his book, seems to recognize this limitation by raising an interesting allegory. For another example
for the multivalent cause is none other than the variegated, dragon-like
form perched across the roof of Antonio Gaudi's Casa Battló in Barcelona
(1904–1906), sometimes referred to as the "House of Bones." Jencks

Figure 3.1   Antonio Gaudi, Casa Battló, Barcelona (1904–1906). Image courtesy
of Romina Canna.

admits he had struggled with the meaning of this design until a clue from the architect David Mackay helped him decipher its anarchist allusion. For here the three-dimensional cross of Barcelona's patron saint – St George – is slaying the dragon of the political body of Spain in warfare, and the bones and skulls below refer to the dead martyrs of the Catalonian separatist struggle. Thus, the idea of revolution obviously remains prominent within Jencks's thinking, but his concluding remarks less militantly draw the reader back to topic at hand:

> For an architect's primary and final role is to express the meanings a culture finds significant, as well as elucidate certain ideas and feelings that haven't previously reached expression. The jobs that too often take up his energy might be better done by engineers and sociologists, but no other profession is specifically responsible for articulating meaning and seeing that the environment is sensual, humorous, surprising and coded as a readable text. This is the architect's job and pleasure, not, let us hope, ever again his 'problem.'[16]

Consummation in Venice

Jencks's book was only the first push in a more strategically planned campaign. It appeared in 1977 almost simultaneously with a special issue of *Architectural Design*, edited by Jencks, which brought together Charles Moore, Paul Goldberger, and Geoffrey Broadbent, among others, to discuss Jencks's book and the new phenomenon of postmodernism. Moore applauds Jencks's analysis of modernism but finds his prescription for "radical eclecticism" incomplete in that it, with its single-minded emphasis on communication, neglects the sensory dimension of the architectural experience, "the way we feel about buildings – how light animates them and the breezes flow through them, and how they engage our bodies and give us a sense of where we are and cause our spirits to soar, as perhaps the spaces themselves soar."[17] Goldberger supports postmodernism's desire for "indulgent complexity," but at the same time he too is hesitant about the "predominance of image, the tendency to let image determine form rather than vice versa."[18] Broadbent, in a lengthy analysis, not only provides a summary of the book but also faults it for both its imprecise terminology and trivialization of architecture, by which one tends "to think of it [architecture] only as a visual matter."[19]

Toward the end of 1977 Jencks followed with a revised draft of the book's final chapter, which appeared in *Inland Architect*. Entitled

"The 'Tradition' of Post-Modern Architecture," the author now finds the roots of the postmodern experience in sources as varied as BBPR's Torre Velasca, Paolo Portoghesi's Casa Baldi, Eero Saarinen's Gothic-inspired dormitories at Yale University, and even in the "semi-historicism" of Philip Johnson, Manoru Yamasaki, Edward Durrell Stone, and Wallace Harrison.[20] The store of postmodernism has also been expanded to include, among many examples, the John Paul Getty Museum in Malibu, images from Rowe and Koetter's *Collage City*, James Stirling, the "*soi-disant* Stalinist" Maurice Culot, the nihilism of Archizoom and Architext, and the poetic surrealism of Hejduk and Tigerman.

It is a rapidly expanding genealogy, so much so that one of the more interesting problems Jencks faces is a "case for the Straight Revivalists" – that is, architects such as Raymond Erith and Quinlan Terry who, in their historical faithfulness to pre-modern prototypes, effectively deny modernism altogether.[21] In this regard Jencks turns to the sociology of Conrad Jameson to resolve the issue. Adopting the latter's plea for an urban architecture as "social craft" (civic architecture for the public realm and removed from the elitist hegemony of professional tastes), Jencks makes the neo-vernacular efforts of the present fall rather seamlessly in line with such past vernacular examples as Joseph Esherick's Cannery in San Francisco. Only the rigidly metaphysical world of Aldo Rossi, who "fails to understand how symbolism works," poses an insoluble taxonomic problem for Jencks, but this issue is also symptomatic of the previously discussed European/Anglo-American divide.[22]

The crowning effort in all of this critical élan, however, was the Venice Biennale of 1980, curated by Paolo Portoghesi. Thematically entitled "The Presence of the Past," the prestigious international event, highlighted by Aldo Rossi's moored Teatro del Mondo, in many ways consolidated the near-delirium of the late 1970s. Portoghesi stepped forth to echo the enthusiasm of his Anglo-American colleagues by proclaiming that "a 'Post-Modern condition' exists, created by the rapid structural change of our civilization," one that seeks the "return of architecture to the womb of history and its recycling in new syntactic contexts of the traditional forms." It was a delicate line that Portoghesi sought to straddle, as his liberal choices of what constituted postmodernism was bound to offend many Europeans. Frampton was so put off by individual participants and even the use of the term "Post-Modern" that he withdrew his participation from the event with sharp words: "I see this Biennale as a pluralist-cum Post-Modernist manifestation; I am not at all sure that I subscribe to this position, and I think I will have to keep my distance from it."[23]

One focal point of the controversy, clearly, was the exhibition *Strada Novissima* (new street) installed within the Arsenale, for which

20 international architects were summoned to design contiguous facades and demonstrate the new style's return to urban themes. Thus, architects as formally diverse as Frank O. Gehry, Allan Greenberg, Hans Hollein, Arata Isozaki, Massimo Scolari, Michael Graves, and Stanley Tigerman were asked to combine their variegated design talents. Within the main exhibition, the works of no fewer than 76 architects were shown in what was, once again, a generous interpretation of the new trend. Portoghesi admitted that his decision to expand upon Rossi's exhibition of 1973 by bringing together work of the Rossi school with the "radical eclectics" championed by Jencks was a legitimate point of contention, but he also defended it on the grounds that differences in theory should not result in omissions.

Essays by Vincent Scully and Charles Jencks, among others, rounded out the catalogue. Scully's genealogy of American postmodernism began with Louis Kahn and Venturi, although he later supported Portoghesi in finding sympathetic chords in the work of the Krier brothers, Maurice Culot, and Rem Koolhaas.[24] Jencks was likewise insistent on the broad nature of the present movement, the two leading ideas of which were, in fact, its plenitude and pluralism.[25]

And if within popular American media the word "postmodernism" needed one final exclamation point, it would be found in Tom Wolfe's best-selling book of 1981, *From Bauhaus to Our House*, which with much flair – echoing the viewpoints of Venturi and Jencks – proclaimed the victory of the new style.[26] The success of the book also documents that by the end of the 1970s postmodernism had moved well beyond the realm of artistic theory and had insinuated itself with the larger academic culture.

European Counterpoints

Not surprisingly, one of the sterner critics of Portoghesi's variegated production at the Venice Biennale was Manfredo Tafuri. Since the Milan Triennale of 1973, the Marxist historian had generally made his peace with the rationalist movement, just as he had lost his patience with aesthetic concerns of the New York Five. In 1980 he was even more adamantly opposed to having Rossi's work paired alongside the postmodern rhetorical productions of Charles Jencks and Robert Stern, two architects whom he would, at a later date, rather disdainfully relegate to the nefarious realm of "opinion-makers."[27] Tafuri was also aware that the regional sensitivities and early "neobaroque experiments" of Portoghesi (who had also written a major history of the baroque period) varied fundamentally in their theoretical roots from the unfettered eclecticism practiced by many Americans. Thus, locutions such as "a hedonistic urge and a taste for citation," "pastiche," "kitsch," and "facile effects" find their way into Tafuri's later chronicle of Portoghesi's Biennale. And Tafuri was equally dissatisfied with the new appellation "postmodern." Alluding to a book of Friedrich Nietzsche, he makes this point forcefully:

> It is not clear that this signifies a true turning point. On the contrary, the most superficial characteristics of the "modern" have been taken to extremes. We are left not with a "gay science," but with a "gay errancy" dominated by a perfect equating of form and meaning, by annulling history in reducing it to a field of visual incursions, and by a *choc* technique informed by television: in the end, a *fiction-architecture* comfortably establishes itself in the computer age. There is good reason to label such a mixture of components as *hypermodern*.[28]

Tafuri was indeed correct on at least one count. Since the Milan Triennale of 1973, the rationalists had pursued an ideological path quite different from that of their American colleagues – other than in their respective concerns with history. Rossi remained at the head of this contingent, as he filled out his portfolio in the 1970s with the completion of the Modena Cemetery (1973–1980), the primary school Fagnano Olona (1974–1977), and the floating theater that came to symbolize the Venice Biennale.

Yet what was indeed changing by 1980 was that the center of the rationalist movement was shifting northward to urban centers in Austria, Belgium, Germany, and England. Leading the way in this regard were the brothers Rob and Léon Krier, natives of Luxembourg. Rob had been trained at the Technical University in Munich and had worked in the German offices of O. M. Ungers and Frei Otto. In 1970, prior to accepting a faculty position in Vienna, he began composing an urban typology, which he published in German as *Stadtraum in Theorie und Praxis* (1975), and in English under the title *Urban Space* (1979).[29] Dedicated to the nineteenth-century urban theorist Camillo Sitte and written with a soft polemical edge, the book was nevertheless a forceful and effective indictment of European planning policies over the previous two centuries, particularly the erosion of historical urban space in areas rebuilt after World War II. Krier countered with page after page of historical and typological schemes for the street and square, all of which supported his argument that building facades should return to the sidewalk and planners should emphasize the morphological definition of urban spaces. Paths for people and automobiles should also be strictly separated, but key to his presentation is the sometimes medieval, sometimes baroque, sometimes neoclassical nature of his spatial conceptions, following upon such pre-ferred urban models as Sienna, Nancy, Bath, and Madrid.

The work and writings of his brother Léon, eight years his junior, dis-play a similar urban passion, albeit with a more militant, quasi-Ruskinian tone. After briefly attending the University of Stuttgart, Léon migrated to London, where he worked in the office of James Stirling in the 1960s and later joined the faculty at the Architectural Association. He entered several competitions with Stirling and J. P. Kleihues (in whose Berlin office he also worked), but the defining event of his early career was his involvement with the Milan Triennale of 1973, which brought his ideas in line with the rationalist movement. As a follow-up, he organized the exhibition "Rational Architecture" for London's Art Net Gallery in 1975, which introduced these tenets to a British audience that – after their own bad experiences with postwar reconstruction – would become quite receptive to them. Krier was also the organizational hand behind the book *Rational Architecture*, which appeared three years later.

The book, in its illustrations, falls only a little short of being a polemical masterpiece. Laid out in a manageable format, it is structured into typo-logical chapters considering the urban themes of streets, squares, and blocks, monuments, motorways, and gardens. Images are generally kept small and densely packed on the pages, but they are powerfully accentu-ated where necessary. For example, one sketch with isolated Corbusian forms populating a landscape is crossed out with two thick red lines; above, a De Chiricoesque scheme for student housing in Chieti, designed by Giorgio Grassi, A. Monestiroli, and Raffaele Conti, is proffered as the preferred urban alternative. In the book's introductory essay, Robert L. Delevoy asserts that the aim of the study is to put forward "a *theory*, the absence of which has been cruelly felt since the decade 1930–1940."[30]

Hyperbole aside – the book indeed offers a well-articulated critique of contemporary planning issues as well as a definition of rationalism. Anthony Vidler takes on the task of the latter with his essay "The Third Typology," an analysis that also appeared as his inaugural editorial for the journal *Oppositions*. His contention was that prior to the 1960s two typologies had appeared within the history of architecture – one the reductive typol-ogy of Marc-Antoine Laugier and J.-N.-L. Durand grounded in neoclas-sical rationalism and the model of nature. The other was the typology of the machine, which emerged out of the Industrial Revolution and achieved its synthesis in the Taylorist views of Le Corbusier and Walter Gropius. Beginning with Rossi and Léon Krier, he goes on to argue, a new rational-ist typology has emerged. It is based on eighteenth-century visions of the city, although now stripped of any positivistic eschatology: "The concept

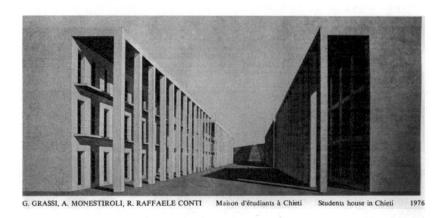

G. GRASSI, A. MONESTIROLI, R. RAFFAELE CONTI   Maison d'étudiants à Chieti   Students house in Chieti   1976

Les bâtiments ne forment pas un espace descriptible. L'espace public est accidentel.

The buildings do not form a describable space, the public space is accidental.

59

Figure 3.2   Page from *Rational Architecture*. Courtesy of Léon Krier.

of the city as the site of a new typology is evidently born of a desire to stress the continuity of form and history against the fragmentation produced by the elemental, institutional, and mechanistic typologies of the recent past." These types are garnered from the past as proven urban elements, but they are not entirely cleansed of their earlier semantic residues. Rather, the older meanings merge and enrich the newly acquired meanings: a self-evident process of dialectic transformation. This new typology, furthermore, is neither nostalgic nor eclectic; it filters its historical "quotations" through a critical modernist lens. Thus for Vidler rationalism trumps the "post-modernism" of the day, including the "collage-city" strategies of Rowe. It also restores criticality to a disdained "public architecture otherwise assassinated by the apparently endless cycle of production and consumption."[31]

Krier followed with a highly combative essay, "The Reconstruction of the City," to which he referred as the "working document" for the new movement. The architecture of the New York Five and the Venturi school, which had been shown at the Milan exhibition, had now been excluded from the London show, Krier noted, so as not to dilute the typological and morphological themes. Also excluded were any references to semiotics, that is, "all pompous attempts of producing architectural meaning without a very clear political intention." Politics also condemns nineteenth-century eclecticism as well as, willy-nilly, the "vast suburban settlements in Anglo-Saxon countries," which for Krier have preempted the class struggle and rendered their political systems inherently conservative.[32] In their place, Krier – somewhat incredibly – holds up the Karl Marx Hof in Vienna and blocks of residential towers in Moscow as "exceptional achievements" for the new city. Yet the greatest obstacle standing in the way of a true reform of the European city is industrialization itself, the results of whose technologies and building techniques (based on profits) simply fall short of the artisanal culture of the architecture that it destroyed. Krier's reconstruction of the city thus depends on a return to proletariat values and manual (pre-industrial) labor techniques.

Rational Architecture was only a part of a larger campaign orchestrated by Krier. Appearing alongside the book was a special issue of *Architectural Design* devoted to the theme, in which the architect seized the occasion to upbraid the RIBA, Nikolaus Pevsner, kitsch, Robert Venturi, and architectural education in general – in what amounted to a paean to the ideas of Laugier, William Morris, Raymond Erith, and Karl Marx.[33] Also taking place that year was an international colloquium of socialist planners, out of which came the "Brussels Declaration."[34] It condemned EEC planning policies, particularly those for Brussels, and went on to demand sweeping educational, technical, political, and historical reforms aimed toward the "repair" of the city. Among the signers were Léon Krier, Pierluigi Nicolin, Bernard Huet, and Maurice Culot. The declaration was published by the Archives d'Architecture Moderne of Brussels, the legal entity that would now take up the political cause through its publications.

Krier and Culot had, in fact, already formed an alliance. Culot, a professor at the Ecole Nationale Supérieure de La Cambre, had for several years been active in Brussels with the ARAU (Atelier de Recherche et d'Action Urbaine). It was an ad hoc political and planning group that opposed large-scale redevelopment schemes for Brussels by conducting neighborhood workshops, organizing local opposition, and proffering less invasive, alternative proposals. In 1978 Krier and Culot teamed up to write a manifesto for *Oppositions*, carrying the determined title "The Only Path for Architecture." Here the anti-modern "urban struggle within the framework of the class struggle" assumes the apodictic moralism of a fire-and-brimstone revival. In the end, architecture's salvation will only come about when the Marxist "reconstruction of artisanry, of manual work" will somehow spawn an "intense social life."[35] Culot would explicate the specific architectural means to achieve this in an essay published a few years later when he rejected large windows and large spans, nuclear energy (particularly serving the production of concrete and aluminum), and indeed the use of any materials other than stone, wood, and brick.[36] Leaving aside the polemical edge, the authors, with their emphasis on urban scale and neighborhoods, touched on a number of issues that were in desperate need of discussion in the 1970s, and Krier in particular would elaborate upon similar themes in the coming years in a very surprising way.

Still another vision of rationalist architecture was emerging at this time in the drawings of Oswald Mathias Ungers. Five years older than Rossi, Ungers had been trained at Karlsruhe Technical University in the late 1940s, and, in practice in Cologne in the 1950s, he drew upon the Brutalist movement in England as well as the criticisms of Team 10. These tendencies began to give way around 1963 when, after taking a position at the Technical University in Berlin, he withdrew from everyday practice. In two competition entries of that year, the Berlin redevelopment project for Grünzug-Sud and student residences for Enschede, Ungers first invoked the idea of morphological transformations by designing a series of articulated forms: the first project linear and differentiated in its street character, the second a collection of rectilinear buildings transforming themselves (at an acute-angle pivot point) into a series of curvilinear forms. A similar compactness of autonomous forms set around a courtyard is found in his competition project for the German Embassy to the Vatican of 1965, which is important because in that year he began his association with Cornell University, where he served as dean from 1969 until 1975.

In 1974 Ungers set up an office in Frankfurt and was moving between his duties in Europe and America. He was still advancing his crystalline morphology on paper through the compositional strategies of assembly from fragments, collisions, coincidence of opposites, and historical adaptation to the *genius loci*. With the commission for the German Architectural Museum in Frankfurt (1979–1984), Ungers suddenly burst upon the international stage as a mature talent with a clear and compelling language. His formal similarities to the work of Rossi are sometimes striking, although nuanced somewhat differently. If Rossi in his holistic thinking generally inclined toward pure geometries, Ungers's neoclassicism is closer in its logic to the looser interpretation of realism of Karl Friedrich Schinkel. Either way, a very distinct rationalist style is evident by the end of the 1970s, one that would also undergo further development in the following decade.

4

Modernism Abides

Notwithstanding the near adolescent infatuation of the popular press with the phenomenon of postmodernism in the late 1970s, the formal language of high modernism did not really recede that much in practice. Technological advancement, following its well-established pattern, continued to intensify its pace, and the visible persona of the majority of buildings put up in this decade for the most part did not change. The aspirations and ambitions of the many modernists persisted under duress, even while many of their underlying tenets were called into question and criticized. What we have appearing during the 1970s, then, is not an easily identifiable counterinsurgency but rather a number of competing approaches to design. In many ways it was a fragmentation of theory opening up along several fronts – thematic, material, generational, and national – one that in many ways recalled the style debates of more than a century earlier. The oil embargo of 1973 and the resulting economic recession and high inflation that ensued in the second half of the decade also played heavily into events. The fact that so many architects were out of work or unable to make the transition from school to practice assured that the debate would remain sharp and intense. The youthful anger of a decade earlier had not abated, but then again significant events with the limits of modernism continued to take place.

The Chicago High-Rise

The continuing faith in technology and progress can be found by considering the work of Skidmore, Owens & Merrill (SOM), perhaps the largest professional firm in the world operating out of New York, Chicago, and

An Introduction to Architectural Theory: 1968 to the Present, First Edition.
Harry Francis Mallgrave and David Goodman.
© 2011 Harry Francis Mallgrave and David Goodman. Published 2011 by Blackwell Publishing Ltd.

San Francisco. The firm, which was founded in 1937, moved to the forefront of architectural visibility in the 1950s with such designs as Gordon Bunshaft's Lever House (1951–1952) and Bruce Graham's Inland Steel Building (1956–1957) – both of which epitomized the sleek style of high modernism. The 19-story Inland Steel Building, for instance, was clad with a curtain wall of stainless steel and green-tinted glass, and its shallow office slab, loosely attached to a 25-story service core, was framed with a clear span of 90-foot girders, supported on columns pulled outside to accentuate the sheen of the metallic finishes.

The same building holds another distinction in that it launched the career of Fazlur Khan, an engineer from East Pakistan (now Bangladesh) who was completing his doctoral studies in 1956.[1] After designing the structural system for the Inland Steel building, he sought work in East Pakistan for a brief period but then returned to Chicago and SOM in 1960. Here he rejoined Graham's team and also met Myron Goldsmith, a recent transfer from the San Francisco office. Goldsmith was also an architect and engineer with impressive credentials. He had been studying at Armour Institute of Technology (now Illinois Institute of Technology) in 1938 when Mies van der Rohe arrived to head the school. After graduating, Goldsmith worked for seven years in his office before going to Italy for another extended stay under the mentorship of Pier Luigi Nervi.[2]

Chicago in the early 1960s was experiencing something of a building boom. Two major projects were underway in the Loop: the 31-story Civic Center of C. F. Murphy, and Mies's Federal Center complex. A few blocks to the north along the river, Bertrand Goldberg's twin 70-story circular towers of Marina City were under construction – yet another future icon of American modernism. In 1961 Bruce Graham had commissions in hand for two tall buildings: the Chestnut-DeWitt Apartments on the near north side, and the downtown Brunswick Building. Both became experiments exploring the notion of a "tube" structure, an idea that was not entirely new to structural thinking but one that at the same time had never been fully exploited.

Conventional framed, rectangular buildings with a curtain wall are structurally and economically limited in size, generally to a height of around 30 stories. This limit exists because the determining factor affecting the design of tall buildings is generally the lateral forces of wind. In essence, tall buildings with conventional framing want to oscillate or sway, a tendency that can only be mitigated by a bracing core (structural service shafts and the like) or interior shear walls that bind the exterior walls to the core. Tube structures take a different approach.[3] Here the main columns are placed close together along the perimeter and are designed to act as a continuous exterior membrane, akin to a birdcage. The Lake Shore

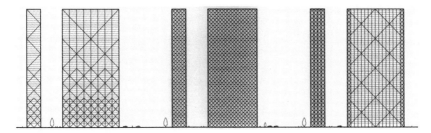

Figure 4.1 Plate from Myron Goldsmith, "The Tall Building: The Effects of Scale," thesis project, Illinois Institute of Technology, advisors Ludwig Mies van der Rohe and Ludwig Hilberseimer. Image courtesy of Edward Windhorst.

apartments of Mies, in fact, suggested such an approach, in that the exterior I-beams (often described as visual ornaments) actually stiffen the curtain membrane. In a tube structure with its much expanded moment of inertia, the width and depth of the building as a whole offsets the lateral forces, and any interior columns have only to satisfy gravity loads. Everything depends on the stiffness of the exterior frame.

With the Chestnut-DeWitt apartments (1961–1964), located immediately to the west of Mies's original Lake Shore towers, SOM decided to challenge their height with a 43-story concrete building. Goldsmith and Khan placed columns along the perimeter every five-and-a-half feet (doubling the span at the base) and connected them with deep spandrel beams, also of concrete. Such thinking owes something to Khan, but also to Goldsmith, whose Master's thesis of 1953, in drawing upon the lessons of D'Arcy Thompson, discussed the limitations of every structural system and how jumps in scale require new structural solutions. For his thesis, he proposed both an 80-story concrete tower as well as several versions of a 60-story steel structure with diagonal bracing.[4] It should also be noted that around the time this building was being designed, Minoru Yamasaki was designing the steel-framed tube structure for the twin towers of the World Trade Center in New York City.

For the design of the 35-story Brunswick Building (1961–1965), across the street from the Civic Center in downtown Chicago, Goldsmith and Khan designed a concrete tube with the exterior columns a little over nine feet apart, joined to a shear service core (a tube within a tube) with a stiff joist and waffle-slab floor system.

In still another interesting and much underappreciated experiment during these years, George Schipporeit and John Heinrich designed the 70-story Lake Point Tower (1964–1967) with a self-reinforcing three-wing or cloverleaf plan, anchored with a strong triangulated core (30 inches of

Figure 4.2   George Schipporeit and John Heinrich, Lake Point Tower, Chicago (1964–1967). Image courtesy of Edward Windhorst.

concrete at the base, 59 stories in height). The angles of the triangulated core are abridged at each vertex for corridor access but beams link the three shear walls. The core, however, also works as a unit with the concrete floor slabs and columns, as well as with the overall configuration of the plan.[5]

As the Chestnut-DeWitt Apartments were under construction in 1964, SOM received a commission that would offer an extraordinary challenge. The developer, Jerry Wolman, had purchased a parcel of land on upper Michigan Avenue, two blocks west of the Chestnut-DeWitt building. Economic studies initially favored a twin-tower scheme with a plaza, but with space again being restricted, the owner decided to consolidate all activities into one tall building of over two million square feet. Goldsmith did not participate in this design, and thus it largely fell to Khan to come up with a structural system for a 100-story tower. Khan, in drawing upon Goldsmith's thesis proposals as well as a recent student project by Mikio Sasaki, responded by designing a diagonally braced tube structure – now the John Hancock building.[6]

The obstacles were numerous, not the least of which was the clayey soil of Chicago, which in this case required no fewer than 239 caissons for the

Figure 4.3 Skidmore, Owens & Merrill, John Hancock Building, Chicago (1964–1969). Image by the authors.

building's foundation. Still another problem was that there was no way at the time to predict accurately the extent of sway or the physiological responses of the building's occupants. Thus Khan, in addition to developing hypothetical mathematical models, undertook a series of empirical lab tests.[7] The mixing of residences with offices was also an issue, in that the former function better with a narrower floor plan than do office suites. The solution in this instance was to place the apartments above and attenuate the overall form of the tower, which lends the building a natural elegance while at the same time creating a more stable form. In a single vertical run of 100 stories, commercial areas, parking, offices, and residences are layered in a tower stretching upward 1127 feet. Only the expression of the intermediate vertical columns impairs the logic of the design.

The Hancock Center opened in 1969, the same year in which Sears, Roebuck & Company commissioned SOM to design a 60-story building in downtown Chicago. Sears envisioned a building with a very big footprint, but Graham convinced the client to build something narrower and taller – in fact the tallest building in the world. When someone at Sears, in Graham's words, declined the use of "those damn diagonal things," the problem thus became one of coming up with another structural innovation.

Khan responded in kind, but once again Goldsmith and IIT were not far in the background. In 1966 another student, A. G. Krishna Menon, had prepared a thesis for the design for a 90-story apartment building, for which both Khan and Goldsmith served as advisors. In elevation, the tube design was similar to the Chestnut-DeWitt scheme, but Menon divided the rectangular configuration of the floor plan into three parts by installing two shear walls.[8] What he had approached was the idea of a cluster tube or "bundled tube" – that is, tubes or structural units that prop up one another so as to achieve greater overall efficiency. Originally, Khan envisioned as many as 15 such tubes for the Sears Tower, each capable of stopping at any height, but in the final design nine 75 × 75ft structural squares (with columns spaced 15 feet along the perimeter of each tube) accommodate 4.4 million square feet of floor space. Two tubes stop at the fiftieth floor, two more at level 66, and two more at the ninetieth floor, allowing the double-square tower, which opened in 1974, to rise up 110 stories or 1450 feet in height. Moreover, the structural steel was held to a remarkable 33 pounds per square foot of gross floor area, whereas in the Empire State Building the steel required over 50 pounds per square foot.[9]

What is remarkable in looking back at the experiments in Chicago during these years is that nearly all of the conceptual thinking and structural calculations had to be carried out without the aid of the computer, which first made its presence felt in architectural offices only as the Sears Tower was under construction. Decisions regarding the use of certain new technologies, such as whether or not to install viscoelastic pads at structural joints to dampen wind forces (they were not installed), had to be made entirely from wind-model testing and with a fair amount of structural intuition.[10] What is also interesting is the context in which these buildings appeared. When the Sears Tower (now Willis Tower) opened in 1974, for instance, it did so in the midst of the oil embargo and on the eve of the great architectural turn toward postmodernism. Thus its striking technological innovations were greeted with relatively little notice or fanfare.

German Engineering

German architecture only recovered slowly from the ruins of World War II. Most of its famed cadre of modern architects had fled their homeland prior to the war, and the country's economic, industrial, and educational infrastructures had been shattered. The severe winter of 1946–1947 led to mass starvation in many parts of Europe, but the recovery efforts in Germany, even with the aid of the Marshall Plan, lagged behind other countries because of the extent of physical damage. And of course there were political factors as well. In May, 1949, the German areas occupied by Great Britain, France, and the United States were brought together as the new Federal Republic of Germany; five months later Joseph Stalin organized the eastern half of the country into the German Democratic Republic. For the next 40 years the "Iron Curtain" would sever the country in two, with Berlin becoming the main stage for the chilling maneuvers of the Cold War.

Thus it is not surprising that one of Germany's leading architects in the postwar era, Frei Otto, would labor through his early years in obscurity.[11] Born in 1925, he had served as a squadron pilot during the war and belatedly took his architectural training at the Technical University in Berlin, where he received a diploma in 1952. He spent the academic year of 1950–1951 in the United States, where he met Eero Saarinen, who directed him to the office of Fred Severud. The structural engineer at the time was designing the suspended roof structure for the new sports arena in Raleigh, designed by the talented Polish émigré Matthew Norwicki. The computational modeling of the Raleigh Arena thus became the subject of Otto's doctoral dissertation and his first book, which he completed in 1953.[12] The book is revealing in what it presages of Otto's later interests. After a relatively extensive historical discussion of suspended roof systems, Otto goes on to discuss membranes, tents, hardware, connectors, anchoring, and indeed provides sketches of several of his own designs. Among the latter was a proposal for a missionary school in East Africa and series of net roofs for a city in Antarctica.

In 1954 Otto joined forces with the "tentmaker" Peter Stromeyer, and from this alliance came a series of open fabric designs for public events: four-point tents and butterfly tents (Kassel, 1955), arch-supported tents, hump tents, and peak tents (all built in Cologne in 1957). In 1958 Otto founded the Institute for the Development of Lightweight Construction in Berlin-Zahlendorf. This interest eventually led, in 1964, to his appointment as director of the newly created Institute for Lightweight Structures (IL) in Stuttgart. The Institute supplied Otto not only with a budget for innovative research but also with a staff of associates to assist him in his research of complex problems. The appointment also underscored how much Otto had quietly accomplished over the previous six years. In 1958 he had met and befriended Buckminster Fuller and Yona Friedman, the latter of whom was directing the Groupe d'Etude d'Architecture Mobile in Paris. All three individuals were exploring the issues of adaptable buildings and the use of thin membranes to enclose large urban landscapes. In 1961 Otto had also begun his collaboration with the noted biologist Johann-Gerhard Helmcke, which advanced Otto's interest in biological principles and systems. The objective of these subsequent biological investigations was not to create biomorphic forms but – following in the lineage of D'Arcy Thomson – to understand the laws of natural formations and their possible application to design (bionics). Also in 1962, Otto, with the assistance of Ludwig Trostel, published the first volume of a book on tensile systems.[13]

It was this background of interests that Otto brought to the IL Insitute, and the research of the center shifted into high gear when Otto, in collaboration with the architect Rolf Gutbrod, won the national competition for the German Pavilion at Montreal's Expo '67. Enclosing 10 000 square meters, the even-net cable structure, supported on a series of masts at varying heights, became the largest such structure in the world and vied with Fuller's Geodesic Dome as one of the engineering wonders of the exposition. A transparent polyester fabric hung from the twisted cable network, lending a light and airy complement to the vast architectural experience. Within the context of German postwar architecture, as Dietmar M. Steiner has noted, it might be seen as Germany's first production of international significance.[14]

The Olympic Games of 1972 provided the second such occasion for structural experimentation. The architectural competition for the event was won by Günther Behnisch and Partners in the spring of 1967. Yet their designs for a continuous roof structure for the stadium, sports arena, and swimming pool were rejected by the jury, which set in motion a lengthy controversy of how such a membrane could be configured and economically constructed. In January 1968 Behnisch brought in Otto as the lead consultant on the design, and it was he who engineered the pre-stressed cable network suspended from a series of masts and pylons.[15] Acrylic panels, sealed with neoprene along the edges, were chosen as the membrane for the system – a decision actually mandated by its transparency and the need to eliminate shadows on the field for the new technology of color television.

Meanwhile, Otto was also expanding his interests along other fronts. In the late 1960s he formed an alliance with the engineers Ted Happold and Peter Rice of the London-based firm of Ove Arup & Partners. They collaborated on a special issue of *Architectural Design* devoted to Otto's work as well as on creating a Lightweight Structures Laboratory in London.[16] The goal was to advance research in cable, membrane, and pneumatic structures with the new possibilities of computer analysis. Otto's other venture during this period was the founding of the journal *IL*, which chronicled the research undertaken in Stuttgart. Each of the 41 issues that ran from 1969 to 1995 focused on a different structural theme. In the first issue (June 1969) Otto related his method of working with soap film strips when designing minimal nets. The second issue (April 1971) featured the "City in the Arctic," a collaborative project of Otto, Ove Arup & Partners, and Kenzo Tange in Japan. Otto and his colleagues were seeking a climate-controlled prototypical city of 45 000 under a shallow inflatable dome two kilometers in diameter and 240 meters in height. A small nuclear power plant was to supply energy to the sustainable ecosystem that featured moving sidewalks, a lake, botanical garden, birds, and animals.

With the third issue (October 1971), Otto began to draw upon the colloquiums of the Institute to widen the stream of contributors. Thematically entitled "Biology and Building," the issue revealed the depth of Otto's collaboration with a team of biologists as well as Otto's own evolution as a theorist. "The relationship between biology and building," he noted in the opening pages, "is now in need of clarification due to real and practical exigencies. The problem of the environment has never before been such a threat to existence. In effect, it is a biological problem."[17] These ecological concerns, following on the heels of the efforts of Fuller and others, have sometimes earned Otto the moniker of "anti-architect," and not unjustifiably so. For his interest in lightweight structures had by now evolved into the belief – later voiced explicitly – that "we put up too many buildings. We squander space, land, mass and energy. We destroy nature and cultures."[18] Otto vehemently opposed the historicism of the day by describing the city first and foremost as an "ecological system," the minimal-mass building as a "biotype," and the minimal energy building as something at peace with the landscape.[19]

Later issues only expanded upon this research. Several issues were based on a colloquium held at the IL in 1973 on the theme of "Pneus," which Otto and his team defined as "a system in which a layer stressed only in tension envelopes a medium."[20] Otto was initially interested in the concept as it related to pneumatic or air-supported structures, but, as he now came to realize, the idea was more far-reaching in its application to any medium (air, liquid, or even gravitational forces): "We were not dealing with a limited area of biological structures, but what we had on our hands was the key to an understanding of all forms and structures of living nature."[21]

The journal *IL* was too rich in content to be fully considered here, as one by one it took on a multitude of issues that have returned to the forefront today – from energy production to wind turbines and solar technologies, geothermal transport and storage, and lightweight adaptable structures. What remains a constant, however, is Otto's hostility toward the "era of concrete bunker architecture" and the "decade of neurotic nostalgia of the past that has been glorified in the mind," which he found so superficially represented in the architecture of the 1970s.[22] The journal ran until the mid-1990s, and in this sense the longevity of Otto's ecological crusade in the end bridged the theoretical divide that in many ways separates these two eras. In this respect alone, his work acquires major historical significance.

British Renaissance

What Frei Otto did for the rebirth of postwar German theory – Ove Arup in many ways did for British engineering and architectural thought. He was born in England to Scandinavian parents, educated in Denmark and Germany, and returned to England to open his first engineering office in 1923. In the early 1930s he drew close to a circle of modernists that included Berthold Lubetkin, Maxwell Fry, and Walter Gropius, for whom he provided the structural design for the ramps of the Penguin Pool at the London Zoo (1933–1934) as well as the concrete flats of Highpoint I and II (1933–1934). After the war, in 1949, Ove reformed the Arup Partnership, but what gained him international prominence was his later involvement with the Sydney Opera House. The architectural competition was won in 1957 in a dramatic way by Jørn Utzon but with a design that was flawed in its execution. Design delays and cost overruns nearly scuttled the project until – in 1961 – Arup reconfigured the roof shells to one and the same radius. Although the attribution of this idea to Arup remains contested, no one disputes Arup's role in bringing the intricate work to a successful conclusion after Utzon resigned from the project in 1966. When the Opera was completed in 1973, Arup's firm, now also enlarged with an architectural division, was a rival to SOM in both staff and influence.[23]

Arup's global accomplishments also inform the work of Richard Rogers and Norman Foster. Rogers, the elder by two years, was born in Florence in 1933 to a British father and Italian mother, and the family later immigrated to England under the pressures of the unfolding war.[24] With the encouragement of his cousin Ernesto Rogers, Richard attended the Architectural Association in the mid-1950s and in 1961 he won a traveling fellowship to Yale. It was there that he met Foster, who had recently completed his architectural studies at Manchester University.[25] The two students studied under Paul Rudolph (for whom Foster briefly worked),

Serge Chermayeff, Vincent Scully, and the visiting critic James Stirling. In the United States, Foster and Rogers were attracted to the ideas of Buckminster Fuller and the work of Louis Kahn, Eero Saarinen, Frank Lloyd Wright, and the Case Study architects.

Back in London in 1963, Rogers and Foster, together with Wendy and Georgia Cheesman, formed up a partnership known as Team 4. Two early commissions, Creek Vean House, in Cornwall (1964–1966), and Skybreak House, Hertfordshire (1965–1966), are transitional designs within the careers of both men. The terraced forms and concrete-block finishes of the former have often been attributed to the influence of Wright and Atelier 5, while the cinematic open-plan and high-modern interiors of the latter prompted Stanley Kubrick to use it to film one of the rape scenes of *A Clockwork Orange*. The defining commission for both men, however, was Reliance Controls in Swindon (1965–1966), an electronic factory, where they began mastering the nuances of industrial detailing – in the tradition of the Case Study architects of California. Designed on a very limited budget, the lightweight, corrugated steel shed was detailed in a minimalist vein. Both men thus embraced naked technology and a coolly efficient style of engineering, but the partners split up after the project's completion.

In retrospect this dissolution would be a happy one, as Rogers first made his mark in a big way in 1971 when – after teaming up with the Italian architect Renzo Piano – he won the competition for the Georges Pompidou Cultural Centre in Paris. The prompt to Piano and Rogers to enter the competition actually came from Ted Happold of Arup, who was seeking a major commission for his structural team after the completion of the Sydney Opera House. And against the backdrop of the postmodern cacophony of the mid-1970s, the opening of the new Beaubourg complex in 1977 struck an almost surrealist chord. Vividly anti-historicist in its glorification of the machine, the glass and plastic envelope consisting of six exhibition halls supported by a double-layered steel skeleton suspended from brackets (*gerberettes*), not only defied all contemporaneous pleas for "meaning" but, with its (originally proposed) moveable floors and exterior video screens, it formed a cross between the constructivists' fantasies of the 1920s and the more recent futurist ideas of Cedric Price and Archigram. Reyner Banham was quick to see this linkage, for he used the drawings and model of the design to conclude his book on megastructures in 1976, pointing out that the "bright colours, keen shapes, inflatables, clip-on gadgetry, giant projection screens and all the rest of the good old imagery of fun and flexibility" were largely the creation of "the Archigram-trained 'Crysalis' group [Alan Stanton, Michael Davies, Chris Dawson]

Figure 4.4 Piano and Rogers, Georges Pompidou Cultural Centre, Paris (1971–1977). Image courtesy of Richard O. Barry.

who had come over from Los Angeles specifically to work on the project in the Paris office."[26] Not all critics were impressed. Alan Colquhoun lamented the fact that this "supermarket of culture" had "no further task other than to perfect its own technology."[27]

Yet within Rogers's development, as well as that of Piano, the Centre Beaubourg remains a transitional work. The two partners broke up immediately afterwards, and Rogers soon secured the commission for Lloyd's Bank in London (1978–1986). Once again the design is an anomaly for the time, and once again Rice was instrumental. After fire-code authorities rejected his desire to use stainless-steel columns filled with water, as had been employed in Paris, Rice turned to slender concrete columns and transformed the *gerberettes* into pre-cast column brackets onto which were mounted the concrete grids supporting the floor slabs. The removal of all stairs, elevators, and lavatories to a series of six satellite towers both enhanced the interior openness and added compositional complexity to the exterior. The stainless steel, articulated pods of lavatories and staircases in fact lend the overall complex its distinctive sheen. Also central to the building's concept is the idea of energy efficiency. The triple-glazed exterior membranes with translucent glass on the outer panel not only reduce solar gain but the recycled heated air from offices is sent to base-ment storage tanks for reuse. The atrium functions as the building's main exhaust stack and operable windows on the interior glass skin allow occu-pants to control ventilation.It was therefore one of the first large buildings at this time to be designed so strictly from the point of view of energy efficiency.[28] In this regard it would within a few years be rivaled by the Hongkong and Shanghai Bank (1979–1986), which of course was designed by his former partner Norman Foster.

Advanced technology in service to both energy and structural efficiency had actually been central to Foster's thinking for some time. In an article written in 1969 he had spoken of new engineering techniques becoming available to architects as well as the possibilities for collaboration with specialists in other fields. If the techniques were then reflected in such phenomena as "lightweight space-frame structures or inflatable plastic membranes," the collaboration – "integrated teams with wide-ranging skills" – would produce "sophisticated components and kits-of-parts" that would radically reform the principles of production.[29] One early test of this thesis was the Willis Faber & Dumas Insurance Headquarters in Ipswich (1971–1975), a building distinguished by its curvilinear forms of mir-rored glass suspended from the roof – as well as by its open floor plan, integrated lighting and mechanical systems, and a roof lawn that resembles a typical English park. The design was conceived when Foster was confer-ring with Buckminster Fuller on the planning of an underground theater for St Peter's College in Oxford. During these talks Fuller proposed the idea of a "Climatroffice," an open, planted "living office" set under a huge lightweight dome.[30] Foster had high hopes of bringing such a solution to Ipswich, but his modest result nevertheless presages his later work.

Another important step in his development was the Sainsbury Centre for Visual Arts in Norwich (1974–1978). Now taking to heart Fuller's frequently posed question "How much does the building weigh?" Foster proposed the radical concept of a museum engineered to the highest standards of techni-cal precision. The prismatic-truss hanger (spanning $30 \times 130\,\mathrm{m}$) is placed on a heath adjacent to the University of East Anglia, where it enjoys privileged views of parkland and a lake. The predominant wall and roof panels are made from a composite of aluminum and foam ingeniously inserted into a network of neoprene, which also acts as the conduit to remove rainwater. Through high insulation-values, mechanical cooling has been dispensed with and natural light is generously admitted through walls and louvered skylights. Inside the open volume, the "Climitroffice" houses the activities of exhibition areas, restaurant, kitchen, coffee areas, limited vegetation, and

Figure 4.5   Norman Foster and Associates, Hongkong and Shanghai Bank, Hongkong (1979–1986). Image courtesy of Russell Edwards.

a school of fine arts. Once again, the building could not have been more incongruous with the postmodern polemics of the decade.

Thus, when Forster designed the Hongkong and Shanghai Bank in 1979, his theoretical program of "more with less" had largely been perfected. The result was one of the more remarkable technical achievements of the century, with the key being the bridge-like structural system engineered by Ove Arup & Partners. The building is in fact three buildings of different heights, supported by eight, four-column, steel "masts," which are open Vierendeel trusses. Two-story, pin-jointed suspension trusses periodically bridge these masts, and intermediate floors are suspended from the horizontal trusses. The steel elements, clad in aluminum panels, are protected from fire and the ocean air with a thin cementitious compound that inhibits rust. Prefabricated, plug-in capsules (139 in all) house the electrical wiring, air-conditioning equipment, and toilets. External louvers protect the south wall of the building, and a programmable sun scoop reflects sunlight into a group of interior mirrors, which in turn send it down 12 stories to the open plaza at ground level.

Foster is a good representative of his generation's mores, a generation groomed in the postwar tradition of Saarinen or Kahn. From this perspective, it is incumbent upon the architect to approach each problem anew and creatively invest the intellectual labor necessary to achieve an exceptional result – technically, aesthetically, as well as from the point of view of a building's usability. In this regard Foster is actually less defined by his acceptance of new technologies or his interdisciplinary teams of consultants than he is by the simple fact that he is at heart a craftsman.

Post-Metabolism in Japan

Japan, like Germany, was a country slow to recover from the war. One early sign of Japan's architectural revival was Tokyo's hosting of the World Design Conference of 1960, a moment that was seized by a group of young Japanese architects who issued a small manifesto, *Metabolism: The Proposals for New Urbanism*. The founders of the movement – Kiyonori Kikutake, Noboru Kawazoe, Masato Otaka, Fumihiko Maki, and Kisho Kurokawa – were all members of what Kurokawa once referred to as the "fourth generation" of Japanese architects interacting with Western culture.[31] The title of the manifesto was concisely defined:

> "Metabolism" is the name of the group, in which each member proposes future designs of our coming world through his concrete designs and illustrations. We regard human society as a vital process – a continuous development from atom to nebula. The reason why we use such a biological word, the metabolism, is that, we believe, design and technology should be a denotation of human vitality.[32]

Metabolism thrived in the 1960s – bred on the same technological fervor as its Western counterparts. Kenzo Tange, who had been active in the 1950s with CIAM, was the acknowledged mentor to the group. In 1959 he had been a visiting studio critic at MIT, where he and his students proposed two curvilinear, A-frame megastructures for Boston Harbor. Back in Japan in the following year, he began work on his proposal for an 18-kilometer extension of the city of Tokyo into the bay. Against the radial expansion of traditional cities, he proposed a linear structure or circulation chain operating on three levels, in which automobiles and monorails would have no barriers. Down the central spine ran a "civic core" consisting of office buildings crisscrossing horizontally between vertical service cores. Running perpendicular to it were a series of ribs supporting housing arrayed with traditional Japanese roofs.

Figure 4.6 Kisho Kurokawa, Helix City (1960). Image courtesy of Kisho Kurokawa Architect & Associates. Photograph by Tomio Ohashi.

The Metabolists followed within this scale of ambition. For the publication of 1960 Kikutake proposed his "Ocean City," consisting of 1250 plug-in, steel units (with a life-cycle of 50 years) to be attached to a concrete core. Kurokawa offered his three-dimensional "Helix City," inspired by the recent discovery of the chromosomal structure of DNA. Fumihiko Maki and Masato Otaka countered what they believed to be the failures of individual building design with their notion of "Group Form," a redevelopment scheme for the Shinjuku district in Tokyo, in which centers for shopping, offices, and entertainment were organized according their own forms and logic. The entertainment center, for instance, was conceived as a system of flowerlike shapes, in which a plaza formed a core surrounded by radiating petals of theaters, a concert hall, and opera.

These visions of the future were distinguished from many of the other megastructural proposals of this period both by the freshness of their ideas and by the fact that the architects followed upon their earlier efforts. For instance, Kurokawa published his "Prefabricated Apartment House" in 1962, in which he joined pre-cast panel construction with the idea of "utility capsules" for kitchen, bath, and nursery units – in his view, an evolution of Kahn's notion of master and servant spaces.[33] In another essay of the same year, he positioned his "Meta-Architecture" alongside NASA's space industry, where building forms "must be precisely organized like a space rocket and at the same time must have free form."[34] And in his "metamorphosis" proposal of 1965 he pushed the idea of a linear city as a way both to enhance social communication and to counter urban loneliness and alienation. This idea became the basis for his Hishino New Town (1967), a city conceived not as a self-sufficient center but as a "network" within the Tokyo–Osaki corridor: a high-density link connected to other urban centers with high-speed rail and a comparable social life.[35] As models, he cited Jean Gottmann's idea of a "Megalopolis" and Constantinos Doxiadis's notion of an "Ecumenopolis," or a cultural and communicational linkage of the world's major cities.

This phase of Kurokawa's thinking culminated in 1969 with his "Capsule Declaration," a homage to "cyborg architecture" and to the new era of electronics and human mobility. Capsule living (which he likened to American mobile homes) eliminates the need for owning land; it allows diversified cities and is aligned with the lifestyles of individuals (as opposed to families), the metropolis, "technetronic" society, prefabrication, and freedom.[36] Conceptually, Kurokawa realized some of his more original architectural creations around 1970 with the "Capsule House" inside the theme pavilion of Expo '70 in Osaka, the Takara Beautillion pavilion, and the Nakagin Capsule Tower, completed in 1972. In this last project, consisting of 144 studio capsules, a half-dozen prefabricated capsules were attached to the concrete service core each day and the full complement of units were completed in one month.

With the oil crisis of 1973, however, the Japanese economy suffered like those in the West, but with one important difference. Although the earlier concern with large-scale projects gave way out of necessity, architects involved with Metabolism never lost their interest in technology, and indeed infused it with a strong Japanese sensitivity toward craftsmanship and detailing. In the second half of the 1970s, Kurokawa embarked upon what he described as an "intercultural" dialogue, in which he mediated his work with traditional Japanese themes of "En-space" and "symbiosis."[37] In describing the latticed courtyard for the Saitama Museum (1978–1982), he spoke of its *engawa* (enclosed veranda), *nokishita* (semi-outdoor passage), and *rogi* (narrow alley). And in his much acclaimed Wacoal Kojimachi Building in Tokyo (1982–1984), he married ideas gleaned from Japanese Buddhism (specifically the "Consciousness Only" school of Nagarjuna) with French poststructural theory in creating a *machine plaisante* (pleasure machine) – that is, "a living, pleasing machine perpetually in kaleidoscopic

Figure 4.7   Kisho Kurokawa, Wacoal Kojimachi Building, Tokyo (1982–1984). Image courtesy of Kisho Kurokawa Architect & Associates. Photograph by Tomio Ohashi.

flux, always producing schisms that resolve into ever new relationships."[38] Such analogies were, however, trumped by the sophisticated detailing of the building's aluminum and synthetic marble exteriors, which can be interpreted as the quintessential icon for Reyner Banham's "First Machine Age." The exquisitely detailed interior finishes are even more high-tech in their overall effect; Kurokawa quite rightfully describes the reception room on the top floor as a "Japanese-decor space shuttle."[39]

Technological expressionism is also found in the work of Maki and Arata Isozaki – two architects who by the late 1970s had been singled out as the leaders of the celebrated "New Wave" of Japanese architects.[40] In the early 1960s Isozaki worked in Tange's office, but he struck out on his own with such early designs as the Otia Library (1962–1966). By the early 1970s Isozaki had clearly claimed a new path, one with a more colorful use of materials and techniques. In the home office of the Soga Bank in Fukuoka (1968–1971), for instance, he dressed the thin, elongated, 11-story tower with Indian red sandstone and complemented it with lower compositional elements of granite and steel. In his much-admired Gumma Museum of Fine Arts in Takasaki (1971–1974), he faced the building with shimmering aluminum panels, occasionally left bare to expose the brute concrete structure underneath. Botond Bognar has described the overall effect of the museum's sparkling skin as illusional and "unreal" in its high-tech effects.[41] Critiquing the work from a contrary postmodern perspective, Charles Jencks described the building's semantic quality as "too cold, clinical, and mechanistic."[42]

Isozaki, however, was quite familiar with the semiotic infatuation of the time, for it was in the mid-1970s that he began to use the Renaissance term *maniera* to describe his allegorical intentions. He saw it as a way to bring historical motifs and regional sensitivities back into design, and also as a way to counter what he described as modernism's failure to maintain "the absolute nature of technology."[43] This last remark is crucial to understanding his work, because even though Isozaki conceived *maniera* as a series of (seven) formal operations, he never denied the relevance of technology itself.[44] Quite to the contrary, he insisted that "contradictorily enough, technology is the only thing the architect today can use." Thus he embraces "*machinelike*" as his preferred metaphor for *maniera*: a mixed, layered, and eclectic metaphor to be sure, but one nevertheless through which architecture becomes "a machine for the production of meaning." This is truly a unique interpretation of postmodern trends, one in which technology (as with modernism) no longer controls expression, but rather – as with the modernism of Otto Wagner – "technology becomes expression."[45]

Maki's embrace of high technology was different only in that he never really departed from his modernist roots. His early emphasis on group-form remained a theme throughout the 1960s and 1970s, and indeed it took on a more developed character as he continued to weave additional patterns into it. In one essay written while at Harvard in 1966, "Movement Systems in the City," Maki emphasized the need for architects to create urban spaces that were legible, poetic, and engaging, in the sense of becoming inspirational stages for spontaneous social events.[46] In another essay of 1973, "An Environmental Approach to Architecture," Maki stressed not only the relationship of the building to its environment but also the appropriateness of its scale, ambience, and symbolism.[47]

Over the next few years, his position continued to evolve. In a revealing essay of 1975 projecting what architecture might be like in the last quarter of the twentieth century, Maki indicated that Japanese architecture had undergone a major shift between 1970 and 1975. Gone were the "capsule" architecture of Metabolism and the more general era of megastructural experimentation. In their place came a more introspective sensualism in design, combined with a desire for low-profile urban settings. Whereas these trends, Maki argued, would lead to a substantiation of non-specific functional space and the detachment of exterior expression from interior functions, the concomitant uncertainty of these unsettled times would also demand a return to pragmatism and craftsmanship to bolster waning self-assurance.[48] The idea of craft is the key term here, a point that Maki also raises in a "New Year Greeting" at the start of 1978, when he notes that "the current period of anxiety seems to have inspired a renewal of age-old interest in the beauty of details, materials, light, color, and compositional elements."[49]

On the surface, this shift in Maki's thought may be interpreted (as it has been in the past) as a merging of the aesthetic influence of Kahn with the tectonic detail of Scarpa, but his architecture, on closer reading, actually reveals a larger mediation of competing ideas. The stepped, pyramidal form of his Central Building for Tsukuba University (1972–1980) not only emphasizes detailing but also radically new "high-tech" thinking and techniques. The building's steel structure supports floors of perforated steel deck plates; the interior walls are cast aluminum panels over lightweight steel studs, while the exterior walls consist of glass-block panels fitted into heat-pressed steel frames, which, as he noted, is a way of contributing "to the development of a new vocabulary for curtain-wall design."[50] Here he also points to Pierre Chareau's Maison de Verre in Paris and to its play on the "romance of the machine aesthetics," or, as he explains the exposed steel of the building's atrium: "At the Center, the interior of the building is open to the sky through a square glass and metal courtyard which contains a stairway inspired by Constructivism; and so the machinist image at its most dynamic is enclosed in a soaring metal cage."[51]

By the early 1980s Maki was describing his poetic interpretation of technology as "industrial vernacular." For instance, the "floating" skin of the two roofs of the Fujisawa Gymnasium (1980–1984) is built of stainless steel, 0.4 millimeters or 1/64 of an inch thick, therefore sufficiently thin to crimple. This decorative effects that ensue, he explains, is necessary not only to repair the "unbearable void" of architecture's lost ornament but also "to give a rhythm and scale to the extensive roof." Maki further points out that the "edge of the roof of the large arena, when seen from below, is transparent like the wings of a dragonfly," while the shape of the roof at the same time evokes "a medieval knight's helmet and a spaceship."[52] The same "floating" quality is sought in the aluminum facade of Maki's Wacoal Media Center – the Spiral (1982–1985) – one of the most compelling architectural designs of this decade. Here the aluminum panels and other metallic finishes engage the differing planes of transparent and translucent

Figure 4.8 Fumihiko Maki, Wacoal Media Center, Tokyo (1982–1985). Image courtesy of Luis Villa del Campo.

glazing in what amounts to a visual symphony of layered effects. Such "a high level of detailing," evoking Rowe and Slutzky's notion of transparency, "can be achieved today only when industrial technology is allied to a devotion to traditional craftsmanship," and for Maki this "transparent romanticism" constituted Japan's rejection of postmodern historicism.[53]

The Special Case of Alexander

Christopher Alexander does not fall within the technological framework of this chapter, but his work does represent the lost trail of modernist anthropological thinking that had risen to such glorious heights in the 1960s. Almost alone among his generation, Alexander focused not on the compositional form or symbolic meaning of buildings, but rather on how their occupants experienced architecture. In this sense, his trilogy of books, which appeared in the second half of the 1970s, questioned not only the

value of technology as a tool for advancement but also the highly conceptualized premises of postmodernism.[54]

The foundational piece of his trilogy is *The Timeless Way of Building*
(1979), which – with its Zen-like literary character and amorphous description of such elusive qualities as aliveness, wholeness, and beauty – indeed
struck many at the time as an exercise in esotericism. When readers discovered that "timelessness" was an attribute found less in contemporary
architectural creations and far more in older buildings and towns, it no
doubt appeared to some as quaint or simple nostalgia. But the book has
important empirical analysis as well as character, and in fact Alexander – a
man who has devoted his life to discerning the "living patterns" of a successful architectural environment – has many thoughtful, if not profound,
insights. Take this seemingly straightforward observation about how the
technological and aesthetic instincts of modern architects have obscured a
crucial aspect of design:

> *And, indeed, there is a fundamental difference between those societies in which
> people are able to make their environment alive, and those in which the towns
> and buildings become dead.*[55]

With all of its simplicity, this assertion calls forth many implications.
How does one design a building or city that is alive, as opposed to one that
is dead? How does architecture or planning enhance or inhibit the well-
being of inhabitants? Alexander approaches such old notions as "beauty"
in a more picturesque manner than most architects, by training, are allowed
to entertain, but he also underscores that just as nature has its underlying
morphology or geometrical structure that endows it with support, so
should architecture. And what distinguishes Alexander's theory from most
others at this time is his belief that this quality of "aliveness" is found not
in formalistic or abstract theorizing but rather in the genome of the human
organism. At its core, then, this is a biological theory of design originating
back in his cognitive studies of the 1960s, although this fact does not
become fully evident until his later and much more intellectually ambitious
quadrumvirate, *The Phenomenon of Life: Nature of Order* (2001–2004).

The culmination of his earlier research appears in *A Pattern Language*
(1977), a book written in close collaboration with Sara Ishikawa and
Murray Silverstein. In this presentation of 253 patterns, Alexander aspires
to nothing less than a comprehensive manual for design – from the overview of a city's layout to the nook-and-cranny of a living space. It is indeed
a Herculean undertaking, which again (despite the counter-cultural influence of Berkeley in this era) stands out from the lax tenor of the time.

One can fault many of these patterns on several levels (one, his nativist abhorrence of buildings of more than four stories), but many of the observations – on home layouts, room features, natural light, views, entries, courtyards, gardens, neighborhoods, and the spatial and anthropological complexity of towns – do indeed strike one as timeless.

Within the sociological wilderness of this time, one distant compatriot to Alexander was the architect Herman Hertzberger, who, in following the earlier efforts of his countryman Aldo van Eyck, produced in 1973 a feature issue of the Dutch journal *Forum* entitled "Homework for More Hospitable Form."[56] Hertzberger embarks on a fairly extensive critique of the failures of the modern city and the cold and inflexible building forms that have led to a general sense of malaise. He counters by suggesting, among other things, a greater respect for the existing urban fabric, a sincere effort to identify more authentic "arch-forms," a breaking down of larger building forms into smaller ones, and an open-ended design of spaces that can be changed or modified by the inhabitants over time.

And then there was the second edition of Hassan Fathy's book *Architecture for the Poor*, which also appeared in 1973.[57] The Egyptian architect had originally been trained in Western practice, but by the end of the 1930s he had come to see the failure of modernism in Egypt – that is, its rampant destruction of traditional forms, its lack of climate-controlling strategies, and its indifference to the cultural hierarchy of living spaces. During the war years, Fathy began work on the Nubian village of New Gourna, in which he, now rejecting entirely the modernist vocabulary, turned to mud-brick construction and indigenous vaulting techniques, traditional shading and ventilation devices, and historical courtyards. The result, he argued, was not only a much happier population now eager to reclaim the vestiges of a nearly extinguished tradition but also far more humane and comfortable housing built at a fraction of the cost of "modern" housing projects. Fathy's case for indigenous techniques was compelling and blatantly anti-modern, although its full implications would not be felt for some years.

Part Two

1980s

5

Postmodernism and Critical Regionalism

Postmodernism Further Defined

Notwithstanding initial resistance, the historicist school of postmodernism continued to gain favor in the 1980s, particularly in the first half of the decade. And as the movement grew, its different permutations also expanded. On the American continent, Robert Venturi, Charles Moore, and Robert A. M. Stern formed a growing cadre of architects exploiting populist notions of history and irony, while the former "Whites" had by now marked out their separate paths. Michael Graves, beginning with the Portland Building and the Public Library in San Juan Capistrano (both started in 1980), devised a highly symbolic and eclectic language, almost painterly in its palette of historical effects. Richard Meier, in his design for the Museum for the Decorative Arts in Frankfurt (1979–1985), may have adhered to his white vocabulary, but with the Bridgeport Center (1984–1989) he too crossed the color threshold by cladding towers in gray porcelain panels and red granite. In Chicago, Stanley Tigerman, Thomas Beeby, and Helmut Jahn often employed a highly ironic use of history, while in Los Angeles a new and highly talented school of architects led by Eric Owen Moss, Thom Mayne, Michael Rotondi – and later Franklin Israel – began to develop a playful and material-based sculptural style that, in its lack of inhibition, complemented the nearby and evolving work of Frank Gehry.

In many European circles the rationalist principles of Aldo Rossi and O. M. Ungers remained strong, but this movement was also moderated by the quasi-regionalism of Mario Botta or even by the outright classicism of Bruno Reichlin and Fabio Reinhart. An exaggerated classicism is also found

An Introduction to Architectural Theory: 1968 to the Present, First Edition.
Harry Francis Mallgrave and David Goodman.
© 2011 Harry Francis Mallgrave and David Goodman. Published 2011 by Blackwell Publishing Ltd.

in the work of Christian de Portzamparc and Ricardo Bofill in the 1980s, yet only with measured success. Meanwhile, in Vienna, Hans Hollein developed a highly personal style with artful wit, while James Sterling was doing the same from his base in England. In Italy Paolo Portoghesi drew upon his broad knowledge of baroque architecture to fashion ever more elaborate and visually rich spatial experiences, at times abstract, at times highly suggestive in their historical overtures. The immediacy of Europe's historical legacy indeed resonated strongly with many architects, as we can glean from the New York exhibition of Emilio Ambasz and Fulvio Irace in 1982, which found precedents of postmodernism's use of columns, pediments, and globes in such seemingly remote sources as the baroque-inspired apartment houses of Milan in the 1920s and 1930s.[1]

In its underlying theory, postmodernism also evolved during the 1980s. At the start of the decade student editors launched the inaugural issue of *Harvard Architectural Review* with the summary editorial "Beyond the Modern Movement." From a rather parochial perspective, they circum-scribed the phenomenon of postmodernism through the five characteristics of use of history, cultural allusionism, anti-utopianism, urban design and contextualism, and formal concerns. Each was described in some detail. For instance, they defined cultural allusionism as an effort "to bring existing symbols and expressive forms, understood and accepted by broad segments of the population, into the realm of architecture."[2] By formal concerns, they named the diminished emphasis on program, a return of symmetry, a preference for closed and static space over open spatial concepts, an acceptance of ornament, and new explorations into the representational value of drawing.

In the same issue Stern published "The Doubles of Post-Modern," in which he argued that the new movement, like modernism, was split into two camps: the "schematic" (those insisting upon "a clean break from Western Humanism") and the "traditional" (those recognizing "the continuity" of the same). The two were represented, respectively and generally, by the work of Peter Eisenman and Michael Graves. He also further divided each group into two subgroups characterized by their attitude toward modernism. Against the anti-humanist and anti-historical attitude of Eisenman, Stern argued on behalf of a "traditional" postmodernism – that is, one that wants a clean break from modernism but at the same one that accepts modernism as a valid source for Western humanism. This form of postmodernism also corrects the social and technological failures of modernism with a new cultural awareness; at the same time it does not present the "falsely monolithic" facade of modernism because of its pluralistic popular support.[3]

Another attempt to define postmodernism can be found in Graves's "The Case for Figurative Architecture," which appeared in the first major monograph of his work in 1982. Here Graves employed a literary analogy of standard language and poetic language to draw out the distinctions between modern and postmodern architecture. If modern architecture, with its machine metaphor, was largely concerned with technical and programmatic expression, rejecting any form of cultural representation in favor of abstract geometries, figurative architecture was an attempt to re-explore a poetic form that was, by contrast, grounded in both nature and anthropomorphic symbolism. This is true for architecture's elements (walls and windows) as well as for its spaces – as seen in the contrasting experiences of standing in the central hall of Palladio's Villa Rotunda versus the abstract dispersion of spaces one finds from anywhere within Mies van der Rohe's Barcelona Pavilion. Therefore postmodernism, for Graves, is nothing less than a necessary correction to modern architecture's lack of anthropomorphic content, one in which "we re-establish the thematic associations invented by our culture in order to fully allow the culture of architecture to represent the mythic and ritual aspirations of society."[4]

Against this definition, we might also consider the view of Charles Jencks in his follow-up study, *What is Post-Modernism?*, Jencks, still a strong advocate for the epochal importance of postmodernism, reiterated his earlier beliefs by defining it in 1984 as "*double coding: the combination of Modern techniques with something else (usually traditional building) in order for architecture to communicate with the public and a concerned minority, usually other architects.*"[5] By contrast, he defined modernism as the "*universal, international style stemming from the facts of new constructional means, adequate to a new industrial society, and having as its goal the transformation of society, both in its taste and social make-up.*"[6]

Somewhat more evolved is Jencks's contemporary assessment of the movement. He first isolated two main strands of postmodernism, represented by the work of James Stirling and Léon Krier – although the latter, he conceded, was in fact only a "borderline" postmodernist.[7] Yet behind these strands lie six main traditions that compose the large palette of postmodernism: historicism, straight revivalism, neo-vernacular, ad hoc urbanism, metaphor metaphysical, and postmodern space. These multiple pedigrees allow Jencks to label a wide swath of architects as postmodernists – architects such as Peter Eisenman, Frank Gehry, Rem Koolhaas, Dimitri Porphyrios, Aldo van Eyck, Josef Kleihues, and Toyo Ito. The one group that Jencks was keen on excluding from this category was composed of those architects whose work represented "Late-Modernism," that is, an architecture that "*is pragmatic and technocratic*" *in its social ideology and from about 1960 takes many of the stylistic ideas and values of modernism to an extreme in order to resuscitate a dull (or cli-chéd) language.*"[8] Members of this group included Norman Foster, Piano and Rogers, Bernard Tschumi, and certain unnamed "Deconstructionists in America."

A few years later Jencks, in a new chapter added to the book in 1989, concluded by discussing postmodernism almost in classic Hegelian terms as something that must evolve dialectically out of more fundamental social and ecological relations. With images of the student rebellion in Tiananmen Square, he argued that China and other non-industrialized countries must first go through a modernist stage in order to arrive at the higher post-modern plateau, and this "paradigm shift," Jencks insisted, may very well take place by the end of the millennium because of the degradation of the ecosphere and the consequent global awareness of the limits of moderni-zation.[9] The postmodern condition, for Jencks, remained profound.

Somewhat less sanguine about the prospects of postmodernism was the German critic Heinrich Klotz, who in 1987 added a postscript to the American edition of his book of three years earlier, *Moderne und Postmoderne* (translated as *The History of Postmodern Architecture*). Klotz, by this date, was frankly ambivalent regarding the future of postmodern-ism. On the one hand, he was critical of the "certain shallowness" in the "decorative embellishments" and "packaging aesthetic" of many design-ers; on the other hand, he was clearly excited by the success of many pub-lic projects, such as Stirling's new gallery in Stuttgart, Rafael Moneo's Roman Museum in Mérida, and Arata Isozaki's Gumma Museum in Japan.[10] While acknowledging what he already saw as a decline in post-modern's "dialectic of historicism," Klotz at the same time was troubled by where the more recent tendencies (such as the excessively ironical atti-tude of Rem Koolhaas toward modernism) were leading. His conclusion was therefore quite guarded if not contradictory: "The result of such dar-ing adventures – trying to reach identity with the historical styles and still stay in the present – necessarily leads to the announcement of the 'end of postmodernism.' The final stage seems to have been reached, yet there is still much to come."[11]

Postmodernism Opposed

Voices raised against postmodern trends also became increasingly evident as the decade advances. One of the more adamant early critics of the move-ment was Aldo van Eyck, who in the late 1950s had been a strongly dissenting voice against the rationalism of high modernism. In a keynote address given the RIBA in 1981, he delivered what the Institute's journal somewhat understatedly termed "a withering attack on Post Modernism and all the architectural fashions that are attempting to supersede functionalism."[12] The catalyst to his remarks was a statement allegedly made by Léon Krier about the tragedy of this "monstrous epoch" – alluding to the modernist period of Le Corbusier, Reyner Banham, Sigfried Giedion, the Smithsons, and van Ecyk.[13] In the sharpest terms, van Eyck defended his interpretation of the modernist tradition of humanism, but not without some bloodletting of his own. Employing the acronym RPP for postmodernists – short for "Rats, Posts and Pests" – he responded with stinging rhetoric:

> I find the RPP's most extravagant fantasies as stale as pornography and certainly as uninventive. And, what is far worse: perversion – even perversion – is rendered distasteful in their hands. But what really excites my anger more than their little flirtations with absurdity, irony, banality, incoherence, contradictions and ugliness is the wilful inclusion of elements that are intended to be disconcerting, intended to aggravate, to pester. Who could ever have thought that one day, buildings, counter to any conceivable kind of logic, would, instead of assisting people's homecoming by helping to ease inner stress, wilfully provoke it.[14]

In a later issue of the same journal, Geoffrey Broadbent responded to van Eyck with "The Pests strike Back!" in which he defended the attempt of postmodern architects to create a "comfortable, human, economic and truly functioning architecture," something the "Machine Aesthetic" was never able to achieve. "The architects of the latter fought battles and crusades against an unwilling public," he goes on to say, "but the 'Rats, Posts and Pests' above all *want* to be liked. They want to do things that ordinary people will love, so we need far better reasons than those of *architects* such as Van Eyck for rejecting it in favour of that architecture of the 1920s which, while it was called 'Functional*ism*' actually functioned very badly."[15]

Another prominent architect generally critical of the postmodern movement in the 1980s was the editor of *Casabella*, Vittorio Gregotti. Although he too had been cool toward the dogmatic modernism in the 1960s, Gregotti subsequently resisted both the rationalism of the Rossi School and what he termed postmodernism's "obsession with history" at the expense of social concerns. "Architecture cannot live by simply mirroring its own problems, exploiting its own tradition," he noted, "even though the professional tools required for architecture as a discipline can be found only within that tradition."[16]

Figure 5.1 Rob Krier, Gateway to IBA Housing, South Tiergarten, Berlin (1980–1985). Image by the authors.

Still another position within this postmodern debate was staked out by Josef Kleihues in his work on behalf of Berlin's IBA or Internationale Bauaustellung (International Architectural Exhibition). This massive housing and rehabilitation undertaking grew out of a proposal by the Berlin government in 1977 to fund a major housing exhibition, in part in celebration of the fiftieth anniversary of the Weissenhof Exhibition of 1927. Opposition – led by Kleihues and others – intervened, with the result that the idea of a single housing estate was rejected in favor of a series of reconstruction projects scattered throughout the still war-scarred areas of the city, particularly adjacent to the Berlin Wall. Kleihues, who oversaw a board of architects and planners for new construction, responded with a multifaceted strategy of competitions, exhibitions, and symposia. His work resulted in hundreds of new housing units being built in South Tiergarten, South Friedrichstadt, Prager Platz, and in the outlying suburb of Tegel. A large number of international architects were brought in to design many of these projects, among them Charles Moore, Rob Krier, Hans Hollein, O. M. Ungers, James Stirling, Vittorio Gregotti, Aldo Rossi, Herman Hertzberger, John Hejduk, and Koolhaas.

Of interest in these endeavors were the theoretical underpinnings that Kleihues established for the projects. While allowing the architects some latitude to experiment with different solutions, Kleihues, an architect sympathetic toward the rationalist movement, was a strong advocate for "critical reconstruction" – that is, design that was both innovative and respectful of Berlin's "memory" of place while also articulating a "a language which can be generally understood."[17] This approach rejected the "tower" solutions of the postwar years as well as the barrack-like tenements found in some of Germany's housing estates; it favored instead the reconstitution of the prewar street system, mixed zoning, green courtyards, and a refocus on neighborhoods in the scale of the early nineteenth century. In this sense, the IBA guidelines might be seen as both an acceptance and rejection of aspects of postmodernism, or rather, as a cross-over point between postmodernism and another regionalist front that was developing at the time.

Critical Regionalism and Phenomenology

The idea of a regional modernism is as old as modernism itself. In the late 1890s the German theorist Richard Streiter espoused a form of modernism that would take into account the local milieu and building traditions.[18] Around the same time, Frank Lloyd Wright was experimenting with the principles of his "Prairie Style," which were also predicated on specific geographic conditions. In the early twentieth century another regional modernism took root in California in the work of Bernard Maybeck, Greene & Greene, Willis Polk, Myron Hunt, and Irving Gill. And in the 1920s we have the regional ideas espoused by Lewis Mumford, Benton MacKaye, Charles Whitaker, and others connected with the Regional Planning Association of America (RPAA). By contrast, European and American modernism after 1925 – following the Weissenhof Exhibition of 1927 and seconded by the "Modern Architecture: International Exhibition" at the Museum of Modern Art of 1932 – largely became a process of winnowing the range of formal possibilities or defining a style that could be deemed universal and international. One of the few exceptions among European countries prior to World War II was Italy, which wrestled with the problem of its own historical traditions and sunny climate.

Yet the idea of a regional modernism in the United States never subsided. In one of the first chronicles of American modernism, *The Modern House in America* (1940), James and Katherine Morrow Ford characterized modernism in the United States as a regional phenomenon, following the geographic and climatic diversity of the country.[19] One year later, Katherine Ford distinguished seven regional styles of American modernism: defined by the areas of New England, Pennsylvania, Florida, the Great Lakes, Arizona, the Northwest, and California.[20] Of these, a California style was certainly the most pronounced, thanks to the work of a first and second generation of modernists that included Rudolf Schindler, Richard Neutra, William Wurster, Gregory Ain, Raphael Soriano, Harwell Hamilton Harris, and Joseph Esherick.

Regional ideas only intensified in the late 1940s and early 1950s, even as New York's Museum of Modern Art continued to lobby on behalf of European modernism – first with an exhibition on Walter Gropius and the Bauhaus in 1938, and second with an exhibition on Mies van der Rohe in 1947. The last event took place in the same year that Lewis Mumford touched a raw nerve at that institution by penning an essay in the *New Yorker* on the "Bay Region Style." The museum, as we noted earlier in this study, responded with the symposium "What Is Happening to Modern Architecture?"[21] This event, in turn, initiated a sometimes shrill debate in the early 1950s on the pages of American architectural journals, in which Elizabeth Gordon and Joseph Barry, among others, supported the idea of an American regionalism as an outlook emanating from legitimate cultural differences between Europe and the North America.[22] The debate only quieted in the mid-1950s when Harwell Harris, who was close to individuals in both camps, attempted to mediate the issue by offering a positive "Regionalism of Liberation" against a less sophisticated "Regionalism of Restriction."[23] The latter with its provincial attitudes tends to constrain creative impulses, while the regionalism of liberation moderates or supplements its regional outlook with a global knowledge of modernism.

During these same years, Europe underwent a similar debate, although one not quite as sharply drawn in its opposing forces. In 1947 the English critic J. M. Richards, in reporting on the recent trends in Scandinavian domestic architecture, noted their more informal compositions, use of natural materials, and the integration of the dwelling into the natural environment. All seemed almost quaint to Richards, who at the time was championing the use of concrete and other industrial materials, and he dubbed the phenomenon "New Empiricism."[24] At the CIAM meeting in Bergamo in 1949 Bruno Zevi applauded both the regional variations of New Empiricism and the work of Frank Lloyd Wright, and went on to condemn the fact that CIAM had for so long been dominated by the rationalist modernist visions of Le Corbusier, Walter Gropius, and Sigfried Giedion.[25] Perhaps partly in response to these attacks, Giedion, a few years later, began to offer up his own vision of a regional modernism.[26] But this concession did not still the eruption that took place at CIAM '59 in Otterlo, when Ernesto Rogers was forced to defend himself against the charge of regionalism.

Thus it should is not altogether surprising that this debate over a regional modernism surfaced again in two essays that appeared 1981. In the first, "Der Frage des Regionalismus" (The question of regionalism), Alexander Tzonis, Lianne Lefaivre, and Anthony Alfonsin recounted the earlier debate surrounding Mumford's article in 1947, and raised the idea of a regional architecture to criticize postmodernism, which in their view was superficially focused on historical themes.[27] In the second essay, written for the Greek magazine *Architecture in Greece*, Tzonis and Lefaivre incorporated the "liberation" theme of Harris and discerned three types of regionalism in Greece over the course of three centuries. The first was tied to nationalistic sentiments in the eighteenth century, while the second, which followed the Greek War of Independence of 1821, was a regionalism deriving from the influence of German neoclassicism. The third phase of regionalism – what they term "critical regionalism" – arose from aspirations of Greek architects to liberate themselves from the dogmatic modernism of the 1950s. One exponent was Dimitris Pikionis, whose humanistic efforts to break with the "abstract universal norms" and the "technological exhibitionism and compositional conceit" of modernism are likened by Tzonis and Lefaivre to the architecture of van Eyck and Team 10.[28] The work of Dimitris and Susana Antonakakis, in particular their use of pathways and terraces (following upon studies of Greek vernacular examples), not only reaffirms "architecture as a cultural object in a social context" but it also offers an alternative to the rationalist typologies of the late 1970s.[29] Critical regionalism is thus at heart humanistic and is opposed the trendy acceptance of historical forms.

The arguments of Tzonis, Lefaivre, and Alfonsin were powerful ones within the context of the early 1980s, and their logic was not lost to Kenneth Frampton. The latter, as we have seen, had ties back to the New York Five and the IAUS, and he was still a persistent critic of the work of Venturi and Scott Brown. The pivotal point in his thinking, however, was the editorial with which he opened his first issue of *Oppositions* in October 1974, entitled "On Reading Heidegger."[30]

Frampton was drawn, in particular, to Martin Heidegger's essay of 1951 entitled "Building Dwelling Thinking."[31] Heidegger was a German philosopher and a disciple of Edmund Husserl, who founded the philosophical school of phenomenology. The latter, in its inception, was an attempt to break away from the philosophical abstractions of nineteenth-century idealism by engaging in a rigorous description of "things themselves," that is, our conscious experiences in the everyday world. It views consciousness not as an abstraction, but always as "consciousness of" something, and therefore something permeated with the moods, emotions, and contextual layers of meaning that we bring to the act of perception. In his late essay "Building Dwelling Thinking," Heidegger considered the etymological connection between the German words *bauen* (to build), the old German *buan* (to dwell), and *ich bin* (I am), from which he concludes that building is a quintessential form of dwelling. Building and dwelling are, in essence, the clearing of a "place" or the marking of locations for human memories, like the bridge that gathers the earth and landscape around a meandering stream. Heidegger, who was also strongly opposed to the influences of technology, was lamenting the "rootlessness of Western thought" that began with the seemingly innocent yet abstract Latin translation of Greek terms, through which language itself lost much of its concreteness.[32] For instance, the English word "space" derives from the Latin word *spatium*, and as a concept is removed from perceptual experience. By contrast, the German word for "space" is *Raum*, which is related to the English word "room," a physical expression of the idea of a "place."

Frampton, too, preferred the word "place" over "space" as a way to counter the conceptual gamesmanship of semiotics. He also drew attention to the more descriptive German word for architecture – *Baukunst*, literally "art of building" – in that it suggests a more material way of thinking about architecture. For if the abstraction of the term "architecture," in his view, leads to the "Charybdis of elitism" (formalist approaches that strip away any ecological, social, or topological concerns), the abstraction of "space" results in the "Scylla of populism" (the "non-place" of Melvin Webber, Venturi, and the commercial strip).[33] Re-centering architecture back on the theme of "place," conversely, demands not only a genuine concern with the tectonic art of building but it also acknowledges that there is a "public sphere" in design that architects must ultimately accommodate. Hence, in this editorial, Frampton first posited his formula of *"place, production, and nature"* as a more vivid "homeostatic plateau" for design.[34]

Frampton's attention to "place," of course, was not entirely new to this decade. Architects such as Aldo van Eyck, Louis Kahn, Kent C. Bloomer, and Charles Moore had earlier emphasized the word "place," yet without the phenomenological underpinnings. In this last regard, Christian Norberg-Schulz had also preceded Frampton by a few years. After his involvement with semiotic circles in the 1960s, the Norwegian architect had, by the end of the decade, come to reject the use of semiotics in favor of a more grounded phenomenological approach. In his book *Existence, Space & Architecture* (1971), dedicated to his friend Portoghesi, he described his "new approach" specifically as phenomenological and distinguished it from the parallel efforts of Alexander, Venturi, and others.[35] He then goes on to differentiate no fewer than six types of space: pragmatic, perceptual, cognitive, abstract, existential, and architectural. It was with the last two types that Norberg-Schulz's main interests resided, as his principal thesis was that architectural space "concretizes" existential space – that is, it is a symbolic form that mediates such spatial features as the place/node, path/axis, domain/district, within the multiple existential dimensions of landscapes, towns, and individual houses.[36] What we should demand from architectural space, he concludes, is "an imageable structure that offers rich possibilities for identification."[37] Norberg-Schulz later expanded his thesis in his two books *Meaning in Western Architecture* (1975) and *Genius Loci: Towards a Phenomenology of Architecture*.[38]

It was from such a base, in 1983, that Frampton put forth his idea of critical regionalism, with his essay "Towards a Critical Regionalism: Six Points for an Architecture of Resistance." The subtitle of the essay underscores the continuing influence of Adorno and Hannah Arendt on his thinking, but Frampton now brought something new to the table. He opened by distinguishing between civilization (a concept ruled by instrumental reason) and culture (a civilization's creative expression), and first to be targeted by his scorn were the avant-garde pretensions of postmodernists, who represented both the "bankruptcy of the liberative modern project" and the "decline of critical adversary culture."[39] Against current neo-avant-gardism, he proffered the *arrière-garde*, or rearguard position, of critical regionalism, one that was able to "deconstruct" the superficial world of culture that it inherited as well as to mitigate the positivist or technological forces of universal civilization.

Critical regionalism, in his view, accomplished these objectives through the menu of place-form, topography, context, climate, light, tactility, and tectonic form. If place-form harkens back to his earlier interest in Heidegger and dampens wanton historicism with a certain conservative or blocking strategy, the considerations of topography, context, climate, and light (which Frampton found especially evident in the architecture of Jørn Utzon and Alvar Aalto) calls to mind the ecological sensibilities that had been languishing for more than a decade. Yet the *pièce de résistance* of these offerings is Frampton's novel emphasis on tactility and tectonics. If the former draws attention to the fact that architecture is much more than simply a visual or semiotic art, tectonics concerns the form or the detailing of construction and thereby serves as both "a potential means for distilling play between material, craftwork and gravity" and as "the presentation of a structural poetic rather than the representation of a facade."[40] In this way, tactility and tectonics counter what he viewed as the scenographic nature of postmodern historicism as well as the emerging school of deconstruction.[41]

Shortly to follow Frampton in this regard was the Finnish architect Juhani Pallasmaa. Since the early 1960s Pallasmaa had been active as a teacher, museum director, and architect, and thus he combined his great respect for the Finnish design tradition with an international sophistication gained by travel, through which he came to question the contemporary loss of cultural authenticity as well as even the possibility of maintaining a "regional architecture in post-modern society."[42] In an essay written in 1985 he also lamented the fact that few modern buildings (in contrast to almost any rural farmhouse) have any emotional appeal, a failing he attributed to the rationalist fixation on formalism in the previous few decades. He embraced the term "phenomenology" as a way to seek out a more "authentic work of art," because phenomenology's role is specifically to probe the deeper structure of human reality and thereby to articulate the "language of metaphors than can be identified with our existence." Phenomenology further emphasizes the fact that architecture is first and foremost a multisensory experience (as opposed to a purely visual or conceptual exercise), and in this regard it "sensitizes our whole physical and mental receptivity."[43] Pallasmaa (against postmodernism) therefore pleaded for a "Second Modernism," or an architecture that is situational, emotional, relativistic, and inclusive of regional sensibilities – characteristics found in the architecture of Barragán, Aalto, Alvaro Siza, Imre Makovecz, and Reima Pietilä. "The human task of architecture," he elaborates, "is not to beautify or to humanise the world of everyday facts, but to open up a view into the second dimension of our consciousness, the reality of images, memories and dreams."[44]

Mérida and Venice

In the mid-1980s, two further events also played heavily into this discussion: one a building and the other an exhibition. The building was the Museum of Roman Art in Mérida (1980–1985), designed by Spanish architect José Rafael Moneo. This native of Navarra had received his architectural diploma in 1961 and worked in the offices of Jørn Utzon and Francisco Javier Sáenz de Oiza. A two-year stay at the Spanish Academy in

Figure 5.2 José Rafael Moneo, Museum of Roman Art, Mérida (1980–1985). Image courtesy of Romina Canna.

Rome also allowed him to meet Bruno Zevi, Manfredo Tafuri, and Paolo Portoghesi. Thus, early in his career Mérida was attracted to the rationalist thinking of Rossi, particularly his typological insights on the city, but he never went so far as to embrace what he (even earlier) had called Rossi's "estrangement from the real" or (later) "tyranny of form."[45] This hesitation on Moneo's part is revealing because his design for the Museum of Roman Art takes a very different approach with regard to history and to architecture.

At first glance the museum appears to be a perfect illustration of postmodern historicism in the early 1980s. Mérida was the site of a Roman town in Spain, in fact, the largest town in Spain toward the end of the Roman Empire. The building is erected over the archaeological site along a different axis to the street plan of the ruins, and its main space if formed from nine interior parallel walls with a linear series of arches cut through them on several levels for circulation. A particularly tall and wide series of arches down one side of the building accommodates the main circulation spine, not unlike the transept of a church. To one side of the building, the parallel walls also protrude from the enclosing wall and become exterior buttresses. It seems as if Moneo has literally built a series of Roman walls with relieving arches and skylights above to house the ruins of an ancient Roman city.

On closer inspection, however, the literalness fades. Moneo on several occasions has pointed out that the walls are not strict imitations of Roman walls (which were always supported with cross-walls), but rather a reference to the Roman construction method of filling hollow brick walls with concrete. He is particularly at pains to note the great care he took in minimizing the mortar joint of the brick – first to make the wall more ahistorical (and therefore removed from Roman walls) and second to emphasize the brick's materiality. Both qualities, he argues, puts one in a better frame of mind to appreciate Roman archaeological fragments.[46] In fact, for the visitor to the museum, the building has two grand themes: light and materiality. The contrast of light is especially vivid between the walls of the upper levels where artifacts are on display, and the darker, almost cave-like atmosphere of the lower level where the urban ruins can be viewed. The theme of materiality is forcefully articulated by the sheer bulk of the massive brick walls. It connotes for Moneo the idea of "lasting," and this objective too, he understands, leads him against the mainstream: "The idea of permanence has for me a value. Architecture is not simply the brilliant expression of an idea."[47]

The second event to play heavily into contemporary discussions in the 1980s – the exhibition – took place in Venice and Milan while the museum in Mérida was under construction. Once again it stands out by virtue of its disconcertedness with its temporal context. The show's focus – Carlo Scarpa – had passed away six years earlier, and up to this time he had received little critical recognition outside northern Italy. The layout was designed by Mario Botta and the exhibition and its monograph – *Carlo Scarpa: The Complete Works* – were curated and edited by Francesco Dal Co and Giuseppe Mazzariol.[48] Almost overnight, a major new figure would appear.

Like his spiritual mentor, Palladio, Scarpa was born in the Veneto and raised in Vicenza. After attending the Academy of Fine Arts in Venice in the 1920s, he worked in the office of Guido Cirilli before starting practice. One of his early projects was the renovation of sections of the medieval Ca' Foscari in 1935–1937. In this same decade he also began his long association with Paolo Venini's famed glass manufacturing firm at Murano, where Scarpa learned the nature of materials, color, and detailing. After World War II, Scarpa focused on architecture, with the bulk of his commissions dealing with museum installations and restorations. Among these was his extension to the Canova Plaster Cast Gallery, Treviso (1955–1957) and the restoration of the Castelvecchio Museum, Verona (1956–1973), which led to his commission for the reorganization of the ground floor of

Figure 5.3 Carlo Scarpa, Castelvecchio Museum, Verona (1956–1973). Image courtesy of Evan Chakroff.

the Fondazione Querini Stampalia, Venice (1961–1963). With these works, Scarpa acquired the reputation of being a master of spatial and visual effects as well as for exploiting materials through an inventive and refined detailing. In 1956 he shared the Olivetti Prize for architecture with Ludovico Quaroni, but the crowning achievement of his career was his design for the Brion Tomb, San Vito d'Altivole (1969–1979), which was finished one year after his death. Throughout these years Scarpa also taught drawing and other disciplines at the University of Venice, and therefore influenced the intellectual development of a number of students.

Given the power of Scarpa's designs, it is not difficult to understand why the show and catalogue so quickly commanded global attention; but not to be lost in the belated recognition of his talent was the particular accord that his designs found at this particular time – that is, at the height of postmodernism's popularity. This is puzzling because Scarpa was in many respects an old-school modernist, and his work thus carried an anachronistic air.

One reason for his new-found acceptance was the seductive power of his drawings, but this can be said only with a major qualification. His drawings are neither in the axonometric style of so many of the conceptual designs of the time nor in the lavish and colorful style of postmodern presentations. They are above all design drawings, that is, *working* drawings in the non-technical sense of this word. A few lines with a T-square might, with the aid of colored pencil, reveal the rough figuration of a floor plan or elevation, but more often than not the content of the drawing is found in the dozens of tiny sketches of constructional details that fill out the sheets of tracing paper – in, around, and through the plan or elevation – like a medieval palimpsest. Scarpa was an architect who not only designed simultaneously at different scales, as some architects are inclined to do, but with an intensity of inventive thought or exploration (using different inks, crayons, and pencils) that literally consumes each sheet of paper like the contents of a weighty tome.

Certainly one of the more compelling aspect of Scarpa's work was his use of light, but here again we run into problems in explaining his appeal. For not only does the lens of a camera notoriously filter out all nuance of lighting effects, but northeast Italy, with its Adriatic climate and Byzantine sensibilities, is fabled for its misty and aqueous atmospheres that continually change over a course of a day or season. In one controversial layout for the Canova gallery, for instance, Scarpa placed Canova's white plaster casts against white walls and illuminated them with the "azure blocks" of indented windows floating above the corners of the room.[49] In another exhibit, in which he attempted to diffuse but not dim the light cast on a fragile painting, he scoured the city until he found the suitable tinted nylon underskirt from a haberdasher. Like his drawings, this thoughtfulness suggests a highly sensual or sensory approach to the experience of architecture.

Still another aspect of Scarpa's architecture that is often discussed was his obsession with detailing. But once again, the explanations and interpretations are many and varied. Dal Co, one of Scarpa's most astute admirers, finds his details "anti-modern" because of their "unruliness" and "display of luxury." As he goes on to point out: "In Scarpa's architecture, on the contrary, richness of display is the form taken by the rushing in of memory. Luxury is thus the manifestation of a deep intimacy with things, elusive and unrepeatable; it does not guarantee possession beyond the passing instant."[50] Marco Frascari, a former student of Scarpa, by contrast, views his "adoration of the joint" as the "perfect realization of Alberti's high Renaissance concept of concinnity," one born of his life-long dealings with the "stonecutters, masons, carpenters, glassmakers, and smiths of Venice."[51] Both interpretations might be considered within the context of the famous image of collected details specifically designed by Scarpa for the Brion Tomb – items that look like they could have been culled from an automotive engine, a candle shop, or an architectural catalogue of exhaust vents. Frascari also relates the story that Scarpa had the unusual habit of visiting his buildings under construction at night with a flashlight, specifically to focus on the expression of details.

But perhaps it was precisely these quixotic visions that made Scarpa's intensely personal and regional designs so attractive to so many architects in the mid-1980s. If ever an era needed its mounted knight errant, seeking adventures for his imagined mistress and architectural muse, it was certainly this period of historical unreality. Scarpa's contribution to the time, like that of Moneo, was that he sought to provide something real, something material, something that would mute the bright light of the stage. The only question is whether it was the Venetian or the architectural world-at-large who had gone completely mad.

6

Traditionalism and New Urbanism

The Prince of Architecture

Every 130 years or so, and not without patrician complicity, British architectural theory erupts into a particularly contentious debate. In the 1720s
it was the Third Earl of Shaftesbury and Lord Burlington who conspired
to curb the baroque indulgences of John Vanbrugh and Nicholas
Hawksmoor with the classical recipe of a Palladian Revival. Around 1850
came the ferocious "Battle of the Styles," a verbal slugfest that pitted the
"eclectics" and supporters of industrialization (such as Prince Albert)
against the medieval sanctimony of Augustus Welby Pugin and John
Ruskin. Thus it was not altogether out of order when, in the 1980s,
another quintessential British disputation should appear. What was a little
unusual, however, was that the furor should be ignited by a speech in the
upscale confines of Hampton Court Palace – on the august occasion of the
sesquicentennial anniversary of the Royal Institute of British Architects
(RIBA). Architectural revolutions have rarely been launched before the
chortles of a Wednesday-evening crowd of such well-dressed ladies and
gentlemen.

   Notwithstanding, the now notorious "Monstrous Carbuncle Speech"
of Prince Charles (the great-great-grandson of Prince Albert) cannot be
overestimated for its influence on architectural thinking, even if in many
respects the speech was rather modest and perfunctory. Both his opening
remarks in praise of Charles Correa (the year's Gold Medal winner),
together with his closing quotation on "taste" by Johann Wolfgang von
Goethe, certainly petitioned no controversy. And even as Prince Charles
entered the body of his speech and referred to accessibility standards for

An Introduction to Architectural Theory: 1968 to the Present, First Edition.
Harry Francis Mallgrave and David Goodman.
© 2011 Harry Francis Mallgrave and David Goodman. Published 2011 by Blackwell Publishing Ltd.

the disabled, the need for architects to consider the "feelings and wishes" of "ordinary people," and the importance of involving these same people in "Community Design," he would scarcely have elicited much protest. Even his plea for a return to "those curves and arches that express feeling in design" was probably seen by many in attendance as little more than the personal opinion of an architectural novice.

But the prince, no doubt looking forward to the fireworks to be later displayed over Hampton's Grand Canal, was throughout these affable remarks being sly, like a fox. Earlier in the day he had circulated the full text of his speech to *The Times* and to *The Guardian*, and (once re-circulated to the RIBA) the architectural institution had the gumption to ask the prince, "through the Palace," to make a different speech.[1] What had particularly offended the hierarchy of this stately body of architects were two brief comments of the prince regarding two on-going architectural proposals. One was the long-stalled design by Ludwig Mies van der Rohe for a tower on Mansion House Square (1964), which, because of leasehold contracts, could not be scheduled for construction until 1986. The other was the planned extension to the National Gallery on Trafalgar Square. It was the last design, the competition-winning project by Ahrends, Burton and Koralek, that Prince Charles famously (or infamously, if you prefer) described as "a monstrous carbuncle on the face of a much-loved and elegant friend."[2] One would have to read through a lot of architectural history to find a design likened to such an unfortunate medical condition.

Reaction to the prince's remarks was swift, as one might expect, but (as one might not expect) strikingly so on the generally temperate pages of *The Times*. Clearly a nerve had been bumped. By Friday, a little more than twenty-four hours after the closing of the event, *The Times* was already running an editorial that encouraged the prince, in his condemnation of modernism, to distinguish between good and bad modern architecture, and cautioned him against pursuing a postmodern "retreat into conservation, replication and pastiche."[3] In the same paper, Peter Ahrends, the designer of the National Gallery extension, contested the prince's remarks by describing them as "offensive, reactionary and ill considered" – before taking solace in the fact that building authorities would not be much influenced by the prince's simile.[4] Such optimism became problematic, however, when the majority of *The Times*'s letters-to-the-editor over the next several weeks not only supported the prince's position on this particular design but also broadened the debate into one concerning the unhappy state of British architecture since World War II. It was as if, somewhere in the basement of the British Museum, Pandora's box had been discovered and unsealed.

Opinions followed from all sides. One journalist covering the RIBA address, Simon Jenkins, conceded that the prince's remarks were "devoid of qualification" and "spectacularly impolite," but he nevertheless took to task the "hypocrisy" of the RIBA, or those "architects living mostly in comfortable Georgian houses" who either "defend their Brutalist monuments – the tower blocks, slabs and comprehensive developments that dot the skylines of most British cities – or they blame their defects on the public."[5] If there was any cure for the current state of British architecture, Jenkins continued, it was just this new start of a conservation movement in Britain as well as the more recent contextual approaches of Quinlan Terry and Terry Farrell – all made possible because the "Modern Movement was not just a phase, it was a mistake. It was architecture torn loose from style, invading politics and posing as social engineering."[6]

Michael Manser, President of the RIBA, responded one week later with moderation and perhaps with some embarrassment. Seemingly now wishing to downplay the controversy, he commended the prince for stirring debate, but he then threw down the professional glove:

> Those who think a line must be drawn at Edwardian times are either geriatric or dictatorial. In a healthy, free society there is room for all points of view: Modern architecture, Post-Modern or pastiche, conservation or rehabilitation. Those who want to patronise and continue the development of Modern Movement architecture should be allowed their freedom amongst the rest, despite the fact that, like the rest, some of it will be good and some bad.[7]

An even more spirited defense of modernism was volunteered by Richard Rogers, whose recently completed Lloyd's of London building was concurrently enduring its share of public criticism. Speaking of the specter of modernism being "obliterated by an indiscriminate wave of nostalgia," he defended the lost honor of Louis Kahn, Alvar Aalto, Frank Lloyd Wright, and Le Corbusier (among others who had not been attacked by the prince) and insisted that "artistic development has never stood still. Consensus alone has never produced a great work of art, though public understanding and involvement, together with enlightened patronage, has."[8]

Notwithstanding these counter punches, the early rounds of this debate (not to mention the later ones) clearly went to the side of the prince. In May 1985 the long-delayed Mies tower project was scuttled by the Environmental Secretary Patrick Jenkin, who also happened to be in the audience of the prince's RIBA address of the previous year. The National Gallery extension would suffer a similar fate. After the first design by Ahrends, Burton and Korelak, upon further review, was rejected, a second proposal was offered in 1984, but it too failed to win bureaucratic approval.

The site was then sold by the original developer to a new patron, John Sainsbury, who stepped in and eliminated the speculative office space that had been part of the original program. All of this led to another limited competition that was eventually won by Venturi, Scott Brown and Associates.

The Paternoster Controversy

Prince Charles, in the meantime, was holding up his side of the debate with lectures, visits to selected sites, and meetings with similarly inclined architects. Little by little he began to fashion a series of themes and organize a visible movement. Early in 1985 he elaborated upon his notion of "community architecture" by praising the advocacy planning of several run-down urban neighborhoods in Liverpool and Macclesfield, all with the "help and expert advice of their own architect."[9] Not wishing to sound too compliant, he soon thereafter vowed to lead a crusade on behalf of the "ordinary bloke" and promised "to throw a proverbial royal brick through the inviting plate glass of pompous professional pride."[10] In a speech given in 1986 he invoked the "mathematical laws of harmony" (citing the fifth-century Greek sculptor Polycleitus) as well as Ruskin's ornamental definition of architecture, in what became another impassioned plea for "reestablishing human scale in street patterns and heights of buildings."[11] Finally, in another well-publicized address given at George Dance the Elder's Mansion House in December 1987, he waded into still another controversy surrounding the competition for the rebuilding of Paternoster Square.

In many ways, the Paternoster debate might be seen as one of the more pivotal events in recent planning theory.[12] The seven-acre tract of urban land lies just north of venerable St Paul's Cathedral, within the old walls of the City of London. The cathedral itself dates back to the seventh century, although it was destroyed by fire and rebuilt several times over the course of its history. A sixteenth-century map shows the narrow streets and tight medieval character of the Paternoster area, originally named for its rosary makers, although it later became a center of London's publishing industry. The Great Fire of 1666 again destroyed the cathedral and the surrounding area, but by 1715 both had been reconstructed along their medieval lot-lines. Paternoster, in fact, remained largely intact until the German Air Force firebombed the area in December 1940. After the war, officials made the disastrous decision to rebuild the area along "modern" principles of planning, and a group of dreary concrete-slab buildings (dreary by everyone's concession) were randomly deposited on the site.[13] Most of the buildings were erected in the early 1960s – that is, less than 20 years before the city and public opinion were united in wanting them removed.

Therefore, in June 1987 the city and a consortium of developers concluded a limited competition for ideas to redesign the district. Seven architectural firms were invited to participate: Skidmore, Owens & Merrill, Norman Foster, Arata Isozaki, James Stirling, Richard Rogers, Arup Associates, and MacCormac, Jamieson, Prichard & Wright.[14] The goal of the competition, which was won by Arup and Associates and Richard Rogers, was not to produce a master plan but to seek ideas for a planning strategy. The prince was privately shown the seven schemes in July and he voiced his firm disapproval of them all.

The stage was thus set for the prince's "Mansion House Speech" of December, in which he took aim not only at the seven schemes but more broadly at Britain's entire policy of urban redevelopment since World War II. He vilified the "1947 Town and Country Planning Act" as well as the majority of postwar planners, architects, and developers for wrecking London's skyline, for losing the dome of St Paul's "in a jostling scrum of office buildings," and indeed for sweeping away the historic lanes, alleys, and hide-away courtyards of Paternoster, "which in most other European countries would have been lovingly rebuilt after the war."[15] He went on to call for the design-review of all new buildings near major monuments, for firm aesthetic guidelines regarding their scale and detailing, and for specific rules for the preservation of London's skyline. Again with respect to the Paternoster area, he made one of his most determined and eloquent pleas:

> So, I would like to see the mediaeval street plan of pre-war Paternoster reconstructed, not out of mere nostalgia, but to give meaning to surviving fragments like Amen Court and the Chapter House, now left like dispossessed refugees in an arid desert of God-forsaken buildings. I would like to see a roofscape that gives the impression that St. Paul's is floating above it like a great ship on the sea. I would also like to see the kinds of materials Wren might have used – soft red brick and stone dressings, perhaps, and the ornament and detail of classical architecture, but on a scale humble enough not to compete with monumentality of St. Paul's.[16]

Yet the prince this time did not limit his action to words. As Charles Jencks has reported, he worked behind the scenes with Léon Krier, Dan Cruickshank, and John Simpson, and set in motion a counter-proposal to the seven schemes, a proposal that would be carried out by the classicist Simpson.[17] With such an act, the lines of the controversy were thus clearly drawn for everyone to see, and many architects once again felt that the prince had overstepped his bounds by taking a particular side on the issue of style.

The competition schemes in themselves are very informative of this period. Izosaki and Stirling produced a "postmodern" montage of individual units, while SOM and Norman Foster countered with geometric schemes still within a modernist planning vein. The entry of MacCormac, Jamieson, Prichard & Wright, with its street layouts, reverted in part to the original texture of the area, while Richard Rogers was somewhere in between with a dense building footprint and a large central square. None of the proposals – in large part because of the enormous square-footage of rental area asked for by the competition brief – paid much attention to the historic character of the area or to the spatial edge abounding St Paul's. Nor did they take into account the scale, modulation, or the hierarchy of the public spaces.

All of this was highlighted in the spring and summer of 1988 when both Arup and John Simpson unveiled their respective proposals. Arup, still regarding its winning scheme as a "Work in Progress," in fact produced three alternative plans: one of which featured a modest amphitheater next to the main entrance of St Paul's, and two of which contained a curving arcade near the original footprint of Paternoster Row.[18] The common denominator of all three proposals, according to Philip Dowson, was the mandate of the competition jury to conceive their design as a series of "routes, alleys and squares," which now brought some of the historic street layouts back into play.[19] In this regard, however, Arup was trumped by the more modestly scaled layout of John Simpson – especially by his oil-renderings and classical designs of extraordinary character and visual seduction. Simpson had also reduced the programmatic requirements and thus was able to revert to the original layout of the streets and squares. Arup countered with its scaled-back final version of its scheme in November 1988 (emulating Simpson's proposal even more closely), but the firm would be unsuccessful in countering the momentum that the prince had generated. When new developers purchased the rights to the site in 1989, John Simpson, together with Terry Farrell and Thomas Beeby, were named the new architects and planners for the area.[20]

Paternoster aside – the publicity surrounding the prince's speech at the Mansion house in 1987 raised the pitch of an already loud architectural debate. London architects were split in two camps, with Léon Krier, Terry Farrell, Jeremy Dixon, and Rod Hackney, among others, rallying to the prince's side. Krier, whose political views had evolved over the years, moved to the forefront of the debate in 1988 when he was commissioned by the Duchy of Cornwall (the private estate of the Prince of Wales) to design the 450-acre, new community of Poundbury, adjoining the town of Dorchester.[21] He took as his model a typical English village and created a town square, market, and civic buildings; he further divided the neighborhoods into mixed-use communities (for education, employment, shopping, and leisure) and therefore made them much less dependent on the automobile. His work with the local population in incorporating their viewpoints also proved to be a major public success.

Opposition to the campaign of Prince Charles nevertheless continued to intensify. Some time between 1988 and 1989 Charles Jencks, a popular critical voice in London, recanted his earlier support for Charles's pluralism and faulted the prince for his ethical lapses.[22] Richard Rogers again renounced the prince's historical nostalgia as well as his politics, in what had now become a battle riddled with politics. Shortly after the Mansion House address, he countered the prince's "rigid classicism" with a defense of individual creativity and the necessity for architects to keep pace with technological change.[23] Norman Foster also contended the prince's position, but in a more modest way. He praised the prince for rallying the people to the issue of the environment and also expressed his opposition to "our appalling legacy of postwar development."[24] At the same time he pointed to the world's economy becoming ever more global and to the crucial need for British firms to participate in this new reality. In the end he suggested a role for the prince similar to that of Prince Albert 130 years earlier, which meant becoming involved with the Royal Fine Arts Commission – not pausing to note that its secretary had recently and harshly criticized Prince Charles.[25]

Prince Charles, however, took a more public tack. In the fall of 1988 he starred in his own BBC television documentary, "A Vision of Britain," which was so successful that in the following year it was extended into a major exhibition at the Victoria and Albert Museum, accompanied with a book. The television documentary attracted six million viewers and 5000 letters: 99 percent of which, the prince later boasted, fully supported his views on the subject.[26] The book, also carrying the subtitle "A Personal View of Architecture," was in some ways even more successful. Whatever position one may hold with regard to the prince's architectural views, the book, very much in the earlier tradition of Pugin, made a powerful statement with its assembled images, clearly written text, and contentious edge. If using photographs contrasting the smaller-scaled, traditional architecture of Britain with some of the worst calamities of its postwar development is almost too easy a tactic, the prince at least humbles his victory by presenting a rather positive vision for the future. The work of Hassan

Fathy is cited when the prince notes that many areas of the world are losing their cultural identity through the endless replication of the modern aesthetic.[27] This is also true of Britain's historical legacy, which he emphasizes by taking to task yet another respected center of postmodernism: "Why, for example, is the Architectural Association's headquarters situated in one of London's most beautiful squares, while some of its graduates have been helping to create ever uglier surroundings for other people to live in?"[28]

The prince moves on to articulate his "Ten Principles We Can Build Upon," his guidelines for future development. The first five – defining architectural place, hierarchy, scale, harmony, and enclosure – could be gleaned by reading Camillo Sitte, as Charles's concern for an urban scale appropriate to pedestrian or human proportions seems to be his foremost concern. The other five principles owe much to the Victorian sensibilities of Ruskin, as local materials, embellished with decoration and art, with limits on signs and building heights, compose the ingredients of an architecture truly responding to the community and indeed taking the community's tastes and aspirations into account. Prince Charles concludes by offering several examples of how this is currently being done by a partnership of community-minded architects, and in this respect it is a positive sense of "nation" that the author leaves with his audience.[29] When these principles are placed against the contemporary debate over Deconstruction in Britain (an issue simultaneously reaching its Derridean crescendo), it is almost impossible to imagine two more contrary architectural approaches being offered to the public. Such is one of the many paradoxes of the 1980s.

Toward a New Urbanism

Near the end of the documentary and the book, Prince Charles discussed the new American beachside community of Seaside. Sandwiched between images of traditional English villages and scenic views of Sienna, the photographs at first seem strikingly out of character, but the prince assured his audience that this sandy beach town on the azure coast of Florida's panhandle was in fact "an extraordinary place – with a modern, classical look," one that had successfully joined the "traditional virtues" of the American small town with the impulse of "the planned English garden city movement."[30] With a stroke, the prince thus put his finger on the project that within the next couple of years would serve the paradigm for the American movement of "New Urbanism." Its two architects – the spousal team of Andrés Duany and Elizabeth Plater-Zyberk – were not the sole instigators of this new direction, but few projects of the 1980s could have put such a sunny face on the initiative.

Duany and Plater-Zyberk were both schooled at Princeton and Yale in the early 1970s under the tutelage of a faculty that included Kenneth Frampton, Michael Graves, Allan Greenberg, and Vincent Scully. Duany, after taking a teaching position at the University of Miami in 1974, worked briefly for another of his mentors, Robert A. M. Stern, while Plater-Zyberk, upon her graduation, apprenticed in the office of Venturi and Rauch in Philadelphia. In 1975 the two architects joined forces to renovate the Wrecker's House in Key West, which served as a prelude to their alliance with Hervin Romney, Bernardo Fort-Brescia, and Laurinda Spear – in the formation of the stylish Miami office of Arquitectonica. In 1980, with diverging directions now evident within the firm, Duany and Plater-Zyberk established their own practice in Coconut Grove under the abbreviation DPZ.

By this date, both had already made contact with Robert Davis – in fact, they met him at a 10-year-reunion honoring the "Five Architects," held in Boca Raton in 1978. The Miami-based developer was at the time experiencing his own change of direction. He had inherited an 80-acre parcel of land from his grandfather on Florida's northern coastline, 30 miles west of Panama City, and was interested in developing it such a way as to recall the childhood summers he had shared with his family in modest, wood-framed cottages in the same area. Owner and architects together embarked on various journeys through the South to explore the regional characteristics of traditional wood-framed housing and the spatial character of small towns. The result was a very bold and untypical decision to create not a typical Floridian development but rather a "community," one that would re-create both the flavor of a small Southern town and its typical architectural features (porches, sloping overhanging roofs, numerous windows, and cross-ventilation). All were chosen in response to the region's hot, humid climate.

Thus, in writing the "Traditional Neighborhood Development" ordinance for Seaside in the summer of 1982, DPZ rather skillfully requested a number of unusual developmental features, among them small lots with minimal setbacks, streets generally oriented toward public spaces and the water, commercial buildings with arcades, and houses with picket fences. The ordinance even encouraged cupolas or small towers atop the houses to vary the (generally metal) rooflines and allow views of the Gulf of Mexico. The fact that it was no more than a 10-minute walk from one side of town to the other neatly downplayed the use of automobiles. The actual design of the houses and buildings was also

Figure 6.1 Seaside, Florida, planned by Andrés Duany and Elizabeth Plater-Zyberk. Image courtesy of Duany Plater-Zyberk & Company.

Figure 6.2 Seaside, Florida. Image courtesy of Helen Haden.

relegated to outside, sympathetic architects – bringing to the project the other essential element of variety.

Little by little, as the elements of the town came to be developed during the mid-1980s, the non-architectural press began to pick up on the uniqueness of the endeavor. In 1986 Roger K. Lewis of *The Washington Post* underscored Seaside's "indigenous traditions and imagery," which for him were "both nostalgic and innovative."[31] The next year Steve Garbarino of the *St. Petersburg Times* rather insightfully portrayed the early houses of Seaside as the "comeback" of the traditional "Cracker" style of Southern architecture, that is, the simple and functional houses of Florida's first settlers before the advent of air conditioning.[32] And in 1987, Joseph Giovannini, an architectural critic writing for *The New York Times*, put the plan of Seaside within the context of a "new urbanism" that was spreading across the country.[33] This point was made even more convincingly in the following year in a lengthy article by Philip Langdon that appeared in *The Atlantic Monthly*, "A Good Place to Live."[34] Langdon featured Seaside and other urban designs by DPZ as the second coming of a "new traditionalism," one being embraced by urban and suburban developers in projects unfolding in Florida, Cape Cod, Princeton, Reston, Battery Park, and Portland. The special appeal of Seaside for Langdon was not only the "old-fashioned, down-home style of its houses," but also its quaint civic character: porches, picket fences, beach pavilions, and public space, but most especially its allegiance to the pedestrian at the expense of the automobile and the resulting "quiet" that results.[35] Through his conversations with the architects, Landon also put his finger on two forces in place with the conception of Seaside: the "studies of British and American suburbs" by Robert Stern, and the urbanism of Krier, "who advocates a return to small cities on a human scale."[36]

Also not overlooked by Langdon was the inspiration of a little-known American planner John Nolen (1869–1937), whose roots lay within the landscape tradition of Frederick Law Olmsted.[37] Nolen, who was in the first class of landscape architects to graduate from Harvard University in 1905, might be called one of the first American town planners with a deep appreciation for nature, although many of his grandest visions (of over 400 projects overall) went unfulfilled. At the larger scale he prepared master plans for the cities of San Diego, Madison, Roanoke, and Charlotte, but his talent is more apparent in some of his smaller executed developments, such as Mariemont, Ohio, and Venice, Florida. Nolen preached "a wiser husbanding of our aesthetic, human and natural resources," and later drew close to the garden-city ideal of Raymond Unwin.[38] In his loosely geometric plan for Venice (1926), for instance, he lined the entire gulf front with a park and planned each of the neighborhoods with green spaces and short streets scaled to pedestrian access. Even the diagonals evident at Seaside, as well as the soft tones used in presentational rendering, suggest a debt to Nolen and his appreciation of the coastline.

If Stern, Krier, and Nolen all played important roles in the rise of New Urbanism in the 1980s, not to be overlooked is the movement's connection with the social and environmental movements of the 1960s and 1970s. Important in this regard were the efforts of Sim Van der Ryn and Peter Calthorpe. Van der Ryn was a graduate of the University of Michigan, where he was influenced in particular by the teachings of Buckminster Fuller. After moving to California and joining the faculty at Berkeley, he – like Alexander – began to search for alternative approaches to conventional modernism and founded the Farallones Institute as a way to explore ecological and recycling issues. In 1975 he helped to devise the new energy-efficiency standards for state office buildings, and in 1977 he designed the much publicized Bateson Building, whose solar courtyard relied entirely on passive climate control. His younger colleague, Peter Calthorpe, briefly attended Yale before returning to his native California to work for Van der Ryn. In 1978 the two formed a partnership and produced innovative redevelopment projects for Sacramento and Marin County (the latter an unexecuted solar community on the site of the recently closed Hamilton Air Force Base), and in 1980 they were instrumental in instigating an important debate on sustainable urban planning on the West Coast.

The venue was the Westerbeke Ranch near Sonoma, where, a group of three-dozen professionals from various disciplines gathered to consider the planning premises of American cities and towns and their patterns of energy consumption. The result of the conference, *Sustainable Communities* (1986), is an early primer on green design – the word "sustainable" in the title may very well be the first use of the term in an architectural book.[39] Van der Ryn and Calthorpe, among others, contributed essays on the urban and suburban fabric, and stressed the need for denser neighborhoods built around public spaces and pedestrian activities. They also called for less dependence on the automobile and for a greater use of mass transit as well as for employing passive and active energy strategies.

It was Calthorpe who would advance this vision within a larger planning context. Working first with Mark Mack, and then with a group of like-minded faculty at Berkeley in the 1980s, Calthorpe turned in particular to suburban development, and he raised the concept of "pedestrian pockets," a notion he first defined "as a balanced, mixed-use area within a quarter-mile or a five-minute walking radius of a transit system."[40] The gist of the idea, and an old one at that, was to concentrate compact suburban developments along rail and other mass transportation lines leading into cities. In the spring of 1988, Douglas Kelbaugh, the director of the architecture program at the University of Washington in Seattle, organized a one-week charrette for his students consisting of four design teams (one led by Calthorpe and Kelbaugh) to implement such a strategy on a site in Auburn, Washington. In his preface to the published book of the proceedings, Kelbaugh rationalized this focus on the suburb as a response to "the dogmatic if convincing urban design theories of Krier" and to the softening of energy prices, which had since the mid-1970s enervated the environmental movement.[41]

Calthorpe's first opportunity to implement this strategy, however, did not come until 1989, when, at a conference at Berkeley, he met the developer Phil Angelides and received the job of redesigning a 4000-acre suburban tract just south of Sacramento, called Laguna West. Although the project would eventually end in financial distress, it was cited in a 1991 article in *Time Magazine*, alongside the work of DPZ, as one of those "Oldfangled New Towns" that were revolutionizing American planning.[42] Calthorpe was shortly thereafter commissioned to prepare planning guidelines for the cities of Sacramento, San Diego, and Portland, which would lead to his important study, *The Next American Metropolis* (1993).[43] Here he transformed the theme of "pedestrian pockets" into the notion of "Transit-Oriented Developments" (TOD). In a manner reminiscent of Alexander's *A Pattern Language*, it was filled with a bevy of design guidelines specifying the details of such an approach.

The year 1993 also became the defining moment for the new movement in several respects. In April of that year Cynthia Davidson organized a roundtable discussion on Seaside that featured Duany and Plater-Zyberk, Diane Ghirardo, and Robert Stern against the opposing forces of Peter Eisenman, Neil Smith, and Mark Linder. All three naysayers, convinced they were witnessing a trip down nostalgia lane, were united in the belief that architecture should never again come to be seen as a social or political remedy, while the more political Smith was especially hostile to the concept of Seaside, calling it both "profoundly pessimistic" and ideologically representative of "trickle-down paternalism" – an apparent reference to the economic theories of the Reagan administration.[44]

In October, before a more friendly audience, Duany and Plater-Zyberk organized the first Congress for the New Urbanism in Alexandria, Virginia, which was attended by 170 people. The need for such a conference was discussed as early as 1989 in Los Angeles, when Duany and Plater-Zyberk

Transit-Oriented Development (TOD)

A Transit-Oriented Development (TOD) is a mixed-use community within an average 2,000-foot walking distance of a transit stop and core commercial area. TODs mix residential, retail, office, open space, and public uses in a walkable environment, making it convenient for residents and employees to travel by transit, bicycle, foot, or car.

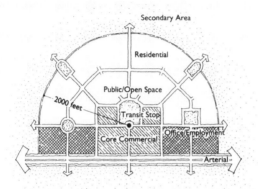

Figure 6.3   Peter Calthorpe, sketch from *The Next American Metropolis* illustrating the TOD. Image and text by permission of Calthorpe Associates.

were collaborating on a project with their Princeton classmates and colleagues Stefanos Polyzoides and Elizabeth Moule.[45] Two years later, in the summer of 1991, the four architects met with Calthorpe at the Ahwahnee Hotel in Yosemite and drafted the Ahwahnee Principles, which set out the founding tenets of New Urbanism.[46] As Moule later noted, the early efforts were a conscious effort to model the charter and organization after the Athens Charter and the CIAM – although philosophically nothing could have been more removed from their own approach.[47] Over the course of three further congresses in Los Angeles, San Francisco, and Charleston (in 1994, 1995, and 1996), and with the participation of Daniel Solomon, a formal charter was written and ratified.

In its final form, the Charter of the New Urbanism was a rather comprehensive document reflecting the differing contributions of more than two dozen people. The brief preamble called for the restoration of existing urban centers and the "reconfiguration of sprawling suburbs," as well as the concomitant "restructuring of public policy" to support these goals.[48] What followed were 27 principles or design patterns that specified, in some instances in precise language, the planning tenets. Earlier thematic definitions and policy concerns had been expanded along a political front. For instance, Randall Arendt spoke to the re-zoning of farmlands, Ken Greenberg to the issue of preservation, and Myron Orfield to the matter of taxation and revenue sharing.[49] Douglas Kelbaugh, who had since assumed the deanship of the architectural and planning program at the University of Michigan, and Mark M. Schimmenti, also spoke to the matter of climate, topography, materials, and natural methods of heating and cooling, thereby drawing New Urbanism closer in line with the sustainability movement of the decade.[50]

This most welcome attempt to describe more definitively the meaning of New Urbanism at the same time carried with it the peril of too narrow a checklist of principles. Whereas the earlier tag of historicist "nostalgia" that many critics applied to New Urbanism in the 1980s had by this time been successfully deflected, other critics, still echoing the mantras of 1968, objected to the movement's desire for social engineering – the belief that architecture can cure society's ills or radically amend personal habits. Notwithstanding its very correct analysis of the social isolation and energy-consumptive habits of many American suburban communities, facets of the charter of New Urbanism carried with them distinct architectural implications along with an air of inflexibility. If the high-rise, for instance, might prove to be more "sustainable" in terms of energy consumption and restoring the density to urban centers, it use had now been precluded seemingly by political fiat.

In any case, one of the more interesting things about the work of the New Urbanists in the early 1990s, in addition to the high quality of much of the work itself, was the messianic spirit of reform that they brought to the architectural profession and its education. Seaside – soon to be transposed into a riveting cinematic stage set – was no longer just sunny; it had by this time become both emblematic of a desire for residential reform as well as a serious challenge to many of the core assumptions of numerous urban developments. People simply liked it – a point that seems to have particularly inflamed many of its detractors. As for the fervor, Vincent Scully perhaps articulated it best in 1994 when he appraised the new movement with no small measure of polemical gloss: "When the great winds rise up out of the Gulf – and the storm clouds roll in thundering upon the little lighted town with its towered houses – then a truth is felt, involving the majesty of nature and, however partial, the brotherhood of mankind."[51] Who, but incorrigible naysayers, could discount such a Pauline experience?

7

Gilded Age of Theory

Based on the number of printed pages in both architectural theory and cultural studies at large, it is not unfair to call the 1980s the Gilded Age of theory. The multitude of theoretical models that had been gathering since the mid-1960s achieve a crescendo in the early 1980s, especially within the ivory towers of academe, and never before in the history of architecture would theory come to be defined in such abstract terms or occupy such a privileged place within deliberations. Marxism, semiotics, phenomenology, Freudian psychology, postmodernism, and critical theory – all play a part in the variegated theoretical palette leading up to this time, and in the 1980s they were joined by the lofty intellectual affectations of poststructuralism and deconstruction. We will distinguish these last two terms from the more general phenomenon of postmodernism, which in this study we will restrict to the movements aligned with historicism and semiotics. Poststructuralism, by contrast, was built on theoretical foundations of German and French theory, best defined, respectively, by the "Frankfurt School" and French structuralism.

Poststructural Theory

The appellation "Frankfurt School" was later applied to a group of political philosophers associated with the Institute of Social Research, a privately funded study group founded by Felix Weil in Frankfurt in 1924.[1] Thus the name refers specifically to a leftist group of intellectuals concerned with social studies, and its political orientation was hardly unusual for this time. The Russian Revolution had taken place in 1917 and Germany's

An Introduction to Architectural Theory: 1968 to the Present, First Edition.
Harry Francis Mallgrave and David Goodman.
© 2011 Harry Francis Mallgrave and David Goodman. Published 2011 by Blackwell Publishing Ltd.

November Revolution followed one year later. Even though this last affair devolved into a somewhat more moderate but still leftist Weimar Republic, the revolutionary impulses (from the Left and Right) that had given rise to it would not soon subside. The economy of Germany lay in ruins in the late 1910s and early 1920s, inflation and unemployment were rampant, and there was a general expectation by many on the Left that a Soviet-styled, proletariat revolution was inevitable. The Institute was conceived as a transitional and educational tool to abet this new revolution.

Yet the focus of the Institute began to change in the early 1930s with the directorship of Max Horkheimer, who had come to reject the economic determinism of orthodox Marxism. He therefore gathered around the Institute an interdisciplinary group of scholars who were much more concerned with the phenomenon of culture. Marxist theory still played a prominent role in the program, yet its influence was now tempered by the iconoclastic thought of Friedrich Nietzsche and the psychoanalytical theories of Sigmund Freud. The ascension of Adolf Hitler and the National Socialists in 1933 closed the doors of the center, but, after a brief stay in Geneva, many of the scholars associated with the school would make their way to the United States, among them Horkheimer, Erich Fromm, Herbert Marcuse, and Theodor W. Adorno. The one person associated with the Frankfurt School who did not cross the Atlantic was Walter Benjamin, who committed suicide at the Spanish border in 1940.

By the 1950s and 1960s the influence of the Frankfurt School was beginning to make itself felt in Europe and North America. Several of Benjamin's writings, among them his highly influential essay "The Work of Art in the Age of Mechanical Reproduction" (1936), first appeared in German in 1955, and in an English edition edited by Hannah Arendt in 1969.[2] In the essay Benjamin speaks of the loss of classical art's "aura" in the age of mechanical reproducibility (film, photography) – that is, art's severance from its traditional ritualistic values or, more recently, its usurpation (in Marxist terms) by bourgeois structures of power. Also appearing in 1955, and exploring a similar theme, was Marcuse's book *Eros and Civilization*.[3] Drawing upon the issues of Freud's *Civilization and its Discontents* (1930), Marcuse examined the competing human instincts of *eros* (life and sensuality) and *thanatos* (death and aggression), and the former's presumed repression by the productive, conformist forces of late capitalist culture. In *One-Dimensional Man* (1964), Marcuse furthered his analysis by arguing that the technological underpinnings of modern culture both exploit and at the same time destroy personal freedom.[4] Based at the University of California at Berkeley in the1960s – the seat of the earliest and most persistent student demonstrations in North

America – Marcuse succeeded in becoming one of the intellectual gurus of America's "New Left."

Nevertheless, it was Horkheimer and Adorno who were destined to have the greatest impact on the decades of the 1970s and 1980s – in particular through their book *The Dialectic of the Enlightenment* (1947).[5] It is the first clear exposition of "critical theory" (a term generally associated with the Frankfurt School) and its intention during the grim war years was to chart the course of Western reason's self-destruction, together with its related Hegelian "myth" of a progressive march toward freedom. Their main argument was that capitalism would not collapse from economic self-destruction, as Marx had predicted, because in fact it had proved to be an extremely resilient economic system by evolving into a mass-consumer society in which individuals were now under the sway of the "culture industry." Through such media as newspapers, magazines, canned-laughter sitcoms, and formulaic movies, these industries were not only pandering to the most uncritical attitudes of the masses, but they at the same time were creating a cultural conformity with their limited range of tried-and-true clichés. Old commodities were simply restyled or repackaged anew for each new shopping season.

What this means for aesthetic theory, as one might suspect, is nothing good. If art is a cultural production and culture has become corrupted by its incessant pandering to the marketplace, then art is seemingly at the end of its road – seemingly, but not absolutely. For Horkheimer and Adorno had one fallback position, in fact a rather classically "modern" one – namely that art should be both autonomous *and* social. It should be autonomous in having its own language of creative techniques and skills, and it should be social in its radical opposition to bourgeois society. Adorno summed up this viewpoint by noting that "art will live on only as long as it has the power to resist society."[6] Hence, art is fundamentally an act of resistance – resistance in the atonal spirit of Arnold Schönberg, in the conscious exaggerations of a Franz Kafka, or in the linear musings Paul Klee. Adorno's critical theory is thus often characterized as a defense of modernism, in the sense that it is a defense of some of the avant-garde strategies of the first decades of the twentieth century.

It was in the 1960s that critical theory joined up with the critiques of French structuralism. In its simplest form, structuralism is an analytical approach to knowledge that attempts to consider phenomena as a complex system of variables operating under certain universal rules. Ferdinand de Saussure's structural approach to linguistics, for instance, considered language as a system of signs (meanings) governed by a greater syntactic structure. Claude Levi-Strauss's structural anthropology of the postwar years was based on the supposition that there was a universal structure to the human mind governed by binary rules, which were the same in all cultures and therefore could eventually be discerned. French theorists in the 1960s, most of whom were educated in structuralist principles, began to dispute such claims. For example, the linguist Roland Barthes, in his essay "The Death of the Author" (1968), questioned the possibility of a truly knowable text, in that the reader inevitably generates a multiplicity of meanings and thereby subverts any one interpretation.[7] Another structuralist to become a dissenting voice was Michel Foucault. In The *Order of Things* (1966), he tried to unravel the taxonomic codes of scientific culture since the Renaissance (the rules by which Western thought is organized) by dividing them into three general *épistemes*, or culturally and historically accepted "givens" that make possible the distinction between what can be said to be true and false within a system.[8] In *The Archaeology of Knowledge* (1969), he dropped the idea of ruling *épistemes* in favor of a more open-ended interpretative process of reading the history of knowledge as a scheme of discourses – that is, as a complex web of human practices defined by society, culture, its institutions, and various other interested authorities. This new archaeology has no particular point of origin and is devoid of any central structure or moral truth.[9]

Foucault's increasing anarchy during these years was not dissimilar to that of Jean Baudrillard, who joined his Marxist critique of structuralism with the insights of the Frankfurt School. In Baudrillard's *The System of Objects* (1968) and *The Society of Consumption* (1970) he argued that all forms of marketplace consumption arise from cultural codes by which we, in choosing one designer label over another, seek to distinguish ourselves or stand out from others.[10] Although this tendency for Baudrillard results in little more than passive conformism, his argument is more expansive in that it is a critique of the traditional Marxist concepts of use-values and exchange values (utility and monetary exchange). The proliferation of consumer goods – their marketing, packaging, and display through the cultural agents of the mass media – all conspire to assign the latest fashions with a certain "sign-value," endowing the purchaser with a coded level of prestige and social standing.

By the mid-1970s, Baudrillard's understanding of reification (defining our self-esteem through the objects we own) discarded the conceptual limits of Marxism altogether. If modern society was predicated on the organized production of goods and services, postmodern society was formed on "simulations" of real work, or the "hyperreality" of television, cyberspace, computer games, and other forms of virtual reality. Images, spectacles, and the play of signs, he argued, were no longer bound to a factual world; rather they were insidiously displacing this world altogether. In *Symbolic Exchange and Death* (1976) Baudrillard described this process as a "third order" of simulacra, that is, the icons and emblems by which society originally defined itself (mass-produced in the modern era through industrialization, photography, and the cinema) had evolved in the post-modern era to the point where the copy has itself become real.[11] For many people this hyper-reality in its vast proliferation has become far more intense and seductive than everyday reality. The binary code of the computer has, in effect, become a symbolic code for our existence, because each decision we make (from selecting a particular soft drink to choosing between two candidates in an election) really changes or alters nothing. Hyper-reality propels itself and we are powerless to slow it down. If this position suggests that we are doomed, as it were, to a technological determinism, Baudrillard's references in the mid-1970s to our dependence on instantaneous images and messaging still uncomfortably resemble life for many in the twenty-first century.

Although Baudrillard was one of the stronger proponents of the new "postmodern" world, Jean-François Lyotard is generally given credit for first popularizing the term. His study *The Postmodern Condition* was written in 1974 at the behest of the Quebec government as a White Paper analyzing the status of science and technology within higher education. The author, however, took a much more general approach regarding the implications of the unfolding computer revolution and predicted that the status of knowledge itself would be inevitably altered. Lyotard reasoned that with the increasing digitalization of knowledge, the liberal arts would become obsolete as a general grounding for education, and information – and more specifically scientific knowledge – would become a hotly contested commodity to be bought and sold in the marketplace. Yet there was an inherent problem to this changed status of knowledge, in that all scientific knowledge has traditionally been supported by two "grand narratives" or "metanarratives" based in the liberal arts. The first is the Enlightenment belief that with increasing knowledge society advances toward a condition of greater freedom. Second is the central premise of the university system itself, which is that one day there will be a unity of knowledge again in the service of humanity. With the collapse of these two narratives and the cultural break they entail, Lyotard defines postmodernism simply as "incredulity toward metanarratives," where metanarratives might be conceived as every grand system of beliefs: whether it be Marxism, liberalism, conservatism, religion, or indeed the utopian political underpinnings of early modernism.[12] Thus the postmodern world is one in which no one grand narrative dominates and we are left only with local or "small narratives" without any pretense of universal legitimacy.

Lyotard's argument for postmodernism was powerful in part because of the very simplicity of his argument, but the same cannot be said for the theories of Jacques Derrida and his strategy of "deconstruction."[13] Derrida's work actually precedes that of Lyotard by several years. Born in Algeria, Derrida's doctoral studies in France centered on the phenomenology of Edmund Husserl, but he also drew extensively on the ideas of Nietzsche, Freud, and Saussure. In his first major study, *Of Grammatology* (1967), Derrida put forward neither a philosophical premise nor a grand narrative but a critical methodology of "close reading" or deconstructing texts by exposing unintended or overshadowed meanings and the absent hierarchies they entail. For instance, he devoted lengthy sections to Saussure, Levi-Strauss, and Jean-Jacques Rousseau to demonstrate that each writer not only worked with terminological dualities but also privileged one term over the other. For instance, Saussure's linguistics was predicated on the idea that speech was superior to writing, while Levi-Strauss's anthropology privileged nature over culture. Rousseau, too, had argued that man in a state of nature was good, but he subsequently became corrupted with the advent of culture.[14]

In these analyses Derrida was not simply pointing out terminological biases; he was arguing something more compelling, namely, that the entire body of Western thought has historically been constructed around the logocentric idea of a "center." Examples of these centers might be a Platonic Idea, an accepted truth or dogma, a grand narrative, or belief in God. Such centers in turn marginalize or repress what is "other," creating opposites by which we conceptualize or apprehend the world. Thus the "presence" of one term (for example, "modernism" in architecture) conceals the "absence" of another (nineteenth-century historicism) – the styles of which might be regarded as "traces." Thus the term "modernism" (privileged for three-quarters of the twentieth century) can only be defined through the idea of historicism (derided as the "other"). Similarly, architectural postmodernism is actually named after its binary opposite by allowing historical eclecticism back into the mix. The entire strategy of Derridean deconstruction, then, consists of destabilizing or decentering privileged terms, thereby overturning the underlying hierarchies on which they are established. In its most extreme form, deconstruction has been accused of subverting all statements about the world, leaving us both silent and stricken with the acute condition of undecidability – a fatal malady in most academic and political circles.

Poststructural Architecture

Derrida's books from the 1960s were only translated into English the mid-1970s, and thus it was only later in that decade that his influence would be felt within the Anglo-American world. This time lag in itself created an interesting divide between European and Anglo-American theory – in that, in Europe postmodernism and poststructuralism were generally (but not always) considered two faces of the same coin, whereas in Britain and North America postmodernism preceded the influence of poststructural theory and the latter, once it arrived, was often viewed as a critique of the former. This was especially the case within architectural circles.

But there were at the same time other issues that complicated the debate of the early 1980s. For instance, when the German philosopher Jürgen Habermas, a former assistant to Adorno, received the "Adorno Prize" in Frankfurt in 1980, he opened his formal address with an attack on the "postmodern" architecture of the Venice Biennale of the same year, labeling it "an avant-garde of reversed fronts."[15] He concluded the same address by going after several camps of "conservatives," among them the "Young Conservatives" of France – the line leading "from Georges Bataille via Michel Foucault to Jacques Derrida." In between, Habermas mounted his defense of modernism and the Frankfurt School: first by decrying the argument that modernism has failed or that its utopian impulses should be surrendered, and second by insisting that the "project of modernity has not yet been fulfilled."[16]

Equating French poststructuralism with postmodernism, however, was not always the norm. For another historian with strong ties to Adorno and the Frankfurt School, Andreas Huyssen, accepted Habermas's overall defense of modernity, but conceded that the intellectual climate of the 1970s had indeed fundamentally changed during the decade. In accepting postmodernism, he insisted, however, that poststructuralism is different, in that its critical strategies are closer to modernism than to postmodernism. He even described poststructuralism as the "*revenant* of modernism in the guise of theory" and concluded his analysis by following Adorno and calling for the two to be combined in a "postmodernism of resistance."[17]

Huyssen's analysis underscores another important issue of the 1980s – the desire of many on the political Left to square the postmodern aesthetics of the decade with the mandate of the Frankfurt School. Lyotard's skepticism regarding grand narratives had indeed been a frontal assault on both Marxist theory and critical theory, as many were quick to see. Hal Foster brought this problem to the fore in the preface to his best-selling anthology *The Anti-Aesthetic* (1983) when he drew the distinction between "a postmodernism which seeks to deconstruct modernism and resist the status quo and a postmodernism which repudiates the former to celebrate the latter: a postmodernism of resistance and a postmodernism of reaction."[18] The first postmodernism is good in the sense that it continues the struggle against bourgeois culture, whereas the latter (which was often associated with the populism of Venturi and Scott Brown) in fact supports or mimics the existing culture.

One writer who certainly took this problem seriously was Frederic Jameson, whose "Postmodernism and Consumer Society" was one of the feature essays in Foster's anthology. In accepting the aesthetics of Adorno as well as the insights of Debord and Baudrillard, Jameson accepts the fact that postmodernism has become a major event, and its aesthetics can be described through the twin strategies of "pastische and schizophrenia."[19] But at the same time, Jameson is uneasy at the fact that postmodernism is not quite as "dangerous and explosive, subversive within the established order" as high modernism. Nevertheless, Jameson seems to be curiously seduced by some images of postmodernism, even by works of Venturi and Scott Brown, and suggests in fact that there should be a way that such postmodern strategies can resist capitalist logic.[20]

K. Michael Hays made this the dominant theme of his important essay of 1985, "Critical Architecture: Between Culture and Form," in which he argued that architecture could occupy a place between autonomy and complete engagement. A new "critical architecture," he postulated, is "one resistant to the self-confirming, conciliatory operations of a dominant culture yet irreducible to a purely formal structure disengaged from the contingencies of place and time." For him one leading practitioner of this critical architecture was none other than the quintessential modernist Mies van der Rohe, whose glass reflective surfaces of his Friedrichstrasse project (1919) were both *"resistant* and *oppositional"* to the dismay and chaos of postwar Berlin and at the same time "intractable to decoding by formal analysis." Hays also read Mies's later plan for a new campus for the Illinois Institute of Technology in a critical way, as "a subtle grafting of an alternative reality onto the chaos of Chicago's South Side."[21]

In any case, by the mid-1980s the critical arguments of poststructuralism had clearly gained an ascendancy over those of postmodernism – albeit only by losing much of its political edge. One theorist to stake out such a position at this time was the Italian philosopher Gianni Vattimo, who (with Pier Aldo Rovatti) edited a series of essays in 1983 entitled *Il pensiero debole* (weak thought).[22] In critiquing the "strong thought" of traditional metaphysics, Vattimo argued on behalf of a mode of hermeneutic or interpretative analysis that makes few judgments, strives not to impose any undue rationality or "Cartesian point of reference," and thus thrives on the Heideggarian virtues of *Verwindung* (healing, convalescence, resignation, acceptance) and *Andenken* (remembrance, recollection, rethinking). If, for example, both Hegelian thought and Marxism demanded an *Überwindung* or "overcoming" of strong dialectical pairs, the less powerful noun *Verwindung*, for Vattimo, suggests a slow and weakened recovery (as from an illness) and, in the end, a good-natured respect for past traditions without trying to supplant them with still another metanarrative.

It would not take long for this idea to be transposed into the architectural discourse. For in 1987 the Spanish theorist Ignasi de Solà-Morales published his influential essay "Weak Architecture," in which the new architecture of resistance (now rendered enfeebled by the loss of any "immovable reference" or epistemological grounding) must also divest itself of its earlier pretensions. Weak architecture, for Solà-Morales, becomes the architecture of "event," of the aleatory, of the "decorative" (ornament lacking any aesthetic system), and of the "monumental."[23] What is interesting in such a formulation is how profoundly the tenor of the times had changed in less than two decades. From the boisterous demands on the riotous streets of 1968 it had been a hard and fast descent to a world more tentative, less certain than it had once been.

Eisenman and Tschumi

The two individuals most responsible for drawing poststructural ideas into the architectural discourse were Peter Eisenman and Bernard Tschumi. The Swiss-born Tsuchumi, after graduating from the Eidgenössische Technische Hochschule (ETH) in Zurich, was living in Paris in 1968 and thus was directly familiar with early poststructural debates, Marxism, and the "spectacles" of the Situationists, with whom he had a particular affinity. Eisenman took a more indirect route, aided in part at least by his friendship with Mario Gandelsonas and Diana Agrest, both of whom had studied in Paris in the late 1960s. Agrest's essay, "Design versus Non-Design," which appeared in *Oppositions* 6 (1976), is, in fact, a poststructural critique of Anglo-American semiotics – that is, an attempt to use semiotics as a basis for analyzing architectural meaning. Instead, she calls for "non-design," or reading architecture through the fluid relations of interacting cultural systems (ideologies). If modernism (from Le Corbusier to Team 10) practiced a form of ideological reductivism by attempting to filter or delimit the metaphors allowed in cultural play, she argues that a more expansive reading of architecture views its images not through a dominant system of selected metaphors (the house as ocean liner, for instance), but rather as a series of "social texts," theatrical fragments if you will. Architecture thus acquires its "densities of meaning" precisely by operating within these open nodes of competing cultural texts – in cafe life, through gazes, gestures, the street, rituals, and "people as decoration."[24]

Agrest's essay was important for Eisenman because around this time (in 1975 and 1976) his thought was undergoing a turning point in response to such events as the Beaux-Arts exhibition at the Museum of Modern Art. He concluded his *Oppositions* editorial "Post-Functionalism" (1976), for instance, by outlining two design strategies. The first was to allow form to be a "recognizable transformation from some pre-existent geometric or platonic solid"; the second was to view form from the perspective of

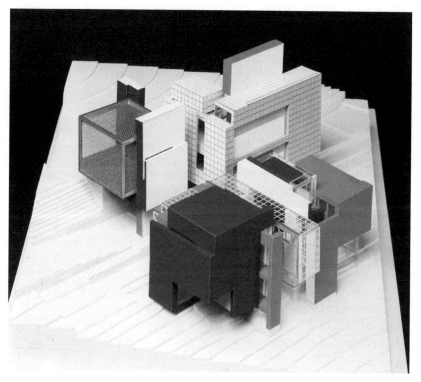

Figure 7.1   Peter Eisenman, axonometric model of House X, Bloomfield Hills, Michigan (1975).

an "atemporal, decompositional mode," or as a series of fragments without reference to a central organizational authority.[25] If Eisenman's "generative" houses of his early years represented the first of these strategies, House X, which was commissioned by a client in 1976, reflected the second.

What is interesting, however, is that Eisenman does not articulate the full rationale for House X until the early1980s – that is, after the ideas of Derrida had become more familiar to everyone. The key to the design concept, he then reports, is the central void, an existential nothingness, a "non-vertebrate," neither hearth, nor stair, nor any humanistic center – hence the "denial of any value-laden origins."[26] Noting that the surrounding parts of the composition also evoke the "metaphoric ideas of ruin, decay, and falling to pieces," Eisenman addresses his house to the modern man who cannot "sustain any longer a belief in his own rationality and perfectibility," and thus the architect's principal design strategy is one of "decomposition," or "an activity analogous to one which literary critics call 'deconstruction.' "[27] He also acknowledges that his earlier process-driven strategy of manipulating the planes and lines of geometric solids is a thing of the past, but this does not entail his renouncing all systems or codes. Design, for Eisenman, remains a heuristic exercise dealing with what Derrida had called "traces" or vestiges of meaning that are not overtly expressed.

Another important shift in Eisenman's thinking is seen in his Venice project of 1978. The project arose out of a competition, and, in addition to Eisenman, five other architects participated. The purpose of the competition was to explore new urban solutions for the Cannaregio neighborhood of Venice, the area just northeast of the train station and defined by two canals and the lagoon separating the city from the mainland. The site was largely industrial in the nineteenth century but its northwest corner also became notable in modernist lore as the spot where Le Corbusier, in the 1960s, had designed a hospital, which was not built. Eisenman responded with three highly conceptualized "texts," by which he criticized what he termed the three nostalgic "isms" of architecture: modernism (nostalgia for the future), historicist postmodernism (nostalgia for the past), and contextualism (nostalgia for the present).[28] In the first text he extended the building grid of Le Corbusier's design over most of the Cannaregio neighborhood, marking it as a series of 18 holes or voids, which he termed "sites for future houses or potential sites for graves" signifying "the emptiness of rationality."[29] The second text he superimposed on the site (generally near or contiguous to these voids) consisted of a series of "solid, lifeless blocks" of different scales so as to defy any contextual relationships. The third text consists of a single diagonal line cut through the site, a "topological axis of symmetry" suggesting

Figure 7.2   Peter Eisenman, model of Cannaregio project, Venice, Italy (1978). Photo by Dick Frank. Courtesy of Eisenman Architects.

that "something may erupt and that perhaps will not stay down: the unconscious or the shadow of memory."[29] Not to be overlooked with these three texts is the fact that Eisenman, in another grand gesture, actually proposed no housing for the site. Everything was conceptual.

If Carraregio discloses Eisenman's new penchant for "fictions," his "City of Artificial Excavation" project for Berlin, submitted in 1981 in partnership with Jaquelin Robertson, takes this theme even further. On a site in Berlin's Friedrichstadt district, he imposes a Mercator grid slightly at odds with the existing street fabric and therefore, in his words, an "anti-memory." The grid defines a network of limestone walls (foundations) and passages 3.3 meters high (precisely the height of the Berlin Wall at the time bounding the site), which he viewed as a way "to erase the physical and symbolic presence of the historical walls."[30] Except for a few buildings around the periphery (one was built), the interior of the site was left open to remain a dissimulated "archaeological site."

Aside from the recondite or highly symbolic nature of these proposals (not unrelated to Eisenman's fascination with psychoanalysis), they are also critical of several competing design strategies. One is the phenomenon of postmodernism, which he condemns for being little more than a craving for "fetish objects."[31] Another is the figure/ground contextualism of Colin Rowe, which again only reinforces "a classical compositional *Gestalt*."[32] Still another factor playing into these designs was Eisenman's desire to extend the scale and reach of his own practice. The Berlin competition, unlike that in Venice, was a real project for which he completed his first major building. In the following year he won the competition for the Wexner Center at Ohio State University, and his architectural trajectory at this point bolted upward. His design strategies of the 1980s – scaling, recursivity, self-similarity, and discontinuity – all were meant to destroy the classical tradition of architecture, or as he explains in poststructural terms, "to destabilize the value of origin, to destabilize the notion of anthropocentrism and to destabilize the aesthetic object."[33] Scaling or the superposing of analogous plans or materials at different scales achieves this end by geometric subdivision (recursivity), by metaphorical change (self-similarity), and by a fragmentation of forms (discontinuity).

All of these terms are perhaps best summarized by the idea of *dissimulation*, the theme of his essay of 1985, "The End of the Classical: The End of the Beginning, the End of the End." Now drawing upon Baudrillard, Eisenman brandishes the term "simulation" – of representation, reason, and history – to characterize architectural development since the Renaissance. What distinguishes our "not classical" age is both the impossibility of any such simulated underpinning or metaphysical support (as found, for example, in postmodernism), or "the possibility of the invention and realization of a blatantly fictional future." What design is left with, for Eisenman, is the idea of "writing" as opposed to "image": writing not as words or signs but rather as Derridean "traces" or fragmentary words with ambiguous meanings.[34] In the Berlin project, for instance, the city foundations he called into play were not real foundations but rather a "fictional reality" and therefore inventive.[35] Similarly, the Wexner Center was placed on a site with existing foundations of the old armory, but Eisenman, of course, did not utilize them.

The textuality found in Eisenman's thought in the 1980s is found in a different form in the work of Tschumi, who, though equally drawn to poststructural ideas, takes a somewhat different approach to design.[36] After his experiences in Paris in the late 1960s, Tschumi moved to London where he joined the faculty at the Architectural Association, then under the leadership of Alvin Boyarsky. The influence of Reyner Banham and Archigram at the school was still quite strong, but the younger faculty and their students constituted a veritable pantheon of future "stars," among them Léon Krier,

Rem Koolhaas, Zaha Hadid, Daniel Libeskind, Will Alsop, and Nigel Coates. Tschumi taught classes on "Urban Politics" and "The Politics of Space" and continued the political activism that he had learned so well in Paris.

The two key essays of this early period were "The Environmental Trigger" and "Questions of Space," both written in 1975. When many British architects were turning either to postmodernism or to Léon Krier's view of Rationalism, Tschumi was seeking an alternative path. In fact, he later described the first essay as "closing a chapter" on his overt political activism, in that he concludes that "the only possible architectural action of a revolutionary nature is rhetorical."[37] This does not mean giving up the struggle altogether, but rather adopting Debord's strategy of *détourné* or diverting the given urban situation through "rhetorical exemplary actions" (sit-ins, street demonstrations), "counterdesign" (the destruction of conventional architectural culture), and "subversive analysis" (aggressive guerilla maneuvers).[38]

In "Questions of Space: The Pyramid and Labyrinth (or the Architectural Paradox)," he built his theme on Denis Hollier's interpretation of the writings of Georges Bataille, in that the "pyramid" (reason) and the "labyrinth" (sensory experience) became the metaphors to guide his discussion of "ideal" and "real" space.[39] Architecture's "paradox" was that while its medium is more spatial than anything else, it is impossible to question the nature of space at a conceptual level while experiencing real space in sensory terms. Sensory space, for Tschumi, in this way becomes the new Adornoesque means for practicing architectural resistance. In elaborating on this objective, he reviewed the conceptual spatial approaches of radical architects (Archizoom) and rational architects (Rossi school), as well as the sensory reflections of Germanic empathetic and Gestalt theorists. Tschumi obviously favored the sensory approaches over the conceptual, and his proffered solution to the current social crisis – "Like Eroticism, architecture needs both system and excess" – is surprising only in its moderation.[40] And erotic spatial design (following the lead of Barthes and Derrida) must therefore become the subversion of what is to be expected, in other words, the pleasure of "excess."

Pleasure and shock indeed became the recurring themes of his work of the late 1970s, which unfolded through a series of exhibitions, writings, and commissions.[41] During 1976–1977 he became a visiting lecturer at Princeton and at the IAUS, which resulted in his essay "Architecture and Transgression" appearing in *Oppositions*. The text reiterates the subversive notion of "eROTicism," and is framed by two of his "advertisements" for architecture depicting the derelict Villa Savoye as it stood abandoned in 1965. Alluding to the building's smell of urine and excrement, together

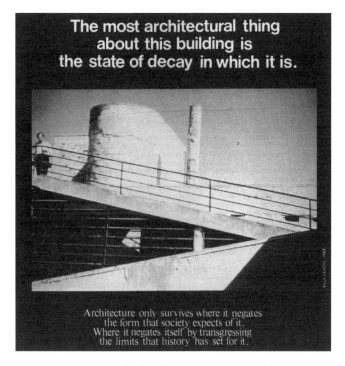

The most architectural thing about this building is the state of decay in which it is.

Architecture only survives where it negates
the form that society expects of it.
Where it negates itself by transgressing
the limits that history has set for it.

Figure 7.3 Bernard Tschumi, the Villa Savoye, from *Advertisements* (1977). Image courtesy of Bernard Tschumi Architects.

with its graffiti, Tschumi's produces two posters that lead with the pronouncements that "The most architectural thing about this building is the state of decay in which it is" and "Sensuality has been known to overcome even the most rational of buildings."[42]

The Swiss architect struck a similar chord with his essay "Violence in Architecture," by which he intended not physical or emotional brutality but rather the use of the term as "a metaphor for the intensity of a relationship between individuals and their surrounding space."[43] People and space were once again the theme of his most important theoretical work, *The Manhattan Transcripts*, a "reading machine" (akin to an "Eisenstein film script" or "Moholy-Nagy stage directions") that he devised through a series of exhibitions between 1976 and 1981.[44] The scenic novel is divided into the episodes of the park, the street, the tower, and the block, and fittingly begins with a murder, perhaps (as Giovanni Damiani has noted) a surrealist allusion to Michelangelo Antonioni's 1966 film *Blow Up*.[45] An act of love, another murder, a fall from a tower, soldiers and acrobats fill out the four sequential (but non-representational) scripts, as stills from avant-garde films are interspersed with plans, diagrams, and axonometric drawings – in what becomes an intertextual attempt by Tschumi not only to accentuate the disjunction between use, form, and social values but also to emphasize the relationship between space, movement, and events. When the first two episodes opened in a Manhattan gallery in 1978, they were observed by few architects.

Tschumi's obscurity, however, would not last for long. Shortly after *Manhattan Transcripts* appeared in a special issue of *Architectural Design* in 1981, the theorist applied his graphic strategies to the international competition for the Parc de la Villette in Paris. When the artist/revolutionary/unpracticed architect was announced as the winner in early 1983 (beating Léon Krier and Rem Koolhaas), he became an instant architectural celebrity. The jury's decision may have proved larger than a fairytale, for Tschumi has since argued that his victory (together with Zaha Hadid's competition-winning design for the Peak Club in Hong Kong) formed a "breaking point between the hegemony of historicist postmodernism and what had up to then been the work of just a minority."[46]

On a purely visual level, the strategies of superimposition and juxtaposition employed by Tschumi at Villette do not seem to differ very much from those of Eisenman, yet their rationales are quite different.[47] Whereas Eisenman purposefully employs recondite themes and extreme formal exercises that Manfredo Tafuri has likened to "formal terrorism," Tschumi focuses on non-programmatic spaces, or rather, in the case of Villette, on the violent and therefore erotic collision of lines, points, and surfaces superimposed as layers over the 125 acres of parkland.[48] The lines are formed by the linear pedestrian pathways and by also of the curvilinear "Path of Thematic Gardens" that randomly weaves its way in and around the "follies." The points are 26 red follies (deconstructed cubes) placed every 120 meters apart at the vertices of a Cartesian grid. The surfaces are the multiple uses seemingly dropped upon the site, among them the museums and halls, lawns and gardens, and the liberal assortment of theaters, restaurants, cafes, art galleries, studios, and playgrounds – all specified by the official program for this "Park for the 21st Century."

Tschumi has referred to his montage of events as a "series of cinnegrams" or contiguous systems already worked out in his earlier theoretical projects.[49] And here is where his approach differs so fundamentally from that of Eisenman. If the latter was simultaneously defining his work as textual in a narrative sense, Tschumi much prefers the notion of "intertextuality," the Barthesian idea that all texts are in effect made up of fragments

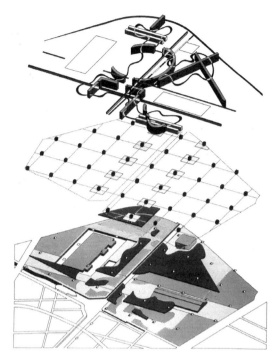

Figure 7.4 Bernard Tschumi, planning grids for Parc de la Villette, Paris (1983). Image courtesy of Bernard Tschumi Architects.

of other texts. In Villette's case, the montage of texts include gestural citations from cinema, literary criticism, psychoanalysis, and even (with the red follies) Constructivist drawings.[50] His very choice of the word "folly" to be the guiding motif of the design (in part an allusion to Foucault) also loads the overall theme with semantic drama. In addition to referring to those garden pavilions once built for aristocratic entertainment, the French word *folie* means "madness."[51] In choosing this word, Tschumi, the urban anarchist, wanted to align the idea of architecture squarely with the aleatory or counter-designed "event." When grids collide, irrational space itself becomes a fount of activity, however rational the madness.

The accidental nature of these inventions also distinguishes his approach from that of Eisenman at Villette. In 1985 the latter was asked by the project manager François Barré to design one of the gardens for Villette in collaboration with the now celebrated philosopher Derrida.[52] Over the next two years the two men labored on "Chora L Works," which in many respects is one of Eisenman's most intriguing designs. Derrida initially restricted his input to proposing the idea of *chora* (receptacle) in reference to Plato's *Timaeus*, but in a letter to the architect he also supplied one sketch.[53] Eisenman struggled to complete the design, in which he joined metonymic elements of the historical site and Tschumi's design with Derrida's script as well as with the metaphor of his Cannaregio project for Venice – all conveniently rescaled into a small corner of the site.

Nevertheless, it was Derrida who had the last (first) word – not about Eisenman but about Tschumi. In 1986, in an exhibition on Villette prepared for the Architectural Association in London, Derrida waxed philosophically about the red follies: their dislocation, destabilization, and deconstruction of meaning. "Do they not," he asks, "lead back to the desert of an architecture, a zero degree of architectural writing where this writing would lose itself, henceforth without finality, aesthetic aura, fundamentals, hierarchical principles or symbolic signification, in short, in a prose made of abstract, neutral, inhuman, useless, uninhabitable and meaningless volumes?" Derrida denies these interpretations, because, he argues, the follies rather "affirm, and engage their affirmation beyond this ultimately annihilating, secretly nihilistic repetition of metaphysical architecture. They enter into the *maintenant* of which I speak; they maintain, renew and reinscribe architecture. They revive, perhaps, an energy which was infinitely anaesthetised, walled-in, buried in a common grave or sepulchral nostalgia."[54] Few young architects throughout history have been conferred with a more esoteric validation by the local philosopher/celebrity, yet never had theory become so utterly difficult to understand.

8

Deconstruction

Notwithstanding the distinctly different philosophical underpinnings of postmodernism and poststructuralism in the 1980s, the view that these two schools of theory differed significantly in their realized designs remains an unsatisfying historical interpretation. For one thing, defining with any precision what is meant by the "historicist" currents of the first half of the decade – historicism in itself – is a tricky task. When, for instance, do simple historical allusions give way to the more nuanced strategies, such as fictive metaphors, narration, or textual apparitions? And when do they become noticeable in design? Where precisely does one draw the boundary between formal decomposition (as an avant-garde strategy of the Constructivists of the 1920s or as advanced by "deconstructivists" in the 1980s) and the increasing formal complexity that is found just about everywhere in the decade? Whereas many humanities professors in universities across Europe and America were reveling in the gamesmanship and terminological affectations of poststructural theory, architects who wanted to keep abreast of things for the most part were struggling to find any solid grounding to support the new formal directions. But we must be clear that this does not mean that they were not also intrigued by the novelty of changing fashions or by the belief that they were creating something that had not existed before. And the question of just who was being poststructural or postmodern remains especially murky when the theoretical bar was not set so high. In this sense, one might liken architectural theory of the late 1980s to that awkward phase of adolescence of which Eisenman had spoken a decade earlier. Confusion, rather than clarity, was the keynote of the time.

An Introduction to Architectural Theory: 1968 to the Present, First Edition.
Harry Francis Mallgrave and David Goodman.
© 2011 Harry Francis Mallgrave and David Goodman. Published 2011 by Blackwell Publishing Ltd.

Postmodernism Undefined

The work of such heralded early postmodernists as Hans Hollein and James Stirling, for instance, display such ambiguity in large part because of their grounding in the aesthetic atmosphere of the 1950s and 1960s. Hollein graduated from Vienna's Academy of Fine Arts and took his graduate studies in the late 1950s at IIT and Berkeley. He therefore returned to Vienna not only knowledgeable of what was taking place in Chicago and California, but also with a deep appreciation for the work of such Viennese-American predecessors as Rudolf Schindler and Richard Neutra. Hollein then took part in various exhibitions during the 1960s, perhaps the most notable one being his show "Transformations," a collection of photomontages he displayed at St Stephan Gallery in 1963. His fine-arts installations soon advanced into product design, furniture, stage design, in short, into every field of design. His two hallmark works of architecture of his early years – the Retti Candle Shop (1964–1965) and the Schullin Jewelry Shop (1972–1974) – further put on display his artistic talent. The former, with its polished aluminum facade and interiors, displays in its detailing a high level of refinement. The latter, with its colorful granite and brass-accentuated fissure down the middle of the facade, pays homage to Adolf Loos and Josef Hofmann, while a few years later it would appear in many publications as a precocious "postmodern" eruption. Hollein's use of gilded palm trees, Oriental pavilions, and Rolls Royce windows in the offices (four in all) of the Austrian Travel Agency in the second half of the 1970s indeed pushed him to the front ranks of the postmodern movement

But looks can sometimes be deceiving, as his other major work of this period – the City Museum at Mönchengladbach (1972–1982) – demonstrates. It is a complex design on many levels. Situated in a historic district of a German town near the Dutch border, it presents itself more as an urban landscape with disparate elements than as a monumental temple to art. The parts in themselves are intriguing: a fractured administrative tower, a stone-clad auditorium, a white marble entrance pavilion, seven zinc-coated galleries turned toward northern light, an urban plaza running atop most of the complex, and a series of curved cascading garden walls, reminiscent of Park Güell, leading down to lawns and gardens. But the leading theme of the design is found elsewhere, in the scenographic phantasmagoria enacted by the lavish interiors of the different rooms, or what Friedrich Achleitner has characterized as Vienna's "tradition of aesthetic heightening of reality," a mode of theatricality that Kenneth

Figure 8.1   Hans Hollein, Museum Abteiberg, Mönchengladbach. Photograph by Marlies Darsow. Image courtesy of Atelier Hollein.

Frampton has likened to episodic "set-pieces."[1] In this sense, it is hard to regard the work as postmodern.

Hollein is, above all, an oblique story-teller with a fondness for meta-phor, but not in a postmodern sense of trying to reinvigorate architecture with "meaning." With a luxurious spirit recalling Vienna's historical con-tacts with the East, he writes performances in which – to cite one of his early lectures – "Everyone is an architect. Everything is architecture."[2] He prefers rhetoric over communication, especially in his choice of materials and tectonics. He also harbors within him that Viennese architectural tra-dition that spans from Fischer von Erlach to Richard Neutra. In suggest-ing the views of the latter in another early lecture, he notes

> Even if architecture is a creation of the spirit, it is also material. It is not only idea but also form, not only empty space but also fullness. It is there. Architecture is primarily seen. But it also felt, heard, and smelled. It speaks not only to the body but also to the soul. Buildings themselves have a soul, a personality, a character. They have emotions and desires.[3]

Still another aspect of Hollein's character is revealed in a sketch he penned in 1978 on Otto Wagner, in which he stressed the architect's affinities with the baroque tradition of Fischer von Erlach. Hollein, in the enriching facets of his own iconography, shares the very same roots. He openly practices a symbolism at times willfully "heterogeneous and whimsical," yet his Viennese gift for performance, like that of Wagner and Loos before him, is also historically tinted with the ironic pageantry and pastiche of a collapsing Habsburg Empire.[4] Fundamentally, his work was actually quite alien to the popular conception of postmodernism at that time.

Stirling's roots are a little more prosaic but no less enigmatic. A native of Liverpool, he graduated from that city's School of Architecture in 1949, and completed his thesis under Colin Rowe, whom he had met during the war in parachute-training school. As for many of his British colleagues in the early 1950s, Le Corbusier was his chosen hero, and the materiality of the latter's Maison Jaoul (1951) became the lodestar for Stirling as he came to embrace the New Brutalist movement in the middle years of the decade.

Stirling's design (with James Gowan) in 1959 for the Leicester Engineering building changed everything. Later in life, the English architect defined his professional development as a march from the "abstraction" of modernism of his early years to the increasing acceptance of "representation" in his later years, and this university building, while compositionally abstract, serves as his first serious critique of high modernism.[5] It is, to begin with, a somewhat awkward assemblage of volumes: vertical shafts for lifts and staircases, a coupling of administrative towers from which canted auditoria protrude in the manner of Melnikov's Worker's Club, and the large horizontal field of laboratories. The tilting of the shed-like skylights of the labs at a 45-degree angle to the rectangular plan results in volumetric terminations with diamond patterns at the perimeter. Brick and tile work, in what amounts to conceptual play, are patterned quite differently. Yet what the offset iconic forms (widely admired at the time) gained by their geometric break with modernist rationality, they at the same time lost in their problematic detailing and in the users' dissatisfaction with the building's functionality. The similarly crisp, geometric volumes of Stirling's university buildings at Cambridge (1964–1967) and Oxford (1966–1971) suffered a similar fate, particularly with their problems of use and detailing.

Around 1970 Stirling's approach to design underwent another evolution – one often attributed to the presence of Léon Krier in the office between 1969 and 1972. Not only was the geometric simplification of *Tendenza* now beginning to become evident in his designs, but so was the historical acceptance of neoclassical typologies. With Stirling, it fully manifested itself in the designs for three German museums in the middle of the 1970s, which in part built upon Hollein's idea of breaking up the museum

Figure 8.2 James Stirling, Neue Staatsgalerie, Stuttgart (1977–1984). Image courtesy of Tim Brown.

box. In the unbuilt project in Düsseldorf for the Museum für Nordheim Westfalen, for instance, Stirling appropriated existing ruins dating from the war (into which he set an auditorium), while the museum itself took on a squared form into which he carved the cylinder of the central court-yard. Off to one side he deposited a classical pavilion for the entrance, which, he noted, symbolized "the whole museum."[6]

The same motif – the circular courtyard – also became the centerpiece of Stuttgart's Neue Staatsgalerie, an extension to an existing museum built between 1977 and 1984. Here the intellectual play begins with the rounded void of the sculpture courtyard enclosed by walls and set on a high podium, surrounded by the U-shaped plan of the museum. Thus it more faithfully recalls Gunnar Asplund's Stockholm library or the rotunda of Schinkel's Altes Museum in Berlin than does the Düsseldorf design. This composition, however, constitutes but one element within what Moneo has called a "diversity of episodes," where "the accidental" entirely predominates.[7] Among the historicist fantasies woven into the fabric are half-buried columns, Egyptian and Romanesque windows, Corbusian forms enacted in plan, and a series of ramps and attached "Constructivist canopies" crisscrossing and flowing into the pedestrian experience. A willful lack of scale, an unusual choice of colors, and feigned exaggeration are everywhere in what seems at first to be simple irony but could also be interpreted as a cerebral exercise carried to the extreme. And here resides the dilemma of the complex. From the perspective of the early 1980s, its numerous historical allusions brand it as a postmodern work par excellence; no building, with the possible exception of Michael Graves's Portland building, received more publicity during this decade. Yet its use of diagonals, sloped walls, and the "slippage" of a few large ashlars that seemingly had fallen out of the wall suggest that it is in fact an early exercise in deconstruction, although one without any apparent theoretical intention.

Gehry

Similar layers of visual complexity are evident in the work of Frank O. Gehry, although this portfolio of designs generally derives from very different premises. A native of Toronto, Gehry, as a teen, immigrated with his family to Los Angeles and studied at the University of Southern California. He served two stints in the office of Victor Gruen, a semester at Harvard, and a year in Paris, before forming a partnership with Greg Walsh in 1962. In some respects, Gehry's early work offers some insights into his later evolution. The Steeves Residence (1958–1959), with its lightness and sense of space, is notable for its confluence of Wrightian motifs (cruciform open plan, flat roofs, use of clerestories, planar extensions), joined with the vernacular of Case Study architects and Japanese design. The Loosian-inspired Danziger Studio and Residence (1964–1965) is a play of two volumes nearly conjoined, one that marries subtle spatial juxtapositions with an introverted disdain for the noise and clutter of Melrose Avenue. Among other projects of the 1960s and 1970s were the Reception Center (1965–1967) and Merriweather Post Pavilion (1966–1967) in Columbia, Maryland as well as the renovation of the Hollywood Bowl (1970–1982).

By the late 1960s Gehry was already experimenting with his design palette – either with the use of inexpensive materials or through "exploding" spatial constructs. On both the O'Neill Hay Barn (1968) in San Juan Capistrano and the Davis Studio (1968–1972) in Malibu, he broke with orthogonal geometries and designed tilted trapizoidal shells sheathed in corrugated galvanized steel and (with the Davis studio) unfinished plywood. In 1969 he designed his first cardboard piece of furniture, and in

Santa Monica Place (1972–1980) he employed chain-link fencing on the garage's south facade. These experiments, aligned with his growing attachment to a number of southern California artists, culminated with the renovation of his own house in Santa Monica (1977–1978), the radicality of which actually bankrupted his firm. It was, as it were, his second "coming-out" party, but this expressionistic play of colliding volumes, layered spaces, and playful lighting effects – what Dal Co has described as an "operation of autobiographical spectacularization" – is arguably still modern in its Merzbau-like compositional elements.[8] Gehry, beginning in 1978, even toyed with postmodernism in his series of buildings and Roman forum for the Loyola Law School in Los Angeles. Yet this cultural influence would be short-lived, and perhaps the most significant factor in its dissipation was his born-again obsession with the emblem of a fish.

Of course, we cannot know the personal reasons for Gehry's repeated adoption of the fish motif during the 1980s, but its use clearly turns a page within his still-evolving architectural outlook. Gehry was not, in fact, the first architect to be attracted to the shape of the fish. In an essay of 1859 on Greek slingshot missiles, the German architect Gottfried Semper, while reflecting on what he termed the "Dynamic Origin of Certain Forms in Nature and Art," argued that the fish's unique form was an evolutionary response to its ecological medium, and then went on to suggest that the ancient Greeks borrowed many of the elastic curvatures of their architectural forms from the organic world – pointing out, for instance, that the Greek word "echinus" had the same etymological root as the Greek word for "sea mussel."[9] Gehry's fascination with the fish seems to have been based more on its symbolism and scaly form. It first appears in a sketch for the Smith House in 1981, and publicly in the same year with Gehry's fish-pylon bridge designed with Richard Serra for the Architectural League of New York. When, in 1983, the Formica Corporation commissioned Gehry to explore the possibilities of Colorcore, the architect morphed the fish (along with a snake) into lamps, and within a few years, to great popular acclaim, the fish appeared in showrooms and sculptural installations around the globe.

The fish, for Gehry, was also metaphorically latent in the spectacle *Il corso del coltello* (the course of the knife), performed at the Venice Biennale in 1985. The play was one of the more interesting architectural events of the decade and arguably Gehry's most definitive artistic statement. Conceived and co-written by Gehry with Coosje van Bruggen, and Claes Oldenburg, it entailed a series of colliding events, and featured an improbable cast of characters that included Dr Coltello (Oldenburg), an unlicensed souvenir vendor who dreams of becoming a great painter; Georgia

Figure 8.3   Frank O. Gehry, fish sculpture for the Olympic village, Barcelona (1992). Image courtesy of Matt Mizenko.

Sandbag (van Bruggen), a retired travel agent who, like George Sand and Calamity Jane, wants to pursue her literary inclinations; and Basta Carambola (Germano Celant), a pool hustler who knows all the angles. Gehry played Frankie P. Toronto, a barber and lecturer who aspires to be a great architect. The principal prop of the drama was a gigantic Swiss army knife that doubled as a gondola; its principal open blade had a fish-like form and an open corkscrew symbolized a coiling snake. In an early scene Gehry, outfitted in a suit of architectural fragments with a fish/ building cap, uses a similar blade to cut his way out of a classical temple scrawled with graffiti. In his ensuing "lecture," he espouses three architectural principles. The first is that "the real order is disorder" (opposing classicism's "sado-mis-machochistic-militaristic order"); the second is that architecture is fundamentally an act of "cutting and slicing, cutting and slicing." After remarking that he was unimpressed with both the Academy and postmodernism, Gehry articulates his third principle of metamorphosis: "Why metamorphosis? The world is constantly changing. People become buildings. Buildings become people. Before people, there were other creatures, other beautiful creatures," chief among them the fish.[10]

These lines not only compose a retort to the historical pretensions of postmodernism, they also reveal how Gehry was beginning to see his own design inclinations changing, and in this regard, the fish also played a very concrete role in Gehry's evolution. For, in proposing a large fish sculpture in 1989 for the Olympic Village in Barcelona, Gehry's office ran into the problem of how to dimension and detail the non-linear forms in such a way that they could be easily fabricated and assembled. The solution was to adapt aeronautical software that was designed for Mirage jets, through which the curvilinear panels could be measured and crafted. This new software was then applied to another project in Gehry's office: the Walt Disney Concert Hall, a competition that he had won two years earlier and for which he was still preparing the final design. Thus the new tool of computer software opened a door (both in Los Angeles and shortly in Bilbao) to a new phase of his practice that would have profound implications for the 1990s. And in both the Disney Concert Hall and the Guggenheim Museum – fittingly – he left the fish scales in place.

The 68ers Come of Age

If Gehry's architectural transformtion was for the most part not motivated by the philosophical infatuations of the 1980s, the reverse was the case with a number of younger architects who were stepping forth at this time. Rem Koolhaas and the Office of Metropolitan Architecture (OMA) stand in the forefront of this group. Koolhaas, a former journalist and (one-time) screenwriter, attended the Architectural Association in the pivotal years 1968–1972, and his stay there was not without its controversial moments. One project that would meet with incredulity from a jury was entitled "The Berlin Wall as Architecture": a study of an "existing building" or psychological no-man's land that rent the still-ravaged city in two.[11] Another, carried out with his future partner Elia Zenghelis, had the no less incarcerating title of "Exodus, or the Voluntary Prisoners of Architecture" (1972).[12] Taking their inspiration from Ivan Leonidov's project of 1930 for a linear town in the Ural Mountains, the two students proposed removing a large swathe of central London and inserting into it two walls that would contain another city. Future residents, or those who were strong enough to love its architecture, could elect to become voluntary prisoners in this new city and endure its highly regimented way of life. The facts that "radios were mysteriously out of order" and the concept of "news" was ridiculed were at least partially offset by such amenities as the bathhouse, where individuals, couples, and larger groups were free to indulge in any and all "private and public fantasies."[13] This project owed much to the fact that Koolhaas had met

Adolfo Natalini in London and became familiar with Superstudio's various projects in the same ironic vein.[14]

Koolhaas split his time in 1973 between Cornell University and the IAUS in New York, where Frampton had invited him to be a visiting fellow. During this year he wrote his essay (with Gerrit Oorthuys) on Ivan Leonidov's three-tower project of 1933.[15] In another paper project with Zenghelis, "City of the Captive Globe," they proposed an urban center of multistory granite blocks on which were mounted competing ideologies in the form of abstract architectonic constructions. The changing skyline of the city was thus defined by the collapsing failure or "speculative ejaculation" of each theory.[16] Both undertakings, however, were little more than foreplay when compared to the archaeological labor of *Delirious New York* (1978), which Koolhaas also wrote while at the IAUS.

This "Retroactive Manifesto for Manhattan" (the book's subtitle) was not only very chic but also notable for the insouciance of its creed of "Manhattanism." Against the long-standing platitudes of academic and professional theory, Koolhaas, to whom Jean-Louis Cohen once referred as the "serene provocateur," proffered a startlingly simple counter-thesis: that congestion moves modern life in a highly positive way.[17] If European theory throughout the twentieth century abounded in manifestoes without evidence, Manhattan's problem was precisely the opposite; not only did it possess "a mountain range of evidence [buildings] without manifesto" but it also "inspired in its beholders *ecstasy about architecture.*"[18] For this last indulgence, Koolhaas insisted, the lessons of Manhattanism had been suppressed, unattended to if not scorned by academe, museums, and professional historians.

The means by which Koolhaas supplied the missing document is especially imaginative, as he provided historical chapters on Coney Island, the skyscraper, Rockefeller Center, Salvador Dali, and Le Corbusier. Not to be lost amid the minutia about amusement parks and dirigibles, however, is the scholarship. His chapter on the skyscraper, for example, tapped into the root of Manhattan architectural culture in the way that few, if any, historical studies had previously succeeded. We not only learn about the catalogue of buildings in considerable detail, but also much more about the personalities driving the bravado and bluster of the 1920s and early 1930s – Hugh Ferriss, Harvey Wiley Corbett, and Raymond Hood. The section on the Waldorf-Astoria and Empire State Building (the idea of the first morphing into the second) is indicative of Koolhaas literary savvy. The rebuilt and much enlarged Waldorf-Astoria is not yet a skyscraper but "a plot – a cybernetic universe with its own laws generating random but fortuitous collisions between human beings who would never have met elsewhere."[19] Its multiple kitchens are staged vertically and culturally to accommodate the world's multiple culinary tastes.

Le Corbusier, too, came in for harsh reappraisal, in particular his obsession with building "the New City commensurate with the demands and potential glories of the machine civilization." It was a dream, however, destined to meet the "tragic bad luck that such a city already exists" in Manhattan.[20] Undeterred, Le Corbusier responded first by waging a campaign of ridicule against American skyscrapers and second by designing the "anti-Skyscraper and the anti-Manhattan" in the form of his Radiant City. In this scheme he placed New York skyscrapers (undressed, amputated at the top and base) at a sufficient distance apart (400 m) to prevent what Krier believed to be the essential urban element of congestion. It was a plan once again doomed to meet with a humiliating response, particularly on his trip to New York in 1935. Even the trip's sponsor, the Museum of Modern Art (which had been waging a similar campaign of anti-Manhattanism for the past three years) could not save him from the fact that the "Capital of Perpetual Crisis" took little note of his designs.

When *Delirious New York* appeared in 1978, Koolhaas and his team were still unknown. Three years earlier he had formed the OMA with his wife Madelon Vriesendorp and Elia and Zoé Zenghelis, but commissions initially were few. In 1981 OMA won first prize in a competition for an extension to the Dutch Parliament in The Hague, although nothing tangible emerged from it. The same was true for the firm's first-place submission (among 10 others) for the park of La Villette in 1982–1983. The latter project, nevertheless, was enormously important for the office, in that it represented OMA's first attempt to invoke the theme of congestion. The office layered the site with horizontal bands, cataloguing "40 or 50 different activities arranged like floors, horizontally over the entire surface of the park," and sprinkled the bands with the "confetti" of kiosks, bars, and restaurants.[21] As this project was being developed, OMA was already at work on its first major commission, the National Dance Theater in The Hague (1980–1987). By the date of its completion, OMA had become one of the largest and busiest offices in Europe and the leader of Holland's architectural renaissance of the 1990s.

Close to Koolhaas in both friendship and interests is Zaha Hadid. This Iraqi-born architect studied at the American University in Lebanon before attending the Architectural Association between 1972 and 1977. In taking the studio of Koolhaas and Zenghelis, she cultivated her interest in De Stijl and Constructivism, as well as the Suprematism of Kazimir Malevich, whose three-dimensional model *Alpha Architekton* (1920), reconfigured as a hotel and placed on a bridge over the River Thames, was the basis for her thesis project of 1977. If Malevich's white-plaster forms are compositionally little altered, they are axonometrically rendered in hues of red, black, white, and blue-grays – not as a recognizable architectural presentation but as an abstract painting. The plan's outline indeed becomes an ornament stamped over the painting's surface.

Upon her graduation, Koolhaas and Zenghelis invited Hadid into OMA as a partner, where she would remain for two years. Her early projects – the Irish Prime Minister's Residence (1979–1980), 59 Eaton Place (1981–1982), and her project for La Villette (1982–1983) – continued to be composed like paintings: without scale, groundless, diagonally aligned, and often shattered before their presumed architectonic reassembly. Her expressionistic tour-de-force was her competition-winning design for the Peak Club in Hong Kong (1982–1983), a victory announced almost simultaneously with Tschumi's winning scheme at Villette. This luxurious private club was to be placed atop Victoria Peak, the highest point of what was then the British colony of Hong Kong. Through a series of paintings, Hadid responded with what she termed a "Suprematist geology," in which excavated rock is reshaped into "a man-made polished granite mountain" while the "building is layered horizontally with architectural beams superimposed upon each other, constituting a series of programmes."[22] The acute sharpness of the design is brought about by a slight splaying of the layered axes as well as by the use of pointed forms. It is "neo-modern," but definitely not in the historicist sense of the early 1980s. Hadid had pushed beyond Suprematism and begun exploring forms with no apparent pedigree, save for her painterly approaches to composition and representation.

Her freshness was also apparent for her first exhibition catalogue, *Planetary Architecture Two*, an exhibit held at the Architectural Association in 1983. It was an impressive showcase for her talent, a large portfolio of six projects with an introduction by Frampton and an interview with Boyarsky. The title derived from a report on her student progress by Koolhaas, in which he described her as a "*PLANET*, in her own inimitable orbit," one for whom a conventional career was "impossible." In her short essay, "The Eighty-Nine Degrees," Hadid modestly defined her task as "reinvestigating Modernity, which entailed the invasion and conquering of "new territories."[23]

Daniel Libeskind also appeared along a similar chronological path of development. A gifted musician, he was born in Poland and immigrated with his parents first to Israel and then, in 1960, to New York City. Five years later he would forego a promising career as a pianist by enrolling in the architecture program at Cooper Union School, where he studied under John Hejduk. Libeskind also took graduate studies at Essex under Joseph Rykwert and Dalibor Vesely and at the Ontario Institute for Advanced Studies in Education, during which time he pursued his interest in phenomenology. In 1978 he received the directorship of the Department of Architecture at the Cranbrook Academy of Art, a private studio that Eliel and Eero Saarinen had created in the late 1930s as a place for architectural meditation.

Libeskind's portfolio of artistic labor during this period is explorative and abstractly mystical. His series of line drawings entitled *Micromegas* (1979) was sufficiently moving to encourage one art-gallery owner – Jeffrey Kipnis – to give up his trade and turn his interest toward architecture.[24] Libeskind described these drawings as "neither a physics nor a poetics of space" but rather the work of a devotee seeking "a radical elucidation of the original pre-comprehension of forms" – a quest, he noted further, that was inspired by Edmund Husserl's essay "The Origin of Geometry."[25] A similar abstruseness is found Libeskind's *Chamberworks* (1983), a series of 28 drawings that was first exhibited at the Architectural Association in 1983. At least here Libeskind conceded that – in lieu of finding any permanent structure, constant form, or universal type for architecture – all that remained was to capture "a trail of hieroglyphs in space and time."[26] More comprehensible are his sculptural machines, *Three Lessons in Architecture*, which he prepared for the Venice Biennale of 1985. Medieval in content and construction, these machines (ordered by Vitruvius and Alberti) display a richness of conception and refinement of execution rare in the art world at large. One (dedicated to Petrarch) features his own version of a monastic "Reading Machine:" two rotating wheels tied together by eight shelves, on each of which is one handmade book. The circular drum, supported within a framework, is propelled by an elaborate series of 92, hand-chiseled gears controlled by the seated reader. The machine, which for Libeskind spoke to "the tautological reality of the architectural text," not only displayed the author's kinship with his mentor Hejduk but also a high sense of craftsmanship.[27]

Of course, Libeskind would begin this practical track in a dramatic fashion in 1989 by winning the competition for the Jewish Museum of Berlin. This is not the place to discuss the story of the acutely-angled, zinc-clad building that was finished only in 2001. With a less determined architect, it would never have scaled the numerous bureaucratic obstacles and seen the light of day. Its elaborate symbolic framework (from Arnold Schönberg's opera *Moses and Aaron* to Walter Benjamin's "One-Way Street") defies any casual decoding, yet it is a work (whose description for the competition was printed on musical paper with the staff lines running through the text) whose simple passion and emotion elides all such intellectual constellations.[28] The fact that it could have sprung from the head of a 42-year-old architect with no previous building experience might in itself be viewed as one of the Eleusian Mysteries of the twentieth century, had it not been augured by his philosophical training and earlier repertoire of compositional labor.

"…a devious architecture…"

Toward the end of the 1980s two things were becoming evident. One was that the phenomenon of postmodernism, which had been proclaimed as an epic event only a decade earlier, was beginning to wear thin as an aesthetic fashion. The second was that there was a general confusion, in American circles at least, as to whether that which was replacing it was yet one more stage within the revolution (a politicized, 1920s-style modernism) or something fundamentally in opposition to it. For instance, when K. Michael Hays, with the support of Kurt W. Forster and Mark Rakatansky, founded the journal *Assemblage* in 1986, he countered – in the inaugural editorial – the "passive, all-accommodating pluralism" with a demand for "oppositional knowledge" that would draw upon "history, literary criticism, philosophy, and politics" as well as suggesting "heterogeneity, collision, incompleteness."[29] Yet how does one square such intellectual abstractions with the culture industry's demand for neat categorization and a tidy accounting of values? If architecture were perpetually consigned to being radically oppositional, would not all values, or even meaning, become as elusive as a Derridean text?

This last point would be made crystal clear by two events later in the decade that sought to define "Deconstruction." The first was a one-day symposium on the theme held at London's Tate Gallery in early April, 1988. The second was the exhibition "Deconstructivist Architecture," which took place at New York's Museum of Modern Art a few months later. Of the two events, the former was intellectually the more ambitious, although it had almost certainly been planned with a view to the New York show.[30] The symposium's organizer, Andreas C. Papadakis, was the editor of Academy Editions. In the late 1970s he revamped the journal *Architectural Design* by issuing a series of "Design Profiles" on topical themes. Moreover, they were lavishly illustrated, heavy on theoretical content, and conceived with the aim of staying on top of the quick pace of change. Papadakis intended to bring no less an authority than Derrida to the Tate gathering to validate the event, but the philosopher reneged on his acceptance at the last moment and the audience had to settle for a taped interview with the Parisian celebrity.[31] And whereas the afternoon session was largely devoted to the theme of deconstruction in philosophy, art, and sculpture, the morning session was given over entirely to architecture, and in fact to a select panel consisting of Eisenman, Tschumi, Hadid, and Mark Wigley. Charles Jencks was the moderator.

Jencks's take on the question of postmodernism and deconstruction is an interesting one because of his earlier ambivalence on the issue. Four years earlier, in *What is Postmodernism?*, he had defined the postmodern movement in such as way as to include such architects as Gehry, Koolhaas, and Eisenman while at the same time excluding others such as Tschumi and Hadid. Yet in a special issue of *Architectural Design* that he had prepared in the first part of 1988 he had concluded that all of these architects were in fact "Late-Modernists" and thus represented a direction different from both modernism or postmodernism. At the same time he was rather sardonic at the prospect of basing any new style on the "emptiness and non-being" of the *nihil* found near mid-town Manhattan.[32]

Yet Eisenman and Tschumi had long been overtly hostile to the semantic focus of postmodernism, and thus the possibility of a showdown at the Tate was quite likely. Jencks fired the first volley with opening remarks entitled "Deconstruction: The Sound of One Mind Laughing." Eisenman reportedly took the podium after Jencks and dismissed him curtly, "I'm quite fond of Charles, but enough's enough. Next time could we have an introducer who knows what he's talking about?"[33] The architect then laid out his theoretical underpinnings for an architecture of Deconstruction – remarks summarized by one editorialist:

> Deconstruction, says Eisenman, is slippery, speculative and difficult. For 400 years it sought to overcome nature, now it has to try to symbolise the overcoming of knowledge. Deconstruction looks for "the between" – the ugly within the beautiful, the irrational within the rational – to uncover the repressed, the real resistant, cut into textuality and displace the system, so that only now does he see his truly Deconstructionist projects emerging, in projects that tackle "the between," bring out the unease, creating an architecture for alienated man much the way Edvard Munch had in painting.[34]

Eisenman also went on to distinguish architectural Deconstruction from the works of such architects as Gehry and James Wines, who in his view do not subvert the larger system as a whole. Tschumi and Hadid followed Eisenman to the microphone – the former discussed La Villette and chose to define architectural Deconstruction as both a break from traditional logics of design and as an alternative to postmodernism and its desperate attempts to salvage meaning. Only Wigley, who was co-curating the New York exhibition with Philip Johnson, stood up to the philosophical barrage by insisting that this new phenomenon in architecture had little to do with Derridean philosophy. The irony here, of course, is that Wigley had completed his doctoral dissertation on "Jacques Derrrida and Architecture: The Constructive Possibilities of Architectural Discourse" two years earlier and he was the one of the few architects in attendance, alongside Tschumi and Eisenman, who was steeped in Derridean theory.[35] But then again, he was also one of the few persons in the audience who knew the particular tack that the forthcoming New York exhibition was taking.

Wigley, however, did not win the day, at least in London. Papadakis followed the symposium with Jencks's Design Profile, *Deconstruction in Architecture*, which, in several essays, underscored its Derridean underpinnings, as found in the work of Emilio Ambasz, Coop Himmelblau, SITE, OMA, Gehry, and Morphosis. The same editor also followed shortly with his *Omnibus Volume* devoted to the theme of Deconstruction, which was an even more ambitious attempt to square philosophy with architecture, and with *Deconstruction: A Student Guide*, which attempted to situate architecture within a philosophical terrain that spanned from Plato to the present.

Meanwhile, the exhibition "Deconstructivist Architecture" opened in early summer in New York. It seems to have been the brainchild of Philip Johnson, although probably in conversation with Eisenman, with whom Johnson was close during these years. For Johnson, who was at this time the Honorary Chairman of the museum's Trustee Committee, the show represented his dramatic return to the Museum of Modern Art, an occasion reminiscent of his "Mies van der Rohe" exhibition in 1947 as well as the "International Style" event of 1932. It seems that Johnson, who in the early 1980s had jumped from the modern to the postmodern camp with the much publicized "Chippendale" top of his AT&T building, had by this time moved on, and the new event was the perfect way to shake-up the institution. He was aided in this regard by Wigley, who in 1987 joined the discussions about the content of the show. In line with his remarks in London, Wigley has described the process of selecting the exhibitors as one of winnowing the field and identifying the movement as one more sectarian than ideological in character.[36]

The formula proved successful because the show was well attended. The architects represented at the event were Gehry, Libeskind, Koolhaas, Eisenman, Hadid, Coop Himmelblau, and Tschumi – all of whom would gain enormous stature by their selection. Gehry displayed his own house, Hadid the Peak Club, Tschumi the Parc de la Villette, and Libeskind his

"City Edge" project for Berlin (1987), which was the forerunner to his Jewish Museum. OMA contributed their project for an apartment building in Rotterdam (1982), while Eisenman displayed his Biocenter for the University of Frankfurt (1987). The Vienna office of Coop Himmelblau, led by Wolfgang Prix and Helmut Swiczinsky, presented three projects, the most interesting of which was the skyscraper project for Hamburg (1985). The design sensibilities of the office, founded in the year 1968, differed from these others participants in its overtly anarchical character.

The exhibition catalogue carried none of the theoretical weight of the London colloquium. Johnson, in the Preface, was adamant that no new style was materializing, no new movement was afoot, and the moniker "deconstructivist" was chosen simply for the formal similarity of this work with the Soviet Constructivists of the 1920s. Hence, the unifying motif to be found in the work of these different architects was "the diagonal overlapping of rectangular or trapezoidal bars."[37]

Wigley in his Introduction followed up on his London argument. Contrasting the "pure form" of the mainstream modernists of the 1920s (the values of harmony, unity, and stability) with the "radical geometry" of the early Constructivists, Wigley interpreted the work of these seven architects as a mediation of sorts: "the cool veneer of the International Style" applied "to the anxiously conflicting forms of the avant-garde."[38] Nevertheless, this was not a conscious revival in the sense that many postmodernists had attempted. As formal exercises operating effectively outside of theory, these works represented both a "decontextualization" and a "defamiliarization" of such time-honored architectural tenets as the idea of enclosure. They are intended neither as something new nor as another avant-garde statement, but rather as forms to shock and purposely evoke a sense of insecurity. Their "disturbance" to the traditional ideas of form was not perceptual but rather cultural, that is, "they produce a devious architecture, a slippery architecture that slides uncontrollably from the familiar into the unfamiliar, toward an uncanny realization of its own alien nature: an architecture, finally, in which form distorts itself in order to reveal itself anew."[39] Interestingly, Wigley concludes by predicting that this "episode" is destined to be short-lived, because each architect will soon go his or her own way.

The 1990s would certainly prove the validity of his last point, but at the same time the New York event was in many ways an architectural embarrassment, in fact a serious one. It was not so much the decoupling of theory from style that offended many ideological purists at the time as it was the unseemliness of the "show" that surrounded the show. Shortly before its opening, the *New York Times* critic Joseph Giovannini wrote a piece for the Sunday edition in which he likened the new movement to the music of John Cage ("intense and purposely 'accidental'"), and to "an unruly world subject to caroming moral, political and economic systems." At the same time he noted that one year earlier, in a book proposal to his editors, he himself had devised the word "deconstructivism" by conflating the words "deconstruction" and "constructivism."[40]

Catherine Ingraham, who later reviewed the exhibition for the *Inland Architect*, took issue with such hubris: not only with "Johnson's and Giovannini's desires to be 'founders of a movement,'" but also with the larger spectacle of the show itself – that is, "the Museum of Modern Art's desire to update its image in the contemporary art/architectural world; New York's desire to be the place where the 'new' is perpetually named and performed first; the architects' desires to be legitimized and so on."[41] Ingraham's comments indeed underscore what an odd theoretical interlude this new and much publicized phase of "Decon" architecture was – if only in the sense that it (with its neo-avant-gardist dismissal of social, ecological, and constructional concerns) was now confirming the worst nightmares of Adorno and Debord and mocking the revolutionary spirit out of which it was presumably born. American theory in the late 1980s, particularly as it emanated from the "elite" schools of the Northeast, was obsessed with its quest for intellectual validation. And like the example of Museum of Modern Art in the early 1930s, it had adopted the uncomfortable pattern of importing the latest "ism" from any or all sources – from Freud to Bataille to Derrida – as long as they were European. Institutions and the suddenly attuned popular media, as well a large part of academe, were uncomfortably complicit and only too eager to follow.

Part Three
1990s and Present

9

Wake of the Storm

The deconstructivist shards of the late 1980s, which had been bound together by little more than loose formal similarities, would continue to fragment in the 1990s. Some architects would focus on the manipulation of geometry or the production of pure effect. Others would turn to techniques of deformation in response to sociopolitical concerns, while still others were perhaps just as technologically deterministic as early modernists in their infatuation with the power of the new digital technologies. All of this work, however, shared an explicit or implicit conviction that deformation, distortion, and formal complexity were the appropriate techniques to confront the turn of a new millennium. Explanations on behalf of these strategies abounded. One was simply the growing sophistication of new computer software and the belief that nonlinear geometries best represented the complexity and contradiction of the post-Cold War era. Others saw these geometries as a way to resist the market forces of consumer capitalism, while still others saw them as expressive and unprecedented spatial forms, which were presumed either to embody the new zeitgeist or to create a fresh one by force.

Fragments of Fragments

What was becoming clear, however, was that these investigations, which had been defined in the second half of the 1980s under the banner of deconstruction or deconstructivism, would in the future no longer be able to use these labels. At least Jeffrey Kipnis raises this point in his essay of 1990, "*Nolo Contendere*," which opens with a judicial plea to unspecified

An Introduction to Architectural Theory: 1968 to the Present, First Edition.
Harry Francis Mallgrave and David Goodman.
© 2011 Harry Francis Mallgrave and David Goodman. Published 2011 by Blackwell Publishing Ltd.

crimes: "On all charges, I, deconstruction, plea: Nolo Contendere."[1]
Kipnis, however, does not come to bury deconstruction, but to praise it.
Deconstruction does not plead guilty, and the essay might be better understood as a plea-bargain agreement in which the underlying principles of
deconstruction are allowed to carry on even though the appellation itself
has wearied. To that end, Kipnis focuses not on what deconstructionist
architecture looked like, but instead on what it had hoped to achieve. He
argues that deconstruction has two primary concerns: first to destabilize
the meaning of previous works, second to produce new projects that avoid
obvious or conclusive meaning. In the first case, Kipnis notes that deconstruction intends to "mobilize the many repressed threads of meaning
within the work" and thereby "expose mechanisms of repression and the
agendas that those repressive mechanisms serve." In the second case,
Kipnis writes that deconstruction aimed to produce "work that, though
not meaningless, does not simply give itself over to meaning." Kipnis thus
suggests the original goals of deconstruction remain important first by
framing the discussion of the work in terms of struggle and engagement,
and second by arguing that projects should still "resist, defer, and destabilize meaning."[2]

One is surprised by the overtly political, and even social and psychoanalytical ends to which Kipnis ascribes deconstruction. The Freudian idea of
exposing the "mechanisms of repression" seems no small task for the hum-
ble work of architecture, and one might be tempted to interpret Kipnis's
social sermonizing as another example of the '68 generation venting its
anger. Indeed, during the late 1980s and 1990s, the pages of *Architecture
New York* (*ANY*) and *Assemblage* – the new critical journals in the United
States that had succeeded *Oppositions* – were stuffed with articles that dealt
with extra-disciplinary concerns: architecture and gender, architecture and
sexuality, and the broader relationship of architecture to power.[3] The idea
that architecture should once again be both engaged and autonomous
echoes the writings of Theodor Adorno, who held that art can only defend
itself against commodity culture by turning inward and focusing on the
techniques particular to the discipline, while simultaneously challenging
consumerism by confronting it directly.

Kipnis's hesitant use of the term "deconstruction" in 1990 evolves into
a rejection of the term in 1993, as we find in his essay "Towards a New
Architecture," which appeared in a special edition of *Architectural Design*.
In the interim, Kipnis's personal circumstances too had changed. In 1992
he had been named director of the newly formed Graduate Design
Program at the Architectural Association in London and – though not a
formally trained architect – he had collaborated with Bahram Shirdel and

Andrew Zago on competitions for Montreal and the Scottish National Museum. In the essay of 1993, Kipnis used these two projects, along with the recent work of Frank Gehry and Peter Eisenman, to describe the appearance of a particular kind of architectural novelty, one based on formal innovation and productive engagement with the site. "In such postmodern practices as deconstruction," he writes, "the project of the new is rejected. New intellectual, aesthetic, and institutional forms, as well as new forms of social arrangements are generated not by proposition but by constantly destabilizing existing forms."[4] Kipnis thus links deconstruction to the strategy of "PoMo" and its historical pastiches – arguing that both had been largely based on the technique of collage as a way to create a heterogeneous architecture and to create new meanings out of combinations of old forms. For now, collage has outlived its usefulness: "From Rowe to Venturi to Eisenman, from PoMo to the deconstructivists, collage has served as the dominant mode of the architectural graft. There are indications, however, to suggest that collage is not able to sustain the heterogeneity architecture aspires to achieve."[5]

Kipnis expands upon this statement by describing two countervailing but aligned tendencies in architecture that move beyond techniques of fragmentation and collage: InFormation and DeFormation. He describes the former as a "collecting graft," in which various programs and forms are fused together into a "neutral modernist monolith."[6] In this category, Kipnis places such projects as Bernard Tschumi's Contemporary Arts Center at Le Fresnoy and OMA's Art and Media Center in Karlsruhe. DeFormation, meanwhile, is where the "new architecture" of the article's title emerges. If InFormation represents the wrapping of novel programmatic combinations in a blank orthogonal wrapper, DeFormation is the generation of novel forms that in themselves lead to new programs, ultimately effecting political and social changes. And, unlike the fragmented and collaged landscape of deconstruction, DeFormation leads to smoothness, continuity, folding, and, in the words of Kipnis, "a new abstract monolithicity that would broach neither reference nor resemblance."[7]

Whereas even a cursory examination of the computer renderings and models accompanying the text will reveal formal innovations (a series of vaguely biomorphic and inflected shapes rendered in a mysteriously glowing and perpetual computer nighttime), the political efficacy of these forms is not immediately apparent. In order to understand Kipnis's claims for this architecture's power of social transformation, we must step back and discuss the broader context of the architectural discourse from which this argument emerged.

From Derrida to Deleuze

Gilles Deleuze's *Le Pli* (The Fold) appeared in French in 1988 and in an English translation in 1993. Its appearance was propitious in that it would provide a framework to build a post-deconstruction platform. The book deals with the work of the eighteenth-century philosopher Gottfried Leibniz, with whom Deleuze seems to align himself and to position as the essential philosopher of the baroque epoch. The Frenchman, however, treats the baroque not as a particular historical period but rather as an "operative function" unconnected to any specific moment in history. The baroque way of thinking, he argues, produced pleats, folds, and twisted surfaces that could be extended into infinity, and thus for Leibniz the "fold" constituted the basic building block of the universe because mass was created through the endless accretion of fold upon fold.

Deleuze concludes from this that through the technique of folding, all contradictions and "divergences" can be synthesized into an inclusive whole – that is, baroque folding synthesizes the purity of "classical reason" with its opposite. The result is not the destruction of the classical but instead an inflection; in the baroque, the classical temple front bends but does not lose its authority.[8] Deleuze describes a folding that is both literal and metaphysical. It is literally found in baroque clothing in the "thousand folds of garments that tend to become one with their wearers." It is metaphysical when it mediates the exterior world of mass and matter with the interior world of the soul.[9] Not surprisingly, architects tended to focus their attention on the literal and physical folding – the idea of formal continuity.

Greg Lynn, who in 1993 edited the special issue of *Architectural Design* entitled "Folding in Architecture," seized upon this idea as the centerpiece of his theoretical agenda. A former student of and assistant to Eisenman, Lynn viewed geometry as a key to generating new form, which for him was closely bound with the new digital software that made possible the precise representation and calculation of complex forms, as well as the ability to manufacture them directly from the digital drawings. In the inaugural issue of the journal *ANY*, for instance, Lynn suggests that new computer techniques will now allow architects, among other things, to "measure amorphousness and undecideability." Responding to Denis Hollier's definition of architecture as a totalizing and exact discipline, Lynn proffers the alternative strategy of making architecture, in a way, more akin to writing. New techniques of geometric modeling, like "random section analysis," allow architects to represent complex and "anexact" form rather than pure or "eidetic" form.[10] The goal, for Lynn, is the conception of architecture as a form of writing that admits uncertainty and indeterminacy.

Underlying this statement is the technological determinism to which we alluded. The new tools exist and should be used, thereby becoming both the vehicle for and the subject of the new architecture. Like the early modernists, Lynn is looking to emerging technologies as a driver of form – in this case, the production of computer drawings, which might then be directly converted into buildings. If Le Corbusier had used ocean liners, automobiles, and airplanes to illustrate the novel technologies being employed in other areas of design, Lynn points to such new computer technologies being developed in the automobile and defense industries – softwares that would allow for the representation and fabrication of complex geometries. Similarly, this Los Angeles-based architect would point to Hollywood to boost his point of a new spirit, citing the liquid, shape-shifting villain featured in *Terminator 2*, and the morphing of Michael Jackson's body in the video for his song "Black or White." In the last instance, video, multiple genders, ethnicities, and races are mixed in a continuous sequence through the digital morphing of images. It is significant that Jackson is not black *or* white but black *and* white, Lynn notes, not male *or* female but male *and* female. His ambiguities are characteristics of a desire for smoothness, to become heterogeneous yet continuous.[11]

This notion of mixture and synthesis would be a crucial one, perhaps the fundamental theoretical basis for much of the post-deconstructivist work. In his own essay for the special issue of *Architectural Design*, Lynn argues that if "there is a single effect produced in architecture by folding, it will be the ability to integrate unrelated elements within a new continuous mixture." Kenneth Powell, in the issue's introductory essay, concludes that deconstruction has succeeded in destabilizing the architectural landscape from both Modernist orthodoxy and Postmodernist historicist pastiche, but that the current task would be to create "an inclusive and organic way of designing which is in tune with the man-made and natural world."[12]

On one level, one might understand this link with the "man-made and natural world" to be a form of neo-Wrightian organicism, as there is a clear biomorphic aesthetic behind much of the post-deconstructionist work, and the literature even sports frequent allusions to human evolution and D'Arcy Thompson's *On Growth and Form*. Powell's suggestion is that work formally resembling natural objects or phenomena or employing a design process analogous to processes of nature (evolution, cellular reproduction, etc.) has a certain claim to truth or universality. The appeal to a higher authority outside the discipline of architecture is not new, but the shift from the post-structuralism of the 1980s in this instance is notable – Darwin has replaced both Derrida and Deleuze.

Quite apart from the formal and metaphorical organicism, however, much of this work aimed at a synthesis with a building's surroundings, in which forces determined to be present on the site would be seen to be pushing, pulling, inflecting, and otherwise deforming an original, and presumably neutral, original form. This technique, with its emphasis on affiliations with the world beyond the individual building or, as in Lynn's Stranded Sears Tower, on "internaliz[ing] influences by external forces" recalls the approach of Peter Eisenman, who was the one architect contributing to the special issue of *Architectural Design* who had significant work on the boards.[13] When the Wexner Center was completed in the late 1980s, Eisenman became involved with a number of projects in which site conditions – found, reconstituted, or, in some cases, metaphorically excavated from history – would play a fundamental role. His project for the Max Reinhardt skyscraper for Berlin (1992), for example, condenses a range of uses into a 34-story Möbius strip. The contorted form creates an inflected and distended triumphal arch of ambiguous scale. For Eisenman, the faceted form of the tower would "represent on one site that which is of many places," and would assemble "the diffuse and unstable bits of the city into a kaleidoscopic array."[14] In the Greater Columbus Convention Center, completed in 1993, Eisenman would overlay the presumably neutral assembly hall volume with a series of strands that traced the splayed network of train tracks once present on the site, creating a serrated and multicolored volume of parallel bars. Eisenman argued that by breaking the building into a fine grain he could both emulate the rhythm of the neighboring buildings along a primary commercial street and provide an engaging experience for the pedestrian. These types of operations, with their superimposition of local conditions (existing or otherwise) and the increased attention to programmatic concerns follow the trail of the Wexner Center in their departure from the highly disciplined formal operations of his early work.

Kipnis perhaps best describes Eisenman's thinking by referring to these transformational site interventions as "affiliations." He argues that, unlike traditional contextual approaches in which the architect simply responds to existing conditions, these transformations emerge from the "intrinsic formal, topological, or spatial character of the design" and thereby create "provisional, ad hoc links" to secondary features found on site. Moreover, this approach does not "reinforce the dominant architectural modes" of a given site, but instead can "amplify suppressed or minor organizations" also found on the site.[15] In effect, the affiliated elements inflect and recon-

Figure 9.1   Peter Eisenman, 1:200 model of the Max Reinhardt Haus proposal, Berlin (1992). Photo by Dick Frank. Courtesy of Eisenman Architects.

figure the context in order to emphasize the secondary elements that were previously ignored.

Geometry and Autonomy

Still another student of Eisenman, Preston Scott Cohen, extends these ideas by applying them to the disciplinary geometrical frameworks and operations of Eisenman's early houses. Cohen's language is not derived from historical excavations or fabrications but through architectural operations: slicing, pulling, bending, and distorting architectural form in response to programmatic concerns. Cohen, who also took a studio under Daniel Liebeskind at the Harvard Graduate School of Design, likens his strategy to the linguistic manipulations of the Renaissance and Baroque, where the architectural style itself guaranteed intelligibility while at the same time allowing a skilled architect to create deformations and subtle distortions for the initiated. These deformations could grow out of the theme itself (as Giulio Romano had done at Palazzo del Te), or alternately, through the application of a language on a building that resisted its regularity.

Cohen's Houses on Siesta Key and Longboat Key were featured in 1990 in an issue of *Assemblage* alongside the explicitly political and surrealist collages of Jesse Reiser and Nanako Umemoto, and the narrative fantasies of Ben Nicholson's "Kleptoman Cell, Appliance House." Viewed alongside these projects, with their desire to "fabricate the mechanisms and the context for an alternative analysis of the house and domesticity," Cohen's houses seem somehow out of step.[16] He represents his work with no-nonsense photographs of basswood models, conventional orthographic projections, and perspective drawings. His designs deal in part with issues of facade composition and decorum (drawing upon readings of Rudolf Wittkower and Colin Rowe), and in part with the distortions and ambiguous readings that Robert Venturi championed. In the House on Longboat Key, for instance, Cohen responded to the real-world code constraints of a pitched roof and elevated floor by overlapping an elongated gable front (which, as Cohen pointed out, might be read either as a rotated, perspectival view of a corner or as a pediment) with a prismatic horizontal volume. These forms jostle with each other for dominance within the whole, so that they can be read either as a pediment or cornice, or both. He also responded to the elevated floor by creating a sequence in which the true entry to the house occurs in the geometrical center of the plan, rotated 90 degrees with respect to the street facade. The end result is a distorted and tightly wound interpretation of the suburban American house with a pedigree recalling both Eisenman and Venturi.

Cohen's House on Siesta Key continued the deformation or transformations of domestic prototypes. This time Cohen began his work with an analysis of Northern Italian Renaissance villas, gradually transforming the original prototype through shifts in plan and section. The starting point is telling, not only because it echoes Rowe and Wittkower but also because the Renaissance facade – as Cohen's reads it – creates a tension between the visual need for a decorous and symmetrical facade and the asymmetrical internal distribution that precluded it. For Cohen, Renaissance buildings provided a catalogue of highly motivated distortions, yet they were created not out of willfulness but rather as occasionally futile attempts to reconcile the bilateral symmetry insisted upon by the classical language and the inevitable asymmetry demanded by the plan. Cohen would call these problems "predicaments" and suggest that, in attempting to resolve them, architects could arrive at a "motivated strangeness," that is, an architecture of unprecedented form as a response to intransigent problems.[17]

Figure 9.2 Preston Scott Cohen, the Torus House (1998). Image courtesy of Preston Scott Cohen, Inc.

In this sense, there is a tragic dimension to Cohen's view of architecture, for it is only through an extreme means that the discipline can "keep itself alive" – in part an effort to conserve the integrity of the discipline from the storm of consumer society. In his projects entitled "Stereotomic Permutations," which date from the mid-1990s, his use of complex geometries provide a cloak of inscrutability for all but the initiated. The drawings are difficult to read: filled with projection lines and markings of the key vertices in a dense variegated web. The computer is incidental, perhaps unnecessary, in Cohen's work. Although these projection drawings, conceived and executed by hand, could much more easily – though less beautifully – be resolved through the computer, it is geometry itself, and not the digital technology, that allows for the deformations of language and form.

By the end of the decade, however, Cohen's manipulative operations would become smoother and more reliant on the computer, such as we find in the Montague House (1997) and the Torus House (1998), both of which were featured in the "Un-Private House" exhibition at the Museum of Modern Art in 1999. In the latter house, an apparently neutral neo-Corbusian volume is lifted off the ground and pierced with a central spiral stairway connecting the ground to the roof. This stair causes a deformation of the original block as its curved contour undulates through the walls and floor. The seductive images of this house, with its rippling, cascading surfaces, were added to the museum's permanent collection and would become icons of the American avant-garde at the turn of the millennium, notwithstanding their intentionally inscrutable qualities. Like Greg Lynn, Cohen would build little in the 1990s, but the Museum of Modern Art show would soon pay off in large commissions.

The Sri Lankan-born structural engineer Cecil Balmond, based in the offices of Arup in London, was also to lead important explorations of geometry and its ability to generate new form. Balmond had been a frequent collaborator of Rem Koolhaas, contributing to buildings like the Kunsthal in Rotterdam, the Congrexpo in Lille, and the project for the Center for Art and Technology in Karslruhe. Balmond's legacy as a key figure in structural engineering would likely have been assured by these innovative collaborations, but his explorations of "informal" structural logics, which he would develop in the late 1990s, would make him a prominent intellectual figure in both engineering and architectural circles in the following decade. Balmond would be seen as a leader in search of complex and novel forms based not on authorly desire or control but on an open-ended application of algorithms and geometric models to develop responsive and supple forms only partially controlled by the architect.

Balmond defines "informal" structures as those that dissolve the knowable and static skeletal structure. Against such, he suggests forms and a structural scheme that would have been unimaginable at the start. Indeed, the only thing that Balmond's structural approach seems to take as a given is complexity and ambiguity rather than certainty, as he calls for an exploration of geometry that allows for discovery and the emergence of solutions along the way, and that creates ambiguity rather than certainty.[18] For Balmond, this point of view represented nothing less than a re-conception of Newtonian physics: "The classical determinism of Newton pictured force as an arrow, straight and true. It bridged the void in unwavering linearity – the fixed link of a rigid chain of logic. Now we see force differently, as a minimum path through a field of potential".[19]

For Balmond, then, an informal structural solution emerges as one option among many for translating a force through a defined medium. The final form is inconclusive, ambiguous, and in some way without an author, as the true invention is the definition of the "field of potential" and the force to be transmitted through it. In this sense, Balmond's work is closely related to contemporary explorations of "parametric" or "algorithmic" architecture in which a detailed, adaptive digital model of a system or structure is constructed and dynamically modified.[20] As one variable in the system changes – a surface profile, for example – all other variables, such as the profiles of individual structural elements, are immediately recalculated according to the established algorithm.

On the most practical level, this technology would have direct application to the management and construction of complex projects, as the dynamic model of all interrelated systems and materials could be immediately and seamlessly updated in three dimensions during the inevitable design changes. Once the algorithm is defined, structural-member scaling, for example, will update accordingly. But there would be a second, parallel tendency in the parametric work – namely, to complicate, or in its most extreme case to eliminate, the role of the architect as author. Parametric design allows for unknowable final results. Its spirit is fundamentally experimental, and if there is freedom in this open-ended approach there is also a possible surrender of agency on the part of the architect. At some point, of course, the architect must step in and direct the algorithm, or at least stop it from endlessly churning. It is at this point that subjectivity and authorship will inevitably reappear.

The End of the Figure: Manipulated Grounds

In contrast to the high conceptualization of so much of American theory in the early 1990s, a series of European projects would soon emerge that aimed at a complete fusion of the individual building with site. These projects would attempt to blur the boundaries between figure and ground, becoming themselves, reconstituted, folded, and punctured versions of the ground surface. It is possible to trace this line of thinking back to Deleuze, as we can see in these projects a continuous surface that folds, like the Liebnizian conception of the universe, if not to infinity, then at least to the very limits of the site. Here, one presumes, the only thing stopping the inexorable spread of the building would be the cold logic of the property line. Yet the intention was not to reveal some hidden or historical forces assumed to be latent in the site, but rather to blur disciplinary boundaries between architecture and landscape.

The work of the Spanish architect and theorist Manuel Gausa is a case in point. During the 1990s he cofounded the highly successful architectural press Actar and served as editor of the Catalan journal *Quaderns d'arquitectura i urbanisme*. And in referring to this new relationship between architecture and landscape as a "hybrid contact," he argues that the mutual inflection of landscape and architecture emanates from a changing attitude toward nature – from a romantic or "bucolic" understanding of the natural to a "mixed and wild" approach.[21] In other words, a new generation of architects and landscape architects had begun to approach the local topology without sentimentality, knowing that it too could be manipulated and this intervention could, in turn, redefine the work of architecture. Gausa describes this process as one of making the landscape architectonic (modeling, trimming, folding it), of creating new topological forms (reliefs, wave forms, pleats, cut-outs), or of facing, wrapping, and enshrouding architecture in an ambiguous synergy with the natural. It is curious that Gausa uses action verbs such as "trimming" and "folding" to describe this architecture, because it is based in large part on actively subjecting nature to artificial processes. The aim here is to exploit nature, not to preserve it.

Perhaps the most influential of the manipulated ground projects was the winning entry for the 1995 Yokohama Port Terminal Competition, designed by the Iranian-born Farshid Moussavi and Spaniard Alejandro Zaera-Polo – operating out of London under the name Foreign Office Architects (FOA). Both were graduates of Harvard and would later work for OMA in Rotterdam. Their project, completed in 2002, aimed to extend the surface of the earth surrounding the terminal up and over the building itself, transforming the roof into a park. Into and upon this undulating park-like surface, they introduced a series of interwoven, looping pathways that would create a nonlinear circulation system for the pier. Thus, what might traditionally have been viewed as a planar progression of the land stepping up and over the terminal to a waiting ship is here transformed into a rolling web. The pleats and folds of the roof create a landscape of varied but continuous spaces, while simultaneously forming the building's structural system, with special attention to the seismic loads.

Here FOA is more interested in continuity and smoothness than in discontinuity and collage. The terminal building itself is subtly indented, folded, bent, and unpeeled along its length, like a progression of CAT-scan images along a body. Yet while Moussavi and Zaera-Polo are clearly interested in formal exploration, they share Koolhaas's preoccupation with use and adjacencies as well as the potential of a continuous surface to create unprecedented programmatic combinations. The continuously modified section of the Yokohama project clearly descends from OMA's Jussieu library project of 1993, with its condensed spiral of continuously ramped floors. Likewise, it makes a reference to Koolhaas's urban design proposals for Yokohama, which called for a reprogramming and transformation of an existing parking lot and market area into "a single warped plane that would be sometimes highway, sometimes ramp, sometimes parking, and sometimes roof."[22]

FOA would continue to explore the idea of the reconstituted ground plane and define these "new grounds" as platforms – not in the sense of a base or plinth, which they argued had traditionally been used to situate a

Figure 9.3 Foreign Office Architects (FOA), Yokohama Port Terminal Competition. Image courtesy of Fang-Yi Lin.

monumental form, but as "fundamentally active, operative" surfaces that were "closer to the contemporary meaning of platforms as 'operating systems.'" In a paper given at a conference in Santander in 1997, the architects summarized the concept of "new grounds" as being artificial, hollow, diagonally structured, constituting neither foreground nor background, and "inseparable from the operation we carry out on them."[23] They defined their operations in so systematic a way that they seemed to be proposing a general strategy of architectural design rather than merely outlining a design tactic they had casually been employing. If so much of this thinking goes back to Koolhaas, it is nevertheless implemented in a surprising and convincing manner.

One might contrast such an approach with that of Zaha Hadid. Beginning in the early 1990s, Hadid would at last have the opportunity to translate into built commissions the dynamic neo-Suprematism promised by her earlier paintings and drawings. Among the more significant of these projects was the Fire Station at the Vitra factory campus in Weil-am-Rhein, Germany (1993), a project in which a series of canted walls is extended beyond the building into the landscape, colonizing a large swath of the industrial park in which it is located, and making this small building seem larger than it actually is. In this way, Hadid argues, the building "sets up a scenario for forthcoming transformations of the site" by providing a framework into which further developments might be attached.[24] But, beyond the pragmatic arguments about phasing and site planning, there is in Hadid's built work a desire to extend the building's sphere of influence beyond the limits of the building itself, either through the tracing of sinuously curved lines and walls into the landscape or through a dynamic formal approach that suggests a magnetic pull to a distant body offsite. These techniques represent the second phase of an investigation that had begun over a decade earlier in drawings; the present challenge was how to translate into inherently static buildings the dynamism promised by the drawings' extreme perspectives and airbrushed vapor trails.

If free-standing buildings like the Vitra Fire Station allowed Hadid to create this dynamism by extending the building's form into the landscape, things would be considerably stickier when working on an urban infill site. In her Contemporary Arts Center in Cincinnati (2003), for example, a concrete "urban carpet" begins as a lobby surface and folds vertically to form a party wall visible throughout the vertically organized museum. Above, the visitor is confronted with this concrete vertical surface, presumably with the memory that this surface had apparently emerged from the ground floor several stories below. Here the folded surface provides a visual representation of continuity, rather than a true programmatic continuity. In short, what began as a means to create fluid relationships between the building's programs became a visual or iconic motif, representing an idea or an image of fluidity impossible in vertical organization.

Form without Rhetoric

While it is difficult to categorize the deeply personal work of the Catalonian architects Enric Miralles and Carme Pinós into any clear school of thought, any review of formal innovation in the 1990s must address the stunning series of projects they completed at the time. One might loosely associate their work at the Hebron Valley Archery Range in Barcelona or the project for Igualada Cemetery with the hybrid landscape projects we have discussed above, although this would misread the very real role that fragmentation, enclosure, and structural expressionism have in their work. One might also view their work in light of deconstruction, but this too would overlook the fact that their bent and curved forms – forms deeply poetic and immediate – may have more to do with the work of fellow

Figure 9.4   Miralles and Pinós, Igualada Cemetery, near Barcelona (1984–1994). Image by the authors.

Catalonians Antoni Gaudí and Joan Miró than with poststructural theory. And if their work can be situated within a rebirth of Catalonian culture and language after nearly 40 years of repression under the Franco regime, there was little political theorizing.[25] A new identity was being formed largely without rhetoric.

It therefore seems useful to approach their work as a personal and expressionistic response to the basic requirements of the projects at hand – that is, as a poetics born of the mundane. Miralles and Pinós describe the curved incisions of the two projects noted above in the most prosaic terms, explaining that they were born out of the need to contain soil.[26] Thus, the retaining wall, which was not an inevitable feature of these two projects, becomes the impetus for a subtle exploration of what it means to hold back the earth and to move through the incisions cut into the ground plane. At Igualada Cemetery, this descent into the earth carries with it an unmistakable reference to burial and the cycle of life. Other allusions also abound, with the wooden planks embedded into the concrete paving suggesting a logjam in a river, whereas the plan's geometry itself is shaped like a womb. The poetry is nevertheless cryptic. "In our impatience to speak and be done with it," Miralles explains, "our reasoning crowds into a single phrase, impulsively spoken and soon swept away."[27] Words thus give way to making, building, and drawing. Their work itself, even with its mass and texture, often has the quality of lines traced upon the earth with the spontaneity and sentiment of the freehand sketch. The twisted structural expressionism of the Rhythmic Gymnastics Training Center in Alicante or the bent tree-like canopies of the Icaria Promenade in Barcelona thereby display an immediacy and directness possible only in a mode of building akin to the physical act of drawing.

Miralles and Pinós ended their partnership in the early 1990s and formed separate practices. Both would continue to explore the themes they had investigated in their collaboration, though the formal and material excesses of Miralles's Scottish National Parliament (in a new partnership) would suggest that something had been lost with the dissolution of the collaboration. The output of the short-lived but extraordinarily productive alliance between Miralles and Pinós inspired near-religious devotion among young architects, a mythology that would only grow after Miralles' early death. If their work resists easy categorization, it is perhaps because it arises from an interest in the power of architecture itself. And if there is a theoretical shard here, it is the unspoken idea that the physical making of architecture is a transformational act in which no rhetoric is necessary.

10

Pragmatism and Post-Criticality

By the middle of the 1990s a few of the primary strands of architectural theory – those which took their start in the politics and extra-disciplinary theories of the 1960s and 1970s – were increasingly becoming seen as suspect or even irrelevant. Pushback would come from several directions, as this and later chapters will show. Interest in critical regionalism and a greater emphasis on tectonics, by contrast, were still gaining in intensity in this decade, and these movements would also manifest themselves in a new emphasis on the urban and regional context and renewed interest in detailing. Against the formal complexity of deconstruction, there also emerged a new appreciation for simpler and more silent forms that at the same time exploited both textures and materiality. Another factor was the changing demographics of the architectural profession itself, which was becoming increasingly diverse in terms of class, gender, and race. Finally, by the mid-1990s there was a new appreciation of the seriousness of environmental issues, which – although largely understated or placed in the background since the early 1970s – galvanized thought internationally around such ideas as global warming, recycling, and ecological sustainability. All in all, the mid-1990s was a transitional period with movement simultaneously taking place along several fronts.

OMA

One of the more significant new developments of the 1990s was a somewhat sudden and unexpected regard for "pragmatism," and the person most responsible for this strategy was Rem Koolhaas. Through a rapid

An Introduction to Architectural Theory: 1968 to the Present, First Edition.
Harry Francis Mallgrave and David Goodman.
© 2011 Harry Francis Mallgrave and David Goodman. Published 2011 by Blackwell Publishing Ltd.

series of provocative buildings, projects, and publications, Koolhaas and his office, OMA, struck at the core of Eisenman's argument regarding the sanctity of autonomous form. In essence, Koolhaas's point was that architects, instead of struggling against or resisting the forces of capitalism, should instead seize and exploit them. Robert Somol and Sarah Whiting have characterized this approach as one of "performance or practice" – that is, architecture as a pro-active discipline that uses its contact with the marketplace as the very source of architecture's vitality and transformative potential.[1] So complete and so rapid would be Koolhaas's conquest of both the academic and professional realms of practice in this decade that by 1996 even Jeffrey Kipnis would admit, with mock admiration (and only three years after having proclaimed a "new architecture" based on the fold) that "there is no other way to put it; Koolhaas is the Le Corbusier of our times."[2]

The reference to Le Corbusier was perhaps more appropriate than Kipnis had initially intended, for on the one hand both architects had been criticized for their occasionally sloppy or indifferent detailing, and on the other because Koolhaas, like the Swiss architect, owed his success as much to his skill as a propagandist as to his ability as an architect. Koolhaas's crisp and provocative literary style, laced with witty aphorisms, rhetorical questions, and short declarative sentences, also recalls Le Corbusier's pithy manifestoes of *L'Espirit nouveau*, with a bemused tone substituting for Le Corbusier's earnest revolutionary fervor. Here was theory for people who lacked the patience or inclination to wade through Derrida or Deleuze, especially when the lure of large commissions beckoned.

The shift from theoretical distance to pragmatic engagement is inseparable from the "irrational exuberance" of the mid-1990s.[3] Such exuberance was fed by a smart recovery from the global recession earlier in the decade, by the "Dot-Com" boom, by the euphoria over a post-Maastricht Europe, and by the rapid rise of economies in both Asia and the Middle East. There was suddenly work on the boards and architects were in demand. Architects jumped to the opportunities, and sometimes were even eager to employ the corporate jargon of the "new economy." The apostate Michael Speaks, who had received his doctorate under Marxist theorist Frederic Jameson, noted in an address to the Berlage Institute in 1997 that the key to "the production of new urban life" was a "focus on animate forms of practice, not on animate forms."[4] He went on to report that that Dutch firms like OMA were transforming the city by exploiting the forces and flows of the city rather than by visually illustrating or imitating these flows, which was the primary mode of working for the "form-driven" American avant-garde. In the last regard he was alluding to the work of Peter Eisenman, Greg Lynn, and, by implication, to the editorial board of the journal *Assemblage*.

At a later date Speaks would make the case that the "business of architecture" – now unabashedly a business rather than a navel-gazing exercise – required a Silicon-Valley style of managerial innovation. The role of academe should be not to teach artistic expression or the generation of form, but rather to produce research for practice. "Architecture should no longer recoil from the degraded world of business and corporate thinking," he noted at a conference in France in the year 2000, "on the contrary, it should aggressively seek to transform itself into a research-based business."[5] The result would be a gradual dissolution of the boundary between the academy and the profession. Think-tank exercises like Koolhaas's "Harvard Project on the City" sought to create a model of academic research in which teams of students, under Koolhaas's supervision, would produce essays, diagrams, and statistics instead of individually conceived and executed design projects. Students would mine phenomena as varied as the ballooning metropolis of Lagos, China's Pearl River Delta, the Roman Empire, shopping, or the command economy of Soviet Communism for the latent architectural lessons assumed to be hidden within. The process here was to investigate conditions as found, suspend judgment for as long as possible, and draw upon what was found to suggest new ways to shape the city by taking advantage of the economic, social, and technological insights.[6]

Such an approach also drove OMA's practice, as well as those of many Dutch spinoffs, whereby the publication of essays and speculations became a fundamental part of professional activity. In fact, for OMA the structure and role of the architecture firm in itself would become an object of study and innovation. In the mid-1990s, for example, OMA entered into a business agreement with a Dutch engineering firm in which OMA would sell a share of its ownership and invite the firm into OMA's management. Koolhaas described the alliance as being less a way to gain access to new markets (though this is very likely true as well) and more a way to enlarge the possible scale of architectural projects – that is beyond the scale of an architectural firm working independently. "What is interesting about this new situation," he observed in a 1996 interview with Alejandro Zaera-Polo,

is that there are clear advantages for both sides. Our association allows us to cover the entire field from architecture to infrastructure, which seems especially attractive in the perspective of certain operations that now occur in Asia. Usually as an architect, it is difficult to deal with planners and infrastructure engineers. There is always an opposition. The way in which our collaboration might become a kind of seamless condition is incredibly seductive.[7]

Such a provocative embrace of marketplace forces should not have surprised those who were familiar with the Koolhaas of *Delirious New York*, but, then again, Koolhaas never viewed himself as a theoretician, rather as "an architect with theoretical interests, with the need to analyze the exact conditions and exact potentials of the profession."[8] Nevertheless, it was not a position at which he arrived easily or quickly. In the mid-1980s Koolhaas had designed a villa in the Paris suburb of St Cloud, not far from Le Corbusier's early villas. The design was effectively a historical pastiche, a re-assembly of Le Corbusier's "Five Points" with overtones of Morris Lapidus. Here a Villa Savoye was split in two and clad in pink and silver corrugated metal, in which the two volumes collide with one other and with a concrete, load-bearing wall. In presenting the design at an architectural symposium organized by Stanley Tigerman in 1986, the notable architects on the panel responded with puzzlement and frustration. Michael Graves was not overly impressed with the project's "nostalgic" content, while Eisenman playfully accused Koolhaas of trying simultaneously to be earnest and a surrealist. It was Rafael Moneo who reacted most sharply to Koolhaas's obtuseness and *detournement* of canonical modernist forms by noting "that you are, at this moment, a bit arrogantly perhaps, alone, and defending a section of modernity that perhaps deserves to be defended. But it should be defended with more intensity." Koolhaas countered that he did not see his work as a defense of modernism, but rather as a "harvesting of some of the remnants that are left in a kind of collective consciousness." Moneo would nevertheless conclude that Koolhaas, despite his talent, was consigning himself to the margins of history by retreating into esoteric in-jokes for the architecturally initiated, and that he should learn to resign himself to "being alone, and being alone a lot."[9]

Moneo's prediction that Koolhaas would toil on the margins of history could not, of course, have been less accurate, but Koolhaas would, by the late 1980s, begin to turn away from historical quotation in favor of "program" – which unfolded within two novel strategies. One was the creation of embryonic, tightly packed skyscrapers, as we find in the competition projects for the Center for Media Technologies (ZKM) in Karlsruhe and that of the Zeebrugge Ferry Terminal, both undertaken in 1989. The second strategy was to produce a microcosm of Manhattan-like urban density on the scale of the mammoth individual building, as first displayed in the competition for a City Hall in The Hague, or less literally, at the Kunsthal in Rotterdam, completed in 1992. Both strategies hark back to *Delirious New York*, and the former in particular to the celebrated chapter on the Downtown Athletic Club – which he described as a vertical programmatic collage "of 38 superimposed platforms" housing varying activities, as well as a "Constructivist Social Condenser: a machine to generate and intensify desirable forms of human intercourse." If, in this all-male club, bachelors could be found on the ninth floor "eating oysters with boxing gloves, naked," it is because they have been shaped by the "anti-natural" program into a new breed of urban dweller, the "Metropolitanite."[10] For Koolhaas, the Manhattan Athletic Club was part of a lost, skyscraper-strewn Eden, and much of his work of the late 1980s and 1990s was an attempt to reconstitute it – that is to say, Koolhaas would at last try to realize in his own work the liberating potential of "Manhattanism" he had proclaimed two decades earlier in *Delirious New York*. He would later call this return to the ideas of his earlier text a "second pregnancy of the same conception."[11] And, with both the individual building and urban planning, it would lead him to pursue the strategies of creative congestion he had documented in the Manhattan of the early twentieth century.

The ZKM builds on the precedent of the Downtown Athletic Club with its "free section" stacking of dissimilar programs and types of spaces within a simple container. Indeed, a side-by-side comparison of the sections of

Figure 10.1 OMA, Center for Media Technologies (ZKM), Karlsruhe (1992). Image courtesy of Office for Metropolitan Architecture (OMA).

these two projects might suggest that Koolhaas had simply translated his earlier studies into a delayed but nevertheless direct application of the same ideas and techniques. Yet Koolhaas at the same time brings to this quotation a more tectonic way of exploring the long-span structure and servant spaces required for the multiple performances and exhibitions. The inhabitable vierendeel trusses spanning two sides of the building create an alternating vertical rhythm of tall, column-free spaces and compressed intermediate stories within the depth of the trusses, within which the vertical members of the vierendeels would have been perceived as columns. The compact, prismatic volume is clad with giant projection screens and with groupings of irregular punched openings that once again recall the Downtown Athletic Club in their evident conflict between exterior decorum and the expression of a varied internal organization.

The Zeebrugge Sea Terminal project continued with this line of investigation, although the model seems not to have been the Downtown Athletic Club but rather the mythical "Globe Tower" project for Coney Island. This fictive project had proposed a formal melding of tower and sphere with a stacking of hedonistic programs above a plinth of transportation infrastructure. OMA's Zeebrugge Terminal, which combines cone and sphere into a mysterious mark on the shore of the North Sea, was a similar tower of earthly delights (casino, swimming pool, cinema, hotel) spiraling up from a base of transportation connections. If built, this project would have become one of OMA's most unique explorations of form, in that Koolhaas proposes a sleek and mysterious object whose compact form and smooth surfaces recall the product design of Phillippe Starck more than the fragmentation strategies of deconstruction.[12] In fact, it recalls some cutting remarks he made in 1993 on his inclusion in the "Deconstructivist Architecture" exhibition of 1988, in which he explicitly rejected the formalist agenda of his supposed confreres, decrying their "naïve" and "banal" analogies of social fragmentation and the architecture of fragmented forms. Koolhaas further argued that a retreat into "an intellectual position for the architect" was misguided, if simply because there was work to be done: "One of the conditions that we enjoy at this moment is the appearance of certain demands made to the profession. It seems very dangerous to me to systematically disappoint these expectations."[13]

The differences between his design approach and that of others in the 1988 exhibit were in fact already evident in OMA's prize winning design for competition for a City Hall in The Hague, which took place in 1986. Here, within a single building, three parallel bands of program were segmented and extruded to varying heights, creating a condensed urban skyline. Similarly, in the design for the Kunsthal in Rotterdam, completed in

Figure 10.2   Zeebrugge Sea Terminal, Belgium (1989). Image courtesy of Office for Metropolitan Architecture (OMA).

1992, OMA arranged a variety of spatial types and programs along a continuous internal promenade. The building is situated between an elevated boulevard and a park with a secondary road traversing the site, and the architects connected both with a public ramp that pierces the building and provides the primary entrance while also allowing the existing road to remain. These individual blocks accommodate exhibition halls and a restaurant, with a spiraling circulation path linking together what Koolhaas has called "a sequence of contradictory experiences."[14] One can also detect here certain remnants of Koolhaas's earlier strategies of modernist pastiche; a neo-Miesian elevation faces the boulevard, echoing the Berlin New National Gallery with its black steel fascia, while a second, roof-mounted truss, sits just behind. This truss, painted traffic-cone orange, is topped by sculptures of a camel and a robed, walking figure; a recollection, perhaps, of the infamous "Arab Village" postcard distributed to protest the perceived foreignness of the Weissenhof Siedlung of 1927.

   Koolhaas's 1990 project for a Hotel and Convention Center in Agadir, Morocco, would trade these Miesian tropes for a mode of working that – with its interrupted constellations of column grids and large circular volumes – loosely resembles Le Corbusier's Assembly Palace in Chandigarh. Here Koolhaas creates an enormous, undulating covered plaza facing the beach, while escalators, an access road, and fields of columns of various diameters dot the exterior space. Below the plaza is a convention center; above it is a hotel slab composed of courtyard apartments, each with a small tower for views of the sea. With its division of the program into three distinct districts, each with its own spatial character, the Agadir project would once again seek to imbue the individual building with the variety of experiences found in the metropolis. In OMA's urban planning work, the references to Manhattan could sometimes be quite literal, as in their 1991 competition for the extension of Paris's *Grande Axe*. In this project, Koolhaas proposed gradually demolishing vast swaths of the area around La Defense and implanting a Manhattan grid. This strategy would reappear in OMA's 2008 project for Dubai Waterfront City, a man-made island upon which Koolhaas would, at last, be permitted to create from scratch the idealized, gridded Manhattan he had been pursuing for years.

By the middle of the 1990s the office of OMA was flooded with commissions, and in 1995 we find the massive catalogue of Koolhaas's writings and projects under the title *S, M, L, XL*. The book, through the collaboration of the graphic designer Bruce Mau, is a graphic tour-de-force, especially with its extensive use of full-bleed images, a heterogeneous mix of typefaces and graphic languages, and a cinematic sense of pacing and rhythm – all of which set a new standard for what an architectural text could look like. The organization of the nearly 1400-page tome is evident in its title, as the projects and essays are presented by their physical size, not by chronology or building type. The projects are also interspersed with essays, graphic non-sequiturs, and a running "dictionary" of terms along the margin. Essays within this encyclopedic volume would range from the results of a fact-finding mission to Atlanta to a comprehensive history of urbanism in Singapore (which Koolhaas terms "a Potemkin Metropolis"), as well as meditations on the phenomena of globalization and the "Generic City."

Though it is difficult to find a centerpiece or guiding thesis in this sprawling book, the essay "Bigness, or the Problem of Large," neatly condensed into a quasi-manifesto much of what OMA had been pursuing over the previous decades. Once again reprising his arguments from *Delirious New York* Koolhaas argues that the technological innovations of the early twentieth century (electricity, the elevator, structural steel, air-conditioning) created the condition of "Bigness" by allowing buildings to grow ever larger, gradually undermining traditional architectural concepts like composition, sequence, and the relationship of a building's facade to its internal organization. Most importantly, he notes that when a building reaches a certain size, it detaches itself from the urban fabric into which it is placed. If architects generally respond to this condition with a strategy of "disassembly and dissolution," or by breaking down large programs into "incompatible fractals of uniqueness" through fragmentation or montage, Koolhaas posited another antidote. He proffers "the Whole and the Real," or an approach that compresses disparate events within a single container, allowing them to interact freely in something resembling a "programmatic alchemy." In their internal richness and variation, Koolhaas argues, these buildings can themselves become urban, internalizing, and perhaps will eventually replace the "classical" city. Koolhaas concludes, rather apocalyptically, that "Bigness" will produce the only architecture able to survive the "now-global condition of the tabula rasa" and that these outposts of architecture will become "landmarks in a post-architectural landscape."[15]

Ultimately, Koolhaas's proclamation on behalf of the architecture of "Bigness" combines a cold acceptance of the market's capacity for creative destruction – the "classical" city is all but left for dead – with a call for architecture's continued relevance in the face of devastating modernization. With a view that would have been deemed political heresy only a decade earlier, Koolhaas is quite satisfied with the view that architecture's newfound "instrumentality" will allow it to sever its association with the "exhausted artistic/ideological movements" of both modernism and formalism. With this mix of idealism and resignation, he proposes a way forward based neither on the aesthetic projects of the past nor on the complete emancipation promised by a turn to the purely digital and virtual.

The Orange Revolution

The publication of *S,M,L,XL* coincided with a general resurgence of architectural practice in the Netherlands in the mid-1990s, as young firms, many of them stocked with veterans of OMA, were to build and publish extensively in the coming years. In large part, this work would follow the example of Koolhaas in its skepticism of formalist strategies and its willingness to work with conditions as found. In a Storefront for Art and Architecture exhibition in New York City in 1999, Michael Speaks would label this emergent Dutch trend as "Big Soft Orange" because of its acceptance of the pragmatics of large projects, its flexibility in the face of demands placed on it by the market, and what Speaks would call a particularly Dutch affinity for the artificial and the commercial.[16] Indeed, the very existence of the Netherlands, a country in large part reclaimed from the sea through the development of dikes and infill polders, has long depended on the artificial, while the Dutch economic model had long valued trade and entrepreneurialism. This combination, along with one of the highest population densities in Europe, had made the Netherlands an important cradle for modernism at the start of the twentieth century and in the 1920s, a place where experimentation became the very face of the vernacular.

Landscape architect Adriaan Geuze and his firm, West 8, would embrace this idea of artificiality, and would use it to create a series of parks, plazas, and urban plans with a playful and unsentimental vision of the natural. In Geuze's landscape work at Schiphol Airport in Amsterdam, for example, he would apply paving surfaces and plant material in a highly graphic way: a blanket of birch trees covering all residual space around the airport and large hemispherical planters (with changing plant material to mark the seasons) populating a plaza at curbside. At Geuze's Schouwburgplein, a plaza set in the middle of a district of theaters in Rotterdam, the only "trees" or plant material would be a series of adjustable, crane-necked lighting standards, an apparent allusion to the city's active port. Perhaps the most influential of West 8's work would be the master plan of the Borneo-Sporenburg peninsulas in Amsterdam's docklands. Here Geuze would reinterpret basic Amsterdam urban typologies – narrow canal houses and nineteenth-century perimeter blocks – transforming them into a dense grid of narrow, attached patio houses interrupted by larger, sculptural housing blocks rotated with respect to the grid. A thin strip of park slices diagonally through the grid, creating a respite from the continuous walls of low-rise, high-density housing.

The work of the offices of Winy Maas, Jacob van Rijs, and Nathalie de Vries (MVRDV) also combined many of the attitudes and formal approaches of the OMA of the 1990s. This was particularly the case in the firm's early work, which repeated the vocabulary of exposed and folded floor-slabs pursued at OMA's Educatorium and Kunsthal. MVRDV's projects were based on the mapping of data and the translation of this empirical information into architecture, sometimes leading to an architecture that directly illustrated the data at hand. Winy Maas, called these physical manifestations of information "datascapes," and his firm would often collaborate with universities in researching population densities and related phenomena. A string of publications followed, including the 1999 *FARMAX: Excursions on Density*, which would propose the further concentration of an already densely distributed Dutch population in order to preserve open space outside the urban areas.[17]

At times, the firm's translation of data into architecture would lead to a playful, almost cartoonish representation of statistical diagrams in built

Figure 10.3   MVRDV, WoZoCo Apartments, Amsterdam (1994–1997). Image courtesy of Daniel de Francisco.

form, as at their WoZoCo elderly housing block outside Amsterdam. Here, zoning regulations dictated a building footprint that would accommodate only 87 of the required 100 units. Rather than placing the remaining 13 units elsewhere on the site, the architects compressed them into a series of enormous volumes that cantilever – impossibly it would seem – off the primary building volume. This decision allowed them to maintain the adjacent open space while still complying with the letter of the zoning ordinance. The relentless "logic" at work – one must maintain open space at all costs – makes the absurd seem reasonable, almost inevitable.

The firm's design for the Dutch Pavilion at Expo 2000 in Hannover would continue this strategy by creating microcosms of the Dutch Ecosystem, one stacked above the other in a literal reproduction of the "1909 Theorem" of stacked ground planes that Koolhaas had illustrated in *Delirious New York*. These platforms, some dedicated to "forest," "rain," or "agriculture" were a direct and unfiltered translation from diagram into architecture, a strategy that Koolhaas had been either unable or unwilling to employ in his own work. In fact, the work of the younger generation of Dutch firms, like MVRDV, would heed Koolhaas's protestations against formalism more that perhaps Koolhaas himself would do. MVRDV's results, however, would often oscillate between the exhilarating and the merely diagrammatic.

Still another young Dutch firm that came to prominence in the 1990s was UN Studio, founded by Ben van Berkel and Caroline Bos. They wasted little time in countering OMA's *S,M,L,XL* with their own massive monograph/manifesto, *Move*, which was arranged in three volumes under the rubrics of Imagination, Techniques, and Effects, or the three "enduring ingredients" of architecture. The authors used these elements to illustrate how architects could transform the organizational structure of their practice, and also how the new media at their disposal could lead to "contemporary architectural effects."[18] In pursuit of the first goal, the transformation of practice, van Berkel and Bos proposed a model of "network practice" closely resembling filmmaking, whereby international teams of experts could be assembled briefly to collaborate on a project within a virtual network and then disbanded. UN Studio would in fact collaborate in this way on large infrastructure projects like the Erasmus Bridge in Rotterdam and the service structures for the Piet Hein Tunnel in Amsterdam, both completed in 1996.

For UN Studio such collaborative projects redefined the architect as an "expert on everyday public information" – that is, as someone who, in leading a team, could process the varied inputs and transform them into "ideas and images for the organization of public life." The end result of this strategy, they argued, is to make architecture more akin to the fashion industry by processing and responding to the latest trends. "Learning from Calvin Klein," they wrote, "the architect will be concerned with dressing the future, speculating, anticipating coming events and holding up a mirror to the world."[19] And if the collaborative model of practice would ostensibly make architects the key figures in "dressing the future" their exploitation of new media would ultimately enable them to direct the content of this new fashion.

One of the principal techniques in this endeavor is nothing less than the old-fashioned diagram, which, as van Berkel and Bos argued, comes from a source exterior to the actual project yet still provides a stable but sufficiently ambiguous map for the development of the project. Whereas OMA and MDRDV also embraced this tool and in fact often literally transposed it into a building, UN Studio would be more focused on exploring it as a generator of novelty or seductive forms. Thus the diagram, in van Berkel and Bos's view, enables the architect to resist established typologies and find interpretations or solutions that might not otherwise have appeared. UN Studio's Möbius House (1998) illustrates this approach. The diagrammatic model of the house is the continuous, interlocked form of the Möbius strip, which connects connects the various elements of the domestic program in a continuous loop. The concrete and glass house is

Figure 10.4 UN Studio, Mercedes Benz Museum, Stuttgart (2001–2006). Image courtesy of Tim Brown.

folded up, over, and back upon itself – a compressed strip transformed from plane to volume.

This approach would be most aggressively tested in UN Studio's design for the Mercedes-Benz Museum in Stuttgart (2001–2006). Based on a DNA molecule, two floors of this corporate showpiece spiral upward in a continuous incremental fashion around a central atrium – with interesting lateral variations. Visitors first ascend to the top in a lift and then make their way down along two alternative paths, with automobiles and trucks arranged in a chronological order. The concrete building differs from the Frank Lloyd Wright's Guggenheim Museum in that no two surfaces of the Stuttgart design are ever arrayed in parallel. None of this would have been possible without the engineering talents of Werner Sobek and the computer consultancy Arnold Walz to plot the geometry. One can look at the extraordinarily elegant design either as one of the great buildings of the decade or as the ultimate exercise in iconic fashion-making.

Like van Berkel and Bos, the Zurich-based Spanish architect and engineer Santiago Calatrava focused his practice in large part on the design of elements of transportation infrastructure – bridges, viaducts, interchanges, and rail stations – not only as responses to the immediate functional requirements at hand but also as catalysts for something more. And whereas van Berkel and Bos positioned themselves as coordinators of a broad, multidisciplinary team of experts, Calatrava's model was that of the inspired and discerning *auteur*, directing teams to complete his structural and often highly sculptural vision. The different approaches signaled different intentions. Whereas the Dutch infrastructural explorations were concerned principally with organizing and choreographing the programmatic energy generated by a mix of programs, Calatrava would focus instead on the fine-grained effects his projects would have on their immediate surroundings, and on an aesthetics that combined structural expressionism with an unapologetically monumental and civic character.

Trained as an architect in Valencia, Calatrava later studied civil engineering at the ETH in Zurich and received his doctorate in 1981. This hybrid training would inform Calatrava's competition-winning scheme for Zurich's Stadelhofen Rail Station (1983). The project, with its sinuous ribbed concrete forms and elegantly tapered steel skeletal canopy forms, established what would come to be a well-developed vocabulary of formal and material strategies in Calatrava's work, often explored in watercolor sketches that transposed the evolution of human or animal forms into structural solutions. The Bac de Roda Bridge (1987), which spanned over a sunken rail yard in a gritty and peripheral zone of Barcelona, displayed another key trait of Calatrava's work: its polemical quality as a symbol for civic enlightenment and modernization. The white, heroically bowing structure of the Bac de Roda Bridge seems excessively dimensioned for the modest span required, and excessively grand for the undistinguished urban context of which it is placed. Yet it is precisely this excess, this gesture of civic grandeur, that would make such a gleaming white bridge a *sine qua non* for a number of urban redevelopment projects undertaken in Seville, Buenos Aires, Manchester, and Milwaukee.

The biologically-inspired forms of these bridges, with their allusions to limbs and flexed muscles, would soon be followed by a shift to the structurally expressive neo-gothic, as we find in architectural commissions for a glass-covered galleria at the BCE Place in Toronto, the commission to complete the Cathedral of St John the Divine in New York City (1992), and the Gare do Oriente train and bus terminal in Lisbon (1998). This marriage of a biologically based structural expression of joints with a Gothic sensibility of pointed, ribbed vaults and glazed infill seems a belated realization of Viollet-le-Duc's ideal of conceptually combining distant structural intuitions with Gothic logic.

Figure 10.5 Santiago Calatrava, Milwaukee Art Museum, Milwaukee, Wisconsin (1994–2001). Image by the authors.

Yet there is also a separate and countervailing tendency in Calatrava's work that seems closer to the *architecture parlante* explorations of a Jean-Jacques Lequeu or Claude Nicolas Ledoux. In projects like the Sondika Airport outside Bilbao (1990), the Lyon Airport TGV station (1994), or the Planetarium and IMAX theater in Valencia (1998), Calatrava would not only use biologically inspired forms to illustrate the distribution of structural loads but would also employ these forms to establish highly legible metaphors that would allude (often quite literally) to the building's program or site. For instance, the theater in Valencia, ascending from a pool like a periscope, takes the shape of an eye, replete with a motorized glassy eyelid. Similarly, the avian roof structure of the Milwaukee Art Museum (1994–2001), perched on the shore of Lake Michigan like a nesting bird, flaps its outstretched wings in response to changing light conditions and perhaps the sight of a meal. These highly metaphorical and sculptural approaches, with their translations of bodies, birds, and trees into architecture, combined with a swoopy and streamlined vision of progress, would make Calatrava that rare species within architecture at the turn of the millennium – a truly popular architect whose work is largely understood and appreciated by the public, on the very terms by which the architect had conceived the work himself. In that sense, the pragmatic dimension of Calatrava lies not only in his attention to infrastructure as a key element of the public sphere but also in his direct appeal to the user.

Post-Criticality

In any case, few would dispute that the phenomenon of Dutch "pragmatism" played a large role in the reformulation of architectural practice during the 1990s. The full dimensions of this shift were cogently brought home in 1996 when Koolhaas, through his work on a series of luxury boutiques and studies of retail strategy for Prada, established the parallel "think tank" of the Architecture Media Office (AMO), which was dedicated to design consulting, branding, media, politics, art, exhibitions, publishing, graphic design, and a loosely defined commitment to "research." Thus, in this rare instant, the "business" of architecture was expanded to include a mode of architectural thinking separated from the actual making of buildings. As Koolhaas later explained its mission:

> Architecture is too slow. Yet, the word "architecture" is still pronounced with certain reverence (outside the profession). It embodies the lingering hope – or the vague memory of a hope – that shape, form, coherence could be imposed on the violent surf of information that washes over us daily. Maybe architecture doesn't have to be stupid after all. Liberated from the obligation to construct, it can become a way of thinking about anything – a discipline that represents relationships, proportions, connections, effects, the diagram of everything.[20]

Koolhaas here makes an emphatic case for the continuing value of theory – for the general "diagram of everything" and the value of architectural thinking "liberated" from practice. This suggests that the shift to the pragmatic was not, at least in Koolhaas's view, intended as an attack on theory, but rather a move to redefine theory in a post-critical fashion. It is a turn toward speculating about the world-as-found rather than speculating about architecture through the coded systems of philosophy, linguistics, or social sciences.

Or course, not all critics involved with architecture were happy with this proposal for a post-critical world. In 1999 Sanford Kwinter, who had ties with the Eisenman circle, likened it to Julien Benda's "*Le Trahison des Clercs*" – that is, to a "breach of trust" or a conservative betrayal of intellectual values. In his words,

The "pragmatism" that the new Dutch work represents, as rich in possibility as it is poor in its present expression, is a pragmatism of the worst kind: it remains little more than ill-digested Koolhaasianism, to which is added the petty bureaucrat's compulsion to justify impotence ("planning is impossible, the market rules!") by inflating his/her ineffectuality into an historical and aesthetic ideal.[21]

Dave Hickey similarly feared that a "post-critical" world would also be post-theoretical and post-intellectual. "If this happens," he laments, "we are lost. We are mere academics and mere businessmen, and there will be no reason henceforth to call anything architecture again."[22]

Others saw this paradigm shift in less cataclysmic terms. Robert Somol and Sarah Whiting, for instance, saw the post-critical world as one in which a "projective" architecture (rather than a "critical" architecture) could thrive, an architecture that is "cool" and easy in its critical role, rather than "hot" in its resistance to society's values.[23] Although Somol and Whiting were quick to note that a projective architecture "does not necessarily entail a capitulation to market forces," it is clear that post-criticality in many cases had already begun to set architects free from many of the taboos that had formerly distanced them from the market. In many quarters there was exhilaration over the fact that Koolhaas had seemingly granted architects a license to play, profit, engage, and learn from the new global economy. Architects, it seemed, were at last freed from the obligation to agonize over the creation of recondite and autonomous form; they were no longer called upon to resist bravely the forces of capitalism by not building at all, or to embed their work in the vagaries of political ideologies or critiques. They would no longer be required to sift through a trove of fashionable theory that few could truly digest or intelligently apply to their work. Indeed, the publication of K. Michael Hays's critical anthology *Architecture Theory Since 1968*, which appeared in 1998, seemed a formal marker defining the end of theory's gilded age; a recognition that the time had come to summarize a movement now clearly on the decline. But within this negatively defined liberty – this freedom *from* historical, theoretical, formal, and political obligations – there was still a nagging sense of doubt or feeling of unease. In the spring of 1999 the "Dot-Com bubble" burst, demonstrating just how fickle the nuances of new economy could be. And two years later, with the destruction of the World Trade Center towers, architects were once again reminded of how tenuous the entire structure of society could be. The earlier sense of euphoria that had pervaded so much of the architectural press of the 1990s would have now to meet a new reality.

11

Minimalisms

While the work of Koolhaas and his confreres represented an assault on exuberant form-making and extra-disciplinary claims, a second, simultaneous strand of work of the 1990s turned the volume down even further. This direction or approach often focused on more primary concerns – namely, the exploitation of new materials and their sensory effects, simple detailing of constructional forms appropriated from high modernism, and the phenomenological nature of the architectural experience itself. Only in a loose way might we group these parallel investigations under the rubric of "minimalism," because to do so would be to posit a relatively elastic definition for a term that more generally refers to a specific movement in American sculpture and painting in the mid-to-late 1960s. Indeed, the art critic Rosalind Krauss has called the application of minimalism to formalist art or architecture "entirely inappropriate," because the term should be reserved for an approach to art centered on how a viewer experiences or receives a work within a specific context.[1]

Nevertheless, we feel the term has some usefulness in the 1990s because in many quarters we find here a significant simplification of form: a shift of attention from form to surface and detailing, from the architecture of programmatic innovation to architecture as neutral container, from authorial intent to the way a work is experienced by the occupant. Collectively, these minimalist projects are generally self-contained, more modest in the intentions than what preceded them, and, for the most part, they are exquisitely crafted. In some respects they also evoke a modernist character or formal simplicity that had been largely been eclipsed by postmodern and poststructural concerns with meaning and syntactic regulation.

An Introduction to Architectural Theory: 1968 to the Present, First Edition.
Harry Francis Mallgrave and David Goodman.
© 2011 Harry Francis Mallgrave and David Goodman. Published 2011 by Blackwell Publishing Ltd.

One clarion call signaling this new direction was Kenneth Frampton's emphatic address of 1990, "*Rappel à l'ordre:* The Case for the Tectonic." This summary "call to order," a re-evocation of Le Corbusier's "Purist" plea of the early 1920s, was in many respects a continuation of his long-standing polemic against the "commodity culture" of postmodern histori-cism and his alternative of critical regionalism. Although this unapologetic "rearguard" argument was clearly a minority view in the 1980s, it now struck a more responsive chord:

> Rather than join in a recapitulation of avant-gardist tropes or enter into historicist pastiche or into the superfluous proliferation of sculptural ges-tures, all of which have an arbitrary dimension to the degree that they are based in neither structure or in construction, we may return instead to the structural unit as the irreducible essence of architectural form.[2]

This return to architecture's ground zero of tectonics and its detailing, which he supported in his essay with the theories of such nineteenth-century architects as Karl Bötticher and Gottfried Semper, was of course amplified in his more ambitious compendium *Studies in Tectonic Culture* (1995), which now cast his theme within a broader a historical perspec-tive.[3] With chapters on such "conventional" architects as Frank Lloyd Wright, Mies van der Rohe, Louis Kahn, and Carlo Scarpa, Frampton proffered a vivid alternative to what was found in most journals of theory. First-chapter images of Dimitris Pikionis's paving stones in Athens and ritual tools used in Shinto ground-breaking ceremonies posed a compel-ling challenge to the intellectual abstractions being bandied about. A new seriousness was clearly discernible, which in 1995 can even be found in the Museum of Modern Art's exhibition "Light Architecture," which – seven years after its much heralded proclamation of "Deconstructivism" – took note of the "new architectural sensibility" taking place in recent work.[4] Terrance Riley ascribed this new sensibility to the lack of strict orthodoxy, a new reticence, and an emphasis on craft. To this we might add a desire to return to basics and avoid either formal or rhetorical excess.

Materiality and Effects

The work of the Swiss architects Jacques Herzog and Pierre de Meuron represents one of these minimalist strands, as they often take particular delight in both materiality and the sensory impact their buildings have on those who come in contact with them – all the while receding into a neutral backdrop for the varied activities of daily life. "The strength of our buildings," Herzog observed in an interview in 1997, "is the immediate visceral response they have on a visitor. For us, that is all that is important in architecture. We want to make a building that can cause sensations, not represent this or that idea."[5] In describing their proposal for four enormous, mute housing blocks adjacent Berlin's Tiergarten, Herzog also remarked that he and de Meuron "wanted the life occurring inside them to be their outside architectural expression."[6] Also present in their work is a fierce resistance to fragmentation and an insistence that each project be only one thing: one essential, closed, and often prismatic form with a homogenous facade treatment, rather than a collage of various formal elements and materials.

It is possible to detect the roots of these guiding concepts in Herzog and de Meuron's earliest formation and collaborations. Childhood friends and classmates who together attended the Eidgenössische Technische Hochschule (ETH) in Zurich during the post-1968 anarchy of the early 1970s, Herzog and de Meuron received an education steeped in planning and political ideology – that is, until the arrival of Aldo Rossi at the ETH in 1971.

> As students," Herzog recalls, "we were fascinated by this charismatic person who told us that architecture is only and always architecture, that social and psychological disciplines can be no substitute for it. This was a shock to us after all the years in which drawing and 'artistic approaches' to architecture were practically forbidden by the severe guardians of the Marxist student movement.[7]

From Rossi, then, they would glean an appreciation for basic typologies and the permanence of building, while their earlier sociological training provided them with a perspective that was largely vanishing from practice. A brief collaboration with Joseph Beuys in 1978, and a longstanding association with Swiss minimalist painter Rémy Zaugg, would add to this mix a sensualist concern for materials and a concern for the nuances of perception. Zaugg's textual paintings tended to address themselves directly to the viewer, implicating one in a dynamic relationship between the viewer and the object being viewed. In his series of 2002 entitled "On Being Blind," for example, Zaugg confronts the viewer with identical lacquered paintings, each reading "*Moi, je te vois*" (Me, I see you), and thus calling into question exactly who was looking at whom. Beuys, who favored unconventional materials like felt, fat, wax, and blood, also emphasized an experimental attitude that in large part would define the work of Herzog and de Meuron.[8]

We can see this emphasis on materiality in one of Herzog and de Meuron's earliest commissions, the rarely-published Blue House, completed in Oberwil, Switzerland, in 1980. The influence of Rossi is immediately evident in the way the house is set beneath a single, sharply pitched gabled roof. Below the gable, the walls are formed of inexpensive concrete masonry units with an irregularly applied coat of Yves Klein-inspired ultramarine blue paint. Overall, the appearance gives one to pause, in that it is conventional with its gabled forms yet also distorted with a gently curving north wall creating a subtly asymmetry on one side of the gable. Similar strategies would be employed in their Plywood House (1984) and House for an Art Collector (1986). In both projects the *gemütlich* gabled forms are enhanced with a rough, almost aggressive materiality.

Yet Herzog and de Meuron's international career would be launched in large part with the mute and scaleless Ricola Storage Building (1986–1987). The architects responded to the simple program (a warehouse for drying herbs) with an equally simple volume: a rectangular prism with a small loading dock attached to one side. What is significant here is the design of the facade, as panels of fiber-cement are attached to a wooden armature, appearing to stack one horizontal layer upon the next. These panels, which grow taller as they reach the top of the building, are interspersed with projecting horizontal bands, with the top band separating from the building volume to become a projecting cornice, supported by a timber latticework entablature. Only at a few places, such as the matter-of-fact interruptions for doors or with the loading dock, does the scale of the object become clear. This is not to say that the details have been suppressed, as each fastener and board has been articulated and exposed fully. Instead, the gradual increase in width of the fiber-cement boards toward the top of the abstract and windowless building creates the illusion that the building is even taller than it is, and the insistent horizontal banding creates a facade that forsakes typical compositional devices (the artful arrangement of windows, doors, etc.) for an overriding material effect. This strange facade has more in common with the paint-scraped canvases of Gerhard Richter than with the regulating lines of Le Corbusier (although some of the boards are cut according to the golden mean), the compositional sheds of Venturi, or the direct expression of interior functions found in some of Koolhaas's contemporaneous work.

Similar strategies were continued at the Auf Dem Wolf Signal Box 4 in Basel, completed in 1995. The six-story building, filled mainly with electronic signaling equipment for the railway engine depot, consists of a concrete shell dressed with copper strips that block out static electrical charges from the outside as well as serving as a unifying exterior skin. As with the

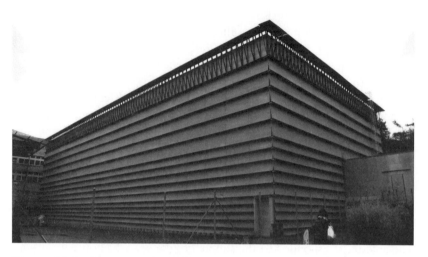

Figure 11.1 Herzog and de Meuron, Ricola Storage Building, Laufen, Switzerland (1986–1987). Image courtesy of Evan Chakroff.

Ricola Warehouse, these copper bands are mounted on a sub-armature protecting an enclosed building volume behind, but here the bands are progressively twisted in areas to admit sunlight. The windows behind the copper cloak thus create blurred zones of semi-transparency – an ingenious means of admitting light to the interior without suggesting the true scale of the building. This brooding copper finish is thus at home in its rusted industrial context and at the same time appears as a hulking intruder.

Such material effects achieve their dramatic culmination (from surface to substance) with the Dominus Winery in Napa Valley, completed in 1997. Once again a simple rectangular volume (445 feet long, 80 feet wide, 26 feet high) accommodates this largely utilitarian facility, but the cladding is now dispensed with altogether in favor of an open wall system consisting entirely of galvanized steel gabions filled with metamorphic basalt rock from a nearby quarry. The intention here – literally – was to make the winery invisible within its majestic viticultural and mountainous landscape, and indeed on an overcast day it is quite easy to drive along Napa's main north–south artery and miss the large building altogether. Again, the logic and sophistication of the design reside in the details. Smaller rocks (therefore more densely packed) are used in areas where temperature control is important (barrel cellar, warehouse, fermentation areas), while the larger rocks in other parts of the building (such as around

Figure 11.2 Herzog and de Meuron, Dominus Winery, Yountville, California (1995–1997). Image by the authors.

the recessed, glazed offices) allow a natural ventilation that minimizes air conditioning. The rough materiality of the jagged rocks is here contrasted with the plan's rectangular geometry, and the building's formal, almost classical setting astride the central axis of the winery.

By the end of the 1990s Herzog and de Meuron would become one of the world's busiest offices, taking on commissions for the Tate Modern in London, a Prada Boutique in Tokyo, the de Young Museum in San Francisco, and most visibly, the "Bird's Nest" stadium for the Beijing Olympics of 2008. Their work in the new century would tend to employ more flexible, if not exuberant, compositional strategies, as one finds in the faceted micro-tower of the Tokyo Prada store, or the curved forms of the library at the Brandenburg Technical University, which recall Mies van der Rohe's Glass Skyscraper project of 1922. This reference to Mies, intentional or not, is in itself telling, because the work of the modern master had – through the writings of K. Michael Hays, Josep Quetglas, Ignasi de Solà-Morales – also come to be appreciated in the 1990s less for his geometric purity or classic universality, but more for his ability to capture changing effects of light.[9] In short, Mies had come to be understood less as a neo-classicist and more a minimalist in the mold of Sol LeWitt or Richard Serra.

The work of the French architect Jean Nouvel would also explore issues of perception and visual effect. While it is difficult to categorize neatly an architect as prolific and varied as Nouvel, several of his projects – with their smooth, polished surfaces, their multilayered glass facades and their complex visual effects – are clearly phenomenological in their playful spirit. His *Tour Sans Fins* project of 1991 – a 350-meter cylindrical skyscraper proposed for the La Defense district in Paris – was intended to be a counterpoint to the cubic mass of Johann Otto von Spreckelsen's Grande Arche, the building that marks the end of the Parisian axis emanating from the central court of the Louvre. Nouvel describes the proposed volume, an apparently "endless" tower, as engaging in an elaborate subterfuge, the illusion of a tower disappearing into the clouds:

> Under the Parisian climate the tower would be mostly indecipherable. From the west, against the light, it would appear like a phantom, ephemeral, immaterial. Visible though from the Tuilleries, it would resonate notably with the Obelisk. The simple, slender form would progressively change in matter from strong, black granite, through gradual tones of grey granite, becoming lighter and with subtle changes of grid, then becoming aluminum, more polished, until it becomes silk-screened glass over several levels, and totally transparent at the top.[10]

Although this idea of the "phantom" building would not be realized, Nouvel would return to the general strategy with the Agbar Tower in Barcelona, completed in 2005. Here the conoidal concrete tower is clad in variegated corrugated metal panels with a secondary facade of translucent glass suspended from it. At the tower's apex, the concrete substructure gives way to a glass dome, in such a way that the building at least intimates its own dematerialization as it meets the sky. At night, an array of colored lights illuminate the intermediate space between the dual facades, creating a vibrant and unmistakable mark on the iconic Barcelona skyline and paying homage to the parabolic towers of Gaudí's *Sagrada Familia*.

Nouvel pursued more restrained effects with his design for the Cartier Foundation in Paris (1994), where delicate scrims of glass extend beyond the limits of the building volume, suspended in place by outriggers. The building, which contains an art museum and institutional offices, is placed among a grove of existing trees, which actually slip between the two extended facades. This creates a visual ambiguity between conditioned space, contained within the building, and exterior space merely trapped between the extended facades. The result is a blurring of the building volume based on the changing light conditions, and at times it is unclear where the building begins and ends. Nouvel here establishes a game of reflection and illusion, one in which the spectator and the changing ambient light are assumed to play a crucial part.

A similar quest for lightness and transparency is found in the work of the Japanese architect Toyo Ito, who began exploiting tectonics, evanescence, and the manipulation of sensory effects in the 1970s. In 1992 Ito described his architecture as "phenomenalism," that is, as "an act of generating vortexes in the currents of air, wind, light, and sound."[11] By this date he was already celebrated for his electronically polychromatic "Tower of the Winds" and "Egg of the Winds." The former was a lighted structure designed to conceal a service tower for an underground shopping mall in Yokohama. It was sheathed with mirrored screens and aluminum panels, and backlit with individual lamps positioned between the two layers. During the day, the tower is mute, a dull grey silo alongside a busy traffic intersection; at night, the computer-programmed lights allow the winds and the nearby noises to "play" the lighting system like a highly sensitive musical instrument. A similar strategy was revisited in the "Egg of the Winds," where he designed a hovering ovoid form that at night became a digital message board for the neighborhood residents.

Both these projects served as a testing ground for the full-scale experiment of the Sendai Mediatheque, a striking multimedia center conceived for a competition in the mid-1990s and completed in 2000. Here, Ito and his engineer, Mutsuro Sasaki, in their pursuit of a new "archetype," vowed not to create joints, beams, walls, rooms, or architecture; instead they reduced the problem simply to plates (composite floor and ceiling panels) and tubes (columns), sheathed in a double layer of ultra-transparent glass. The overarching metaphor for its conception, as the architect himself as noted, is an aquarium, and thus the vortex created here is not only the transparency of the piscine "current" of human movements and activities, but also the fact that it takes place around the series of 13 open, nonlinear "columns" constructed out of tubular steel and canted at odd angles (for seismic purposes) as they progress from one floor to the next. Ito has defined this modulation as a search "differentiated spatialities," and in an exhibition of 1999 he even referred to it as a "blurring architecture" – blurring in the sense of "the interpenetrability between divergent programs."[12] At night, the building, with an illumination scheme and color palette that varies dramatically from story to story, fully comes alive. Ito complements the projection with exquisite detailing.

Figure 11.3   Toyo Ito, Sendai Mediatheque, Sendai-shi, Japan (1995–2001). Image courtesy of Chie Rokutanda.

The collaborative projects of Kazuyo Sejima and Ryue Nishizawa pursue similar objectives with their airy and light volumes of metal and glass, combined with exceptionally thin and refined detailing. Sejima, of course, had worked in Ito's office, and in projects like the O-Museum in Nagano (1999), the circular 21st Century Museum of Contemporary Art in Ishikawa (2004), and the Glass Pavilion for the Toledo Museum of Art (2006) she, and her partner, carry Ito's philosophy of phenomenalism almost to an extreme with their transparent spatial envelopes placed within glazed envelopes. In the Toledo Museum, the spaces between these curved individual glass figures were left empty, a sort of transparent poché allowing visitors to see from one end of the building to the other though several different enclosed spaces. The reflections and distortions of the glass, with other museum patrons seemingly trapped between distant panes, create a disorienting and captivating sensory experience. By contrast, the New Museum in the Bowery, in yet another strategy of minimalist logic, simply stacks six aluminum-mesh boxes in an asymmetrical fashion – all in response to avoiding the monolith form suggested by zoning regulations.

Figure 11.4 Rafael Moneo, Kursaal Auditorium and Congress Center, San Sebastián (1989–1999). Image courtesy of Romina Canna.

Finally, under the theme of materiality, we might also consider Rafael Moneo's Kursaal Auditorium and Congress Center in San Sebastián, a complex conceived and built on the Bay of Biscay between 1989 and 1999. As with Nouvel, it is sometimes difficult to give an overarching definition of Moneo's work, because each project is so thoroughly conditioned by the network of particularities. One might argue, in fact, that these particularities become the distinguishing characteristics of his work. At the Kursaal we are confronted with forms similar to others mentioned in this chapter: a pair of canted auditoria sheathed in concave fluted panels of translucent glass. The two enigmatic volumes sit atop a plinth clad in precast concrete panels with rough shards of slate embedded in the surface. Like musical instruments in their cases, the wood-paneled halls float freely within the glass blocks, and are entered through a system of hanging stairs and platforms. These volumes act as buildings-within-buildings, as users navigate the space between the two-layer translucent exterior skin and the opaque interior mass. The primary sensory impression here is a hazy and mysterious luminosity, transmitting the exterior conditions through a gauzy filter; although the building is sited on the beach, visitors can only find direct views of the ocean through a series of small, strategically-placed openings, each framing a postcard view of the dramatic site.

Yet there is more at work than the creation of effects. From the exterior, the mysterious volumes, one larger than the other, lean subtly forward, as though they were about to drift out to sea. The allusion to natural phenomena is intentional. In the text accompanying the competition entry of 1989, Moneo noted that the extraordinary building site, at the intersection of the Urumea River and the Bay of Biscay should not be treated merely as one more city block. "Today the Kursaal site is a geographic accident," Moneo wrote, "and to my mind, it is crucial that it remain so. This condition must not disappear when site becomes city and loses its remaining natural attributes." Moneo went on to argue that his project would be a rupture with the urban fabric – not a building at all, but instead a geological event that allows the site to belong more to the coastal landscape than to the city. Moneo even called the twin volumes "two gigantic rocks stranded at the river mouth," and, once stated in such explicit terms, it is difficult to see them as anything else.[13]

But it is how he resolves these intended effects that make the work especially interesting. The stone plinth in which the "rocks" are embedded (in which are exhibition and meeting rooms, offices, and restaurants) forms a low and continuous wall along the urban edge, a well mannered and articulated facade. Yet the triangular plazas atop the plinth and the residual spaces claimed along the river (spaces created by the rotation of the auditorium volumes) allow one to perceive the building simply as a pair of free-standing objects. Thus there is a productive tension between the pair of abstract, monolithic objects and the urban plinth that links them.[14] This fragmentation, however, does not challenge the primacy of the two charged volumes; indeed, the overall formal strategy of plinth and dual, rotated objects has less to do with deconstructionist fragmentation than with the general approach of Jørn Utzon's Sydney Opera House, a project in which Moneo was involved while working in Utzon's office in the 1960s. With the San Sebastián complex's similarly dramatic site, its poetic metaphor, and its formal strategy of plinth and rotated objects, Moneo revisits some of Utzon's basic operations, adapting them to a different and in some ways more complex urban situation. The Kursaal and Congress Hall, in short, is a difficult building to categorize, but it is surely one of the Moneo's best works, bringing together phenomenological thinking with both urban and poetic concerns.

Not far removed from the poetry of the Kursaal are the frequent nautical metaphors of Renzo Piano. As the co-designer with Richard Rogers of the Pompidou Center in the mid-1970s, Piano was launched into fame as a provocative and discomforting architect par excellence, but this appellation never really fitted. The sense for detailing evident there was correct, but, as his succeeding commission for the Menil Collection in Houston demonstrated (1982–1987), Piano is a man who prefers contemplation and peaceful surroundings, as his glazed Genoese studio steeply cascading down a hillside toward the Mediterranean makes explicit. At the Menil, a dull gray cedar cladding is the foil he employs against the roof's curved louvers and tectonic structure regulating both light and ventilation; and the control of light, as one might expect, is the recurring theme of his many museums buildings and additions. Sometimes a good metaphor to describe Piano is that of a toolmaker, or rather, of a Stradivari addressing a particular material with of a minimalist functionalism – nautical lightness. At other times he is decidedly a materialist with a fondness for an expressive range of rich tonalities of metal, stone, and terra-cotta. With his fantastical Cultural Center for New Caledonia his selected material is a local wood called iroko, which he employs with laminated struts, glass, aluminum, and stainless-steel paneling. From the sea – if one would dare to undertake the voyage – one might imagine that the dramatic splendor of the 10 thematic headdresses peering above the exotic landscape is seemingly unparalleled in all of twentieth-century architecture.

Neo-modernism

A second trajectory of minimalist design to emerge in the 1990s – once again in response to the postmodern era – might simply be described as neo-modernism. These projects focus on the most basic elements of building, and in that sense they are more grounded in the traditional discipline of architecture than some of the other projects mentioned above. What is also different, and in fact what is reminiscent of the neo-modernist movements of the late 1960s, is the extent to which some architects return to the purist forms of the modern architectural vocabulary. In some cases this appears as a polemical reaction to the formalist exaggerations of postmodernism, in others it comes about because the lineage of modernist forms had never entirely been extinguished.

The austere work of the Swiss father-and-son team of Marcus and Roger Diener represents the latter case. After studying at the ETH in Zurich, Roger Diener joined his father's office, which had been established in the early 1940s. The younger Diener's education had been shaped in part by the Ticinese Rationalist architect and educator Luigi Snozzi, whose pedagogical "Twenty-four Commandments" combined a hard-edged modernist vocabulary with a search for the essential typological conditions.[15] The Diener partnership, which also included architects Wolfgang Schett and

Dieter Righetti, produced a series of projects in Basel that pieced together urban collages out of what seemed to be found fragments of the early modern movement. At the Riehenring Housing and Office Complex (1985), for example, three faces of a U-shaped parcel are lined with a continuous low-rise band of buildings, whereby each leg is given a subtly different architectural treatment. Some are formed with continuous projecting balconies, others with ribbon windows or allusions to Erich Mendelsohn.[16] Even the Modernist trope alluding to naval architecture makes an appearance here in that the facade of an internal courtyard sports a grid of porthole windows, pipe-rail balustrades, and a ship's ladder leading to the roof. By contrast, the firm's stark cubic extension to the neoclassical Swiss Embassy in Berlin (2000), with its unadorned rows of windows, aspires toward a silence worthy of Giuseppe Terragni. At the same time, the series of blind windows applied to the older building's west end, in an odd way evoke the monumental simplicity of Michelangelo's niches and recessions in the vestibule of the Laurentian Library.

Like Diener and Diener, the Spanish architect Alberto Campo Baeza continued with earlier Modernist traditions, which had persisted in Spain despite the imperial pretensions of the Franco dictatorship. Before beginning his independent practice, Campo Baeza had apprenticed with Julio Cano Lasso, who was known for his combination of severe massing strategies and traditional masonry construction with subtle reinterpretations of regional architectural traditions. Campo Baeza's work would continue this tendency toward monolithic forms but often now reduced to detail-less plastered volumes and enormous frameless panes of glass. In approaching the Gaspar House near Cádiz (1992), for example, one observes nothing more than a blank white volume with an entry and garage door centered on one facade. This mute exterior wall forms a perfect square within which a slightly taller, rectangular volume has been inserted. All the functions of the house are located within this contained volume, and the remaining residual spaces are given over to internal courtyards with four ceremonial lemon trees – a reinterpretation of the traditional Andalusian patio house. The detailing throughout is abstract, with connections and any suggestion of materiality suppressed entirely. The abstract composition of patios, openings, water, and vegetation recalls Luis Barragán's own house in Mexico City, with the eclecticism and vibrant color washed away by the southern sun.

Campo Baeza's modernist sources, however, are more far-reaching. In his much publicized De Blas House (2001) he updates the strategy of Philip Johnson's Wiley House of the early 1950s. The stone base in which all private spaces are housed is turned into a rough, cast-in-place concrete plinth, on top of which is now perched a white steel-and-glass frame that defines a

Figure 11.5 Alberto Campo Baeza, Granada Savings Bank Headquarters, Granada (1992–2001). Photograph by Duccio Malagamba. Image courtesy of Estudio Arquitectura Campo Baeza.

small ceremonial living space. The metallic superstructure differs from Mies's Farnsworth House, for instance, in its atectonic qualities, as the columns and roof are joined into a single monolithic frame of the same horizontal and vertical thicknesses. In fact, the form ultimately displays a greater resemblance to Sol LeWitt's white geometric sculptures than to a Miesian exoskeleton. In his Granada Savings Bank Headquarters (2001), Campo Baeza seems to draw upon both I. M. Pei and Le Corbusier with his geometric purity and *brise-soleils*. The one distinction here, and it is an imposing one, is the extraordinary play of light (what Campo Baeza calls an "impluvium of light") that takes place in the building's atrium. It is a masterful orchestration of direct and indirect sources of light that splashes down upon the alabaster walls and floor, endowing the surrounding office spaces – as in Moneo's Kursaal – with a hazy glow. If one were to describe it in terms used by Louis Kahn, the material itself is now reduced to spent light.

Modernist minimalism is also found in the work of such British architects as David Chipperfield and John Pawson, the latter of whom was particularly influenced by Donald Judd. Pawson's book *Minimum* (1996), with its white-on-white cover, assembles brief, aphoristic essays with photographs of "minimalist" architecture and with details from his own work. While not rising to the level of a working manifesto, it is an ethic espousing the virtues of light, structure, ritual, landscape, order, repetition, and simplicity. For Pawson minimalism, which he defines as "the perfection that an artefact achieves when it is no longer possible to improve it by subtraction," is less a formal style than "a way of thinking about space – its proportions, surfaces, and the way that it admits light."[17] Nevertheless, it is clear that a consistent formal and material language can be found in his work. It is seen in a series of exquisite London interiors carried out in the late 1980s and early 1990s, including the Faggionato Apartment of 1999, and Pawson's own houses of 1994 and 1999. It also in the quasi-classical, quasi-modernist, but suddenly fashionable vocabulary of the Calvin Klein stores that Pawson designed in New York, Paris, Tokyo, and Seoul. Indeed, modernist minimalism had, in the 1990s, become something of a symbol of cultivation and good taste, and not just in commercial design. Pawson's minimalist design for the Cistercian Monastery of Our Lady of Novy Dvur in the Czech Republic, completed in 2004, is not simply spare but intensely spiritual in its baroque forms. This project reveals that the architect's vocabulary, which had always carried with it a renunciation of surface luxury or decorative pleasure, ostensibly in exchange for a deeper focus on the spaces contained within, has always been monastic.

The self-trained Japanese architect Tadao Ando, who began his independent practice in 1969, made a name for himself on similarly spiritual ground, as we find in his iconic designs for the Church on the Water in Hokkaido (1988), and the Church of the Light in Osaka (1989). Both projects, and indeed nearly all of Ando's *oeuvre*, employ a similar idiom: velvety cast-in-place concrete, glass, water, and most especially light, combined with a minimalist geometry and aural resonance that, earlier in his career, he drew from the work of Kahn and Le Corbusier. Ando is also well known for his sensitivity to the landscape and this aspect of his work is fully on display in his design for the Stone Hill Center, the gallery extension and conservation center of the Clark Art Institute in Williamstown, Massachusetts (2008). It is judiciously placed on a wooded hillside, a modest but carefully designed uphill walk from the older neoclassical structure housing one of the world's most prestigious Impressionist collections. As with so many of his buildings, Ando employs outrigger walls to stage the experience of approaching the entrance to his buildings, and in this case it also entails framing the ensuing view toward the Berkshire foothills from the lobby. The materiality and detailing everywhere are masterly.

At first glance, the work of the Portuguese architect Álvaro Siza might seem to be very much in line with the modernist minimalism we have outlined thus far – that is, if we look back to much of his earlier work. Still, the roots of Siza's varied and deeply personal output cannot be so easily characterized as his designs are often a blend of several traditions: the vernacular of the Portuguese Alentejo region combined with his longstanding fondness for the varied work of such early modernists as Le Corbusier, Walter Gropius, Adolf Loos, and Alvar Aalto. This mixture of influences is clearly on display in his campus design for the Oporto School of Architecture. The initial phase of Siza's work on this project was the Carlos Ramos Pavilion of 1985, a small U-shaped building that initially served as an annex to the school. Siza's three-sided cloister created a clear differentiation between the building's exterior surfaces, which were coated in white stucco, and an interior courtyard with its floor-to-ceiling glazing.

Shortly after its completion, Siza was commissioned to design an entirely new complex for the school, for which – over the next 10 years – he built a miniature city of individual studio pavilions, together with a core of buildings that housed auditoria, administrative offices, and a library. The complex of joggled volumes, linked by a network of underground corridors, formed an informal acropolis of white stucco pavilions somewhat reminiscent of Weissenhof. Although each of these independent volumes offered a variation on the theme of punched openings and brow-like canopies with which Siza had begun the original pavilion, here he also experimented with subtle optical illusions, slanted windows, and rhetorical games in the detailing. For instance, he fashioned elaborate forced perspectives by angling the building volumes outward along the primary axis of movement. His use of sloped roof planes and long ribbon windows also created the illusion that the buildings are either larger or smaller than they actually are, depending on how one approaches them. These are modernist exercises but always with a historical twist. With his frequent mix of precedents and more personal (and at times perceptual) explorations, Siza aspires to a minimalism that transcends the merely tasteful or well pedigreed. At other times his work unfolds against a regionalist or even a surrealist backdrop, deceptively cloaked in the trim white finery of early modernism. Underlying both interpretations is a turn to more stable forms and to a reduced theoretical (or even programmatic) agenda for the architect. "I am a conservative and a traditionalist," Siza once noted in reflecting on his work, "that is to say, I move between conflicts, compromises, hybridization, transformation."[18] Such an outlook is pragmatic theory in its barest form.

Figure 11.6   Álvaro Siza, Oporto School of Architecture, Portugal (1985–1993). Image courtesy of Romina Canna.

Phenomenological Architecture

Much of the architecture discussed in this chapter has on occasion been described as phenomenological, but this is a term that needs some clarification. In earlier chapters we have discussed the references made by architects like Kenneth Frampton, Christian Norberg-Schulz, and Juhani Pallasmaa to phenomenology, but this discussion was generally somewhat isolated within other, more popular strands of theory. This situation began to change in the 1990s when phenomenology, still growing in influence, offered architects a serious critique of dominant trends. As a philosophical discipline, phenomenology is a well-defined approach to considering the "phenomena" of human consciousness or experience, and in more recent times, with the new scanning technologies directed to studying the brain, it has evolved into such esoteric realms as neurophenomenology – that is, it has largely been fortified by the insights and discipline of the biological sciences. As an architectural term it has never been so precisely defined, yet it nevertheless offers architects something different as a critical perspective. If architectural theory over much of the last quarter of the twentieth century had been focused on politics, meaning, and the formalist composing of buildings, phenomenology returns the focus to the human experience – that is, how we perceive or understand the built environment. In this way, as an approach to design, it is naturally aligned with a experiential point of view translatable into architectural terms.

The work of Steven Holl is an interesting case in point. In his early monograph, simply entitled *Anchoring* (1989), he evoked much of the language of phenomenological description without specifically using the word. He pleaded strongly for the interplay of a building's materiality with its site: the need for the architect to consider selected materials in relation to local lighting conditions, historical memories, and characteristics of the site.[19] In the second volume of the monograph, published in 1996, Holl now spoke in explicit phenomenological terms by addressing architecture metaphorically (following Maurice Merleau-Ponty) as an "intertwining" of "structure, material, space, color, light, and shadow," of which the most suggestive is perhaps the "metaphysics of light."[20] In between these two studies lay "Questions of Perception: Phenomenology of Architecture," a special edition of the Japanese journal *a + u* that Holl edited in 1994 along with Juhani Pallasmaa and Alberto Pérez-Gómez.[21]

The journal edition, later republished as a book, was in many respects the tipping point in bringing phenomenology to a broader audience. It opened with a thoughtful essay by Pérez-Gómez on "Meaning as Presence and Representation," which emphasized architecture's essential metaphoric values. Holl followed a series of meditations on the "Phenomenal Zone" or the artistic impact of such things as spatiality, color, light, time, water, sound, hapticity, proportion, scale, and perception in design. In the essay "An Architecture of the Seven Senses," Pallasmaa emphasized architecture's more recent loss of plasticity, in his view largely the result of the way in which contemporary architects privilege the visual over the other senses:

> Every touching experience of architecture is multi-sensory; qualities of mat-
> ter, space, and scale are measured equally by the eye, ear, nose, skin, tongue,
> skeleton and muscle. Architecture involves seven realms of sensory experi-
> ence which interact and infuse each other.[22]

Not only does Pallasmaa underscore the fact that we touch, scent, hear, and viscerally feel the spaces that we inhabit, but also that we interpret them in terms of our own bodies: what he calls images of muscle and bone, and bodily identification. For Pallasmaa, as his later writings make explicit, buildings and their craftsman-like acts of making are profound rites of a culture that shapes our connection to the world and our collective past, and the vehicles of their mediation are principally our perceptual experience and the memories they reignite in a neurological sense.

We measure buildings with our bodies in more ways than we generally imagine; as he points out (and as brain scans now demonstrate) visual perception cannot be separated from tactile feelings. He also underscores how – viscerally and somatically – our emotions and feelings interact with and bring positive and negative values to our perceptual experience. In this way, perception is not just a form of thinking, it is the very act of thought. In the end, Pallasmaa lays out a psychological and physiological framework for architectural design that builds upon the earlier efforts of Richard Neutra and Steen Eiler Rasmussen.[23]

Holl was also one of the first architects to explore a phenomenological perspective in practice, as we find in his Chapel of St Ignatius on the campus of Seattle University, completed in 1997. In one of his early sketches for this project, a series of colored and twisted "bottles" with distinct overtones of Le Corbusier's Ronchamp are set within a masonry frame – each bottle representing an aspect of Catholic worship. The idea is, in fact, carried out with a series of roofs with tinted clerestories, which sporadically splash the interior walls with episodes of colored light. The single space of the chapel is subdivided into smaller areas through highly articulated and textured ceiling planes, which gently bend over the differing width of the spaces.

In his addition to the Cranbrook Institute of Science (1998), Holl articulated the building's entrance with what he would call a "Light Laboratory," in essence, a sample board of different types of glazing: clear, reflective, bent, and translucent. These panes of glass again impress the interior surfaces with varying reflections, shadows, and textures over the course of the day. Therefore what this work most evidently shares with the architects we have described earlier in this chapter is the attempt to exploit sensory effects – in most cases, effects first intimated by Holl in his skillful watercolor sketches.

He also likes to work with the experience of space. In his contemporary design for the Kiasma Museum of Contemporary Art in Helsinki (1998), Holl sought to "intertwine" two existing axes within the building: one axis, a line linking the site to Alvar Aalto's nearby Finlandia Hall; the other, defined by the site's relation to nearby Töölö Bay. Holl used these imagined axes to structure a series of dramatically lit interior spaces in which pieces of the building's curved metal roof are sliced open to admit the geographically sparse, low Nordic light. This folding of a building upon itself, as promised in one of his sketches, is found in the building's top-lit central lobby space with its textured walls and curving ramp.

Another architect whose work is often described as phenomenological is Peter Zumthor. He came to international prominence in the mid-1990s with two dramatic works: the exquisitely detailed Art Museum in Bregenz and his masterful paean to material and the senses, the Thermal Baths at Vals. Zumthor often describes his work in terms of sensations recollected from childhood, sensations involving primary experiences of smell, touch, and sound:

> When I work on a design, I allow myself to be guided by images and moods that I remember and can relate to the kind of architecture I am looking for. Most of the images that come to mind originate from my subjective experience and are only rarely accompanied by a remembered architectural commentary. While I am designing I try to find out what these images mean so that I can learn how to create a wealth of visual forms and atmospheres.[24]

Zumthor's mode of working, then, is to search for the architectural means to create intense sensations or "moods" that linger in one's memory. Yet these sensations and the buildings that produce them are not meant to be fleeting experiences. Zumthor seeks to compose "buildings that, in time, grow naturally into being a part of the form and history of their place,"

Figure 11.7 Peter Zumthor, Thermal Bath at Vals, Switzerland (1990–1996). Image courtesy of Tim Brown.

and to that end he not only places a high priority on the treatment of the selected material but also seeks out a certain timelessness, rootedness, and attachment to the site.[25]

The Thermal Bath at Vals, completed in 1996, is emblematic of this approach in that, here, Zumthor began his design with his reflections on "mountain, rock, water."[26] Built of precisely cut horizontal slabs of local gneiss, the severe rectangular building block erupts from the sloping site like a natural outcropping, while a planted roof harmonizes the building from above with the pastoral valley landscape below. Within, the palette is minimal: thin strata of rock, water, and light. The procession through the building leads one from light to dark, hot to cold, from a protected to an exposed climate. A series of cave-like chambers with colored light creates a sequence of intense sensory experiences. Icy blue light filters into the coldest bath in a darkened chamber, and a metal cup is provided for visitors to sample the healing waters. Other rooms contain heated baths and jasmine-scented waters for visitors to ponder what might be called the primordial conditions of existence. Throughout the building the ceiling is segmented to admit cracks of light that wash the stone walls, highlighting their subtle texture and color variation. The craftsmanship throughout is precise and controlled, and the overall impression is that of an indestructible stone mass.

Zumthor would continue to explore the basic operation of stacking in such projects as the Swiss Pavilion for the 2000 Expo in Hannover, where he bound planks of wood with steel (recalling freshly-cut lumber on drying racks) to form a temporary enclosure. Zumthor's work – as well as the thoughtful explorations of Glenn Murcutt, Tod Williams and Billie Tsien, and Patricia and John Patkau – not only emphazise the primacy of sensations but also the timeless sense of simple craftsmanship. These architects make no reference to earlier architectural languages, because the allusions they offer the sensitive occupant seem to predate those languages by mining the basic intimations of shelter and refuge. Effects are vague and visceral rather than conscious or focused, and this condition clearly sets their work apart from that of many of their contemporaries.

12

Sustainability and Beyond

The turn toward more pragmatic concerns that we witnessed in the 1990s was not only a response to the abstractions of poststructural theory or the collapse of postmodern sensibilities. Nor did it simply reflect a strengthening of economic conditions that would lead to a global building boom. Driving it from below, so to speak, was the profession's response to a number of social and cultural issues that – with the profession's previous assertion of autonomy – had largely gone unattended since the activism of the 1960s. It is important, however, to note the very different contexts in which these issues once again came to the fore.

Architecture's response to such global problems of poverty, for instance, remains an issue for the twenty-first century, much as it was in the 1960s, except that the world of the 2010s is quite different, and even considerably more affluent than it was then. With the collapse of Communism in the 1980s and the widespread shift to market-based economies and freer global trade, many countries of Asia, South America, the Arabian Peninsula, and Eastern Europe began to experience significant economic growth; indeed, many have attained standards of living that rival those of the traditional economic powers. And although advanced technologies followed these economic trends, poverty did not entirely disappear. It simply transformed itself as an issue, as the once-acute problem of how to feed the world's growing population morphed into the problem of how to accommodate people (physically and economically) migrating from rural to urban centers. On the one hand, this trend resulted in the tremendous growth of populations in many global capitals, building booms, and urban over-expansion that often have had severe consequences with respect to pollution and quality of life. On the other hand, governments were also

An Introduction to Architectural Theory: 1968 to the Present, First Edition.
Harry Francis Mallgrave and David Goodman.
© 2011 Harry Francis Mallgrave and David Goodman. Published 2011 by Blackwell Publishing Ltd.

forced to take dramatic steps to address the housing problem, such as building entirely new cities and new economies to accommodate the influx of rural migrants. Since the turn of the millenium, the huge increase in the scale of such international events as the Olympics has led to major increases in infrastructural spending in the countries selected, also contributing to large architectural and planning undertakings.

Of course, what we are talking about here is the phenomenon of globalization, the ramifications of which are myriad and filled with architectural implications. We are simply no longer living in the politically and economically fractured world of the Cold War era, and global economies as well as their cultures are becoming ever more closely interconnected. And if the internet and the ease with which people can interact with one another have tended to bring artistic tastes and fashions into a kind of global concordance, it has also forced changes within the profession. Architecture of the twenty-first century, quite simply, has become a global activity practiced across borders with relatively few cultural or national restrictions. This trend will no doubt continue and many architectural offices have already undertaken the necessary re-orientation. "Bigness," as Rem Koolhaas suggested a few years ago, has become the new "normal," and the idea that a building might be assembled from different specialists on two or three continents is no longer an unusual occurrence. The fact that many students today take at least a part of their training internationally of course feeds this sense of global cultural unification.

Still another significant social factor has changed the practice of architecture in recent years: the demographics of the profession itself – that is, the number of minorities and women engaged with architectural practice. In the first regard, one can go back to the pioneering journal *APPEND-X*, founded in 1993 by Darell Fields, Milton Curry, and Kevin Fuller. Whereas this journal dealt largely with issues of African-American identity and architecture, its stated goal was to broaden the range of voices and concerns within the discipline, not solely those dealing with race.

Feminist voices also became prominent in the early 1990s, beginning with Beatriz Colomina's *Sexuality and Space* (1992) and *Privacy and Publicity: Modern Architecture as Mass Media* (1996). Also notable was *The Sex of Architecture* by Diana Agrest, Patricia Conway, and Leslie Kanes Weisman, which also appeared in 1996. Feminism as a movement, of course, had resurfaced at various times over the course of the twentieth century, and perhaps most visibly in the street demonstrations of the 1960s, but the inroads evident around the turn of the millennium were quite dramatic. If, in the architectural schools of the 1960s, females generally constituted less than five percent of students, by 2010 their numbers in many countries had reached near or full parity with those of males. Yet the full impact of the transformation will only be realized in the coming years as women pass into the senior ranks of the profession, potentially new or different perspectives on design will become manifest.

The Green Movement

One of the most significant changes that the architectural profession has witnessed since the beginning of the twenty-first century has been the resurgence of environmental concerns and the commensurate demand for the efficient use of clean energy.[1] To be sure this issue – the interrelationship of global resources and their wise husbanding – never completely disappeared since entering into mainstream consciousness in the 1960s. And, in response to the earlier concerns, many governments, particularly in Europe and the Americas, initiated a series of code and ordinance reforms that, little by little, began to alter the practice of design. If the pace of change has at times been discouragingly slow, significant progress has nevertheless been made in many of the industrialized countries of the world. The quality of air in most urban centers in Europe and North America in 2010 has dramatically improved over the conditions of a few years earlier, even as the problem has become exacerbated in other areas of the world.

A number of international agencies have also taken up the cause, although with varying degrees of success. In 1987 the United Nations launched its World Commission on Environment and Development and requested a report from its "Brundtland Commission." The report, also issued as the book *Our Common Future* (1987), was a wide-ranging call for global coordination to protect the natural environment, and it defined sustainable development as an activity that "meets the needs of the present without compromising the ability of future generations to meet their own needs." The report also argued that the next few decades will be decisive for the course of humanity: "The time has come to break out of past patterns. Attempts to maintain social and ecological stability through old approaches to development and environmental protection will increase instability. Security must be sought through change."[2]

The Brundtland Commission resulted in a number of international conferences to consider solutions, mostly funded by the United Nations. The immediate successor was the Conference on Environment and Development held in Rio de Janeiro in 1992 – the first "Earth Summit" – which produced the somewhat far-reaching document known as *Agenda 21*. Later summits, such as the Kyoto Summit of 1997, the Johannesburg Summit of 2002, and the Bali Conference of 2007, continued this process, although at best with modest success. The reasons are many. The Kyoto Accords, for example, committed industrialized countries to the reduction of four greenhouse gases to a level 5.2 percent below the 1990 level – a goal that few countries had attained by 2010 or were likely to attain in the near future. Moreover, it excluded many large, developing countries, where the problems of air pollution are often most acute. Also, political realities have delayed or prevented its ratification in several other countries, such as in the United States. If these problems were not bad enough, some of the scientific premises for these studies have been called in to question – leading to charges of exaggerated claims about climate change and its effects.

Far more effective from an ecological perspective has been an expanding network of national and local building codes that are directed to green architecture and planning. In 2003 the European Union passed its Energy Performance of Buildings Directive (EPBD), which led to the Green-Building Programme. These efforts were matched or even preceded by initiatives in many other countries, such as BREEAM in the United Kingdom, Australia's Green Star, Japan's CASBEE, and LEED (Leadership in Energy and Environmental Design) in the United States. As with the political initiatives, there are many critics of these efforts from both sides of the issue. One objection is their restriction to narrowly defined criteria for individual buildings, such as energy consumption or indoor air quality, while ignoring larger systemic, planning, or regional issues. Nevertheless, such codes and guidelines have been quite effective in raising the question of a building's environmental impact among architects, clients, and the public at large. Many larger architectural offices have also in the last few years written their own proprietary systems for evaluating a building's greenness. Notable in this regard is ARUP's four-quadrant Sustainable Project Appraisal Routine matrix (SPeAR), which is used internally to evaluate the environmental performance of projects, ranging in scale from the individual building to the planning of entire cities.

McDonough and Yeang

As these international concerns for the environment were reemerging in the 1990s, many individual architects, landscape architects, and planners also stepped to the forefront. In 1995, for instance, Victor Papanek, who had long been interested in ecological design, poverty, and their connection with social change, updated his earlier principles with *The Green*

Imperative, which reformulated the designer's task (and fiercely attacked trends in theory over the previous 20 years) in rather stark terms:

> This dismaying visual pollution signals the imminent emergence of a new aesthetic, and most designers and architects will readily agree that, after Modernism, Memphis, Post-Modernism, Deconstructivism, Neo-Classicism, Object-Semiotics, and Post-Deconstructivism, a new direction – transcending fad, trend or fashionable styling – is long overdue. New directions in design and architecture don't occur accidentally, but always arise out of real changes in society, cultures and concepts.[3]

In the year in which this book appeared, work was advancing on Norman Foster's 53-story Commerzbank in Frankfurt (1991–1997). With its central atrium, natural light and ventilation, and 10 oxygenating sky gardens, Foster provided a high-tech demonstration that the notion of sustainability, even at a corporate scale, could also encompass energy efficiency or eco-friendliness. Also in this decade, we find a veritable revolution in the field of landscape design, as this profession began to redirect its focus from aesthetic to ecological concerns. In the mid-1990s, for example, Mario Schjetnan and his interdisciplinary Grupo de Diseño Urbano completed the much heralded Xochimilco Ecological Park in Mexico City. Working with modest materials and a low budget, he demonstrated in very vivid terms what landscape architecture and urban planning – what he termed "metropolitan ecology" – could contribute to the restoration of urban ecological balance.

Certainly one of the more articulate champions of ecological issues in recent years has been William McDonough. Not only has he been a consistent advocate of "Cradle to Cradle" design, but he has also long argued that the idea of sustainability should encompass a more comprehensive approach than simply limiting itself to environmental damage. This argument reflects his belief that human activity can be productively and seamlessly integrated into natural processes – that is, the ideal relationship between the natural and the artificial would be, like nature itself, productive and mutually reinforcing, not merely sustainable.

In 1992 McDonough wrote the "Hannover Principles," a document that in the short run was intended to provide a set of operating guidelines for the sustainable development of Expo 2000 in Hannover. These principles referred to the "rights of humanity and nature to co-exist," to the notion of "interdependence" of the natural and manufactured worlds, and to the relationship of material production and spiritual well-being. This succinct list of seven axioms was accompanied by a detailed explanation of best practices dealing with earth, air, water, energy, and, perhaps most subjectively, the human spirit. In describing this last concern, McDonough equates the spiritual aspect of sustainability—"the most effable of elements" – with a deep understanding of our place on earth. "Concern for sustainability is more than a matter of compliance with industrial regulation or environmental impact analysis," he wrote, "it embraces a commitment to conceive of the work of design as part of a wider context in time and place."[4]

McDonough extended this line of reasoning in his paper "Declaration of Interdependence," which he delivered at a symposium at MIT in 1996. Here he argued that sustainability had up to this point been little more than "a code word for maintenance," and that what was needed was a true "restorative agenda" for architecture and urbanism, one in which the built environment would actually purify soil and water and act as a net producer of energy, thereby returning something to the ecosystem.[5] This agenda was most directly illustrated in the principle of "waste equals food," a statement that placed architecture and urbanism within a metabolic chain of energy consumption and re-absorption. McDonough would eventually label his approach of connecting production, consumption, and re-use a "cradle to cradle" strategy, which became the title of his best-selling book of 2002, coauthored with the chemist Michael Braungart. Here the authors argue not for an abandonment of industrial processes, but rather for a creative application of technology, an "industrial re-evolution" that would create a functional link between the built and natural environments:

> Natural systems take from their environment, but they also give something back. The cherry tree drops its blossoms and leaves while it cycles water and makes oxygen; the ant community redistributes the nutrients throughout the soil. We can follow their cue to create a more inspiring engagement – a partnership – with nature.[6]

The fundamental idea behind such a statement is that manufactured environments can be designed to emulate the logics of the natural ecosystem ("waste equals food"), and therefore to interact productively with it. McDonough thus defines the role of the ecologically driven architect to be a creative one; the architect is the designer of both an individual product and its productive relationship to its physical context.

McDonough also implemented these principles in his many designs for industrial objects and buildings, as well as master plans. His "GreenHouse" office and manufacturing facility in Holland, Michigan (1995), for instance, incorporated both biophilic and "phylogenetic" approaches to

Figure 12.1   William McDonough + Partners, Herman Miller "GreenHouse" Office and Manufacturing Facility, Holland, Michigan (1995). Image courtesy of Herman Miller, Inc.

design. He restored the surrounding prairie and wetlands and amply endowed the interiors with an abundance of natural light and the sensory richness of garden and water features. He also created devices for orientation and social interaction within the complex, and designed spaces that were intended to perform a regenerative function for its occupants, much as the building itself was intended to do with respect to its immediate physical context. Another step to the notion of a "restorative" architecture was taken with the Adam Joseph Lewis Center for Environmental Studies at Oberlin College (2001), which draws much of its energy from the sun, uses geothermal systems for heating and cooling, and filters wastewater through a greenhouse-enclosed "living machine" of wetlands for re-use in toilets and landscape. More recently the building has become a net energy exporter to other buildings on campus.

Beyond these functional efficiencies, however, McDonough has argued that one of the more important benefits of these efforts in conservation and regeneration is in fact their educational value. A building, in this view, might perform the dual functions of saving and regenerating resources on its limited site while it provides an instructive example of how this can be done. Leon van Schaik, architect and professor of architecture at the Royal Melbourne Institute of Technology, has expressed a similar view in commenting on the expressive value of buildings like McDonough's, arguing that their overt display of sensitive environmental strategies and technologies is useful "when a government or a corporation wishes to let people know that *something* indeed is being done."[7] For van Schaik, then, the aesthetic or expressive dimension of a sustainable architecture might either emerge organically from the very forms and strategies that allow architecture to be energy efficient, or a sustainable building might instead be designed in part to further the notion of sustainability. In the latter sense, van Schaik notes, the strategies employed in some of the more expressive sustainable works resemble Konstantin Melnikov's constructivist "emotion-activating" architecture of the 1920s, where a style of exaggerated industrial forms was promoted to symbolize the Soviet Union's aspirations of industrialization, notwithstanding the country's weak industrial base. In doing so, this rhetorical approach would ostensibly spur the creation of progressively more developed ideas of sustainable architecture, until it became the rule rather than the exception.

Like McDonough, the Malaysian architect Ken Yeang has been working with ideas of sustainability since the 1970s. Once a student of Ian McHarg at the University of Pennsylvania, he completed his doctorate at Cambridge University with a dissertation on ecological design and planning.[8] In both his practice and his writings, Yeang has largely focused his attention on sustainability in tall buildings, an area that he believes is necessary to explore because the skyscraper, though ubiquitous and necessary for the growth of our cities, is inherently "un-ecological" because of the added energy and material needed to ensure its proper functioning. In his book *Eco Skyscrapers* (1994), Yeang countered the hostility of many environmentalists toward tall buildings with the argument that the architect's goal should be to "mitigate" the negative environmental effects of the skyscraper and create "humane and pleasurable" interiors for the user.[9]

Yeang is therefore is somewhat more pragmatic than McDonough, although he too argues for a symbiotic relationship between the natural and built environment, a relationship he terms "benign and seamless bio-integration."[10] For Yeang, the best way to achieve this relationship is not necessarily through the application of novel technology, but instead through passive or "bioclimatic" means, a strategy he applied to the design of the IBM tower in Kuala Lumpur (1992), which lies just north of the equator. This building – with its permeable exterior facade, landscaped "skycourts" spiraling along the tower's length, solar shading, and naturally ventilated elevator lobbies – presents an object lesson in an environmentally sensitive architecture that returns to passive environmental strategies (an attention to solar orientation, deep overhangs, etc.). This salute to the indigenous architecture of Malaysia, however, is also combined with a high-tech vocabulary. Indeed, the search for a sustainable architecture points directly to the re-establishment of regional typologies based on responses to the local climate. In this sense, this is an evolution of the idea of critical regionalism that aims for an organic synthesis of a building's form and performance within its particular biosystem. Yeang has long argued, in fact, that this approach is analogous to the development of surgical prosthetics; like the prosthetic, the building must be integrated "both mechanically and organically" within its host system, lest it results in the "dislocation" or rejection of the prosthetic by the host.[11]

Yeang's work has both its supporters and its critics. His principal design manual, *Ecodesign* (2006), remains one of the most comprehensive guides to sustainable design and is an intelligent (even invaluable) translation of the idea of a pattern language to green design in that it is both informative and helpful without being overly prescriptive. At this same time, his more recent study, *EcoMasterplanning* (2009), is less convincing in the social vitality of urban spaces that his designs suggest. This point reflects a larger consensus that is now emerging that "green architecture," as defined in recent years, has given too little attention to the human dynamics of a truly sustainable built environment. In simpler terms, ecology needs to be recast in broader human terms.

Green Urbanism

Urban planners, like their counterparts in architecture and landscape architecture, have seen their profession undergo a revolution since the 1980s. European cities, in particular, have been leading the way – both in preserving their historical centers and in initiating a number of model "ecological" projects in the effort to revitalize them as well. Cities like Helsinki and Copenhagen, for instance, have not only preserved the forested areas that historically have penetrated deep into the downtown areas, but in many instances they have expanded them and planned future growth with a view to their preservation and accessibility. In the case of Copenhagen, the city's "five finger" master plan, first proposed in the 1970s, has limited all suburban development to the fingers emanating from the town center, organized along mass-transit arteries. In between the fingers the lie of the land has been preserved not only as rural landscapes but also as wooded areas in close proximity to the urban residents who may avail themselves of them at leisure. Similarly, Helsinki, in two master plans issued in 1978 and 2002, has not simply protected the limits of its Central Park but extended it to a much larger geographic area of connected parks and waterways that now encompasses the whole of Töölö Bay.[12] This is significant because, since the 1980s, planning theorists and psychologists have been gathering evidence about the stress-reducing and restorative effects of natural environments in close proximity to urban residents. In this regard the notion of "green space" of which many planners speak has in the process taken on a grander and more literal interpretation.

Europe's many demonstration housing projects have also often struck a sustainable theme. One of the more prominent is the new community of Kronsberg outside Hannover, Germany. Set on 1200 hectares and expected to house 15 000 residents in non-detached units, it was an ecological development planned for Expo 2000, and it combines such features as a strict land management plan with an ecological farm, green schools, and a street system that minimizes the use of the automobile. The town is largely powered by wind turbines, an extensive system of PV panels, and a number of heat recovery methods. The town plan also incorporates the surrounding rural countryside and wooded areas, and gray water is recycled through a series of reclamation features and scenic ponds. Housing units, which in both scale and style recall the *Siedlungen* of the 1920s, are built to the strictest standards of natural light, passive design, and energy efficiency.

Alongside Germany, both Holland and the United Kingdom have been in the forefront of large-scale sustainable design and experimentation. One of the many new demonstration communities in Holland is the new suburb of Amersfoort, which is powered by an integrated PV system generating a full megawatt of power. All community amenities are within walking distance, and ponds are once again a prominent feature. England has also built a number of ecological communities, such as Greenwich Millennium Village and the Beddington Zero Energy Development, both in London. Among the many features of the latter upscale community, designed by Bill Dunster Architects, are the use of colorful rooftop wind cowls to ventilate the units, the discouragement of non-electric automobiles, and the fact that most construction materials for this zero-carbon development were obtained locally.

On a regional level, the naturally scenic city of Vancouver, British Columbia, has been exemplary in its sustainable policies. Land ordinances have been put into place that preserves farmland, integrate large sections of green areas into the metropolitan areas, and channel all building development into compact neighborhoods (62 percent of the city's population), with housing oriented toward the street to enhance urban vitality. Thus, a city of two million people has been structured in part into a city of smaller towns connected to each other through an elevated rail system. Even design elements such as impervious surfaces for roads and parking lots have been carefully limited. Walking, cycling, and mass-transit usage flourish.

Little by little, such policies are having a significant global effect. China, which initially powered much of the expansion of its new and existing urban centers with coal-fired plants, considered its first eco-city in the late 1990s – Dongtan, on the island of Chongming. Designed by Arup, the projected city of 500 000 people featured the very best of intentions: protection of local agricultural areas, wildlife habitats and biodiversity, zero carbon emission, water recycling, and zero waste. Arup even designed an electric automobile for this town at the mouth of Yangtze River. Although it is now unlikely that the city will be built in its original form, the publicity it has received has resounded through the country's bureaucracies and will no doubt have a major influence on future planning. Similarly, the Olympic Games of 2008 held in Beijing, a capital that remains plagued with significant air-quality problems, brought home to the public and to governmental officials in the most poignant terms the unacceptable and unhealthy level of air pollution.

The gold standard of sustainable urban ventures is the new city of Masdar, now being constructed on the outskirts of downtown Abu Dhabi. The self-contained walled city, designed by Foster + Partners, has the ambitious goal of being the first zero-carbon and zero-waste city, but what is unusual is the way planners have gone about achieving this. It is a high-density, mixed-zone city for 50 000 people, anchored with a university and energy development research park, yet at the same time it is remarkably low-tech in many of its features. It is largely powered by a solar farm, receives its desalinated water from the Persian Gulf, and is supported by local agriculture. Yet the scale of construction (no buildings more than six stories), together with the cultural sensitivity that was considered in the fashioning of neighborhoods, make it seem like little more than an updated version of a historic Arab town. Automobiles are removed entirely from a city and replaced with tram lines and a personal rapid-transit system; pedestrian streets are narrow and aligned to remain in shadow during the warmest parts of the day, and larger urban squares are in part shielded from the desert sun by louvered screens. Water and its evaporative cooling effect is a prominent feature. Air-movement patterns

Figure 12.2   Foster + Partners, residential street from the proposed city of Masdar. Image courtesy of Foster + Partners/Masdar.

have be carefully considered with two green shoots breaching the north-west wall to allow breezes into the town from the nearby gulf: individual building scoops and interior courtyards channel it through the units with simple convection currents. The urban density is akin to Venice, which in itself remains a viable model for an automobile-free town. In short, Masdar is masterful mediation of the new with the old and will no doubt be extensively studied.

Biophilic Design

One critique increasingly being voiced against the environmental movement is that its idea of what constitutes sustainable design has been too narrowly formed. Certainly the architect has the responsibility to use resources wisely and not denigrate the biology of the planet on which future generations will depend, but one issue often absent from the discussion of sound ecological design is how people respond to the built environment. More specifically, this is the issue of whether built environments contribute to or detract from the health and well-being of their human inhabitants. Much of this reluctance derives from the patterns of past theory. For as we have seen, with the fall of the late-modernist worldview in the late 1960s also collapsed the belief that the architect could in any meaningful way improve the human situation. Architects were not entirely to blame in this regard. If coursework in sociology, anthropology, and psychology was very much a part of the architect's education in the 1960s, many of the premises upon which the social sciences were based lacked any genuinely scientific grounding. The sociological assumptions leading to the colossal failure of urban renewal programs across the globe during this decade reveal in a cogent way the misery that can ensue when planning and architectural decisions are based on false or incomplete premises.

But the scientific backdrop against which we function in the twenty-first century, as many architects are beginning to realize, is vastly different. The architect now has at his or her command a bounty of new insights into the psychological and physiological nature of the human organism – from the biological and microbiological understanding of our genetic codes to the enormous strides that have been made since the 1980s in the cognitive sciences. Entirely new fields, such as evolutionary psychology and neuroscience are at the moment creating compelling evidence-based models of how we perceive and experience the world, and the implications for architects are manifold. The design interests of such earlier individuals as Lázló Moholy-Nagy, Richard Neutra, and Christopher Alexander are now coming full circle and being supported with a new biological platform.

One of the new areas to have gained traction since the turn of the millennium has been biophilic design, also related to evidence-based design. It is a field that has grown out of the insights of evolutionary psychologists and biologists – the realization that the genetic structure by which we respond to the world is older, in fact millions of years older, than the constructed environments that we have fashioned within the past 10 000 years.[13] In short, human behavior is not just a phenomenon of will or cultural training but also of genetic proclivities and behaviors that have long been in place with our hominid ancestors. We are born not with a "blank slate," a premise upon which many of the social sciences of the 1960s were based, but with distinct preferences for how we would like the world to be structured.

Parallel with this realization has been the rise of a number of habitat-selection theories suggesting that we have a particular fondness for environmental conditions that in an evolutionary sense have favored our biological survival.[14] If, as we now know, we have evolved over the course of millions of years from a particular hominid line that thrived on the savannahs of eastern and southern Africa, might we not have a genetic preference for such landscapes? And what were the characteristics of these landscapes? For one thing they offered "prospect" (shielded visibility favorable to hunters) and "refuge" (providing security after the chase). African savannahs are also characterized by spatial openness, visible ground textures, stands of mature trees, and water – much as we might find in a picturesque garden, an urban park, or indeed in many suburban backyards.

Beginning in the 1980s these hypotheses began to undergo empirical testing, and the results have since become rather conclusive. Even brief exposures to natural landscapes have a variety of notable health benefits, among them a reduction of stress, the lowering of blood pressure, improvement in our ability to focus, and, indeed, giving us a brighter outlook on life.[15] In 1984 the sociobiologist Edward O. Wilson defined this component of our biological make-up as "biophilia."[16] And in one classic study of the mid-1980s, the psychologist Roger S. Ulrich underscored its architectural implications. In studying the records of 46 patients who had undergone gall-bladder surgery, he found that those patients recovering in a room with a view of a few trees had fewer complaints, took less medication, and were discharged one-day earlier than patients with a similar condition yet whose room had a view of an adjacent brick wall.[17] Since this realization, the field of hospital design has become ever more specialized in its use of evidence-based design.

On an urban scale, biophilia suggests that the central parks of Helsinki or New York do more than simply serve as the city's "lungs"; they provide an accessible outlet for people to find relaxation and relieve themselves of the pressures of urban life. It also suggests, as Timothy Beatley has noted, that if sustainability concerns suggest higher urban densities, these densities should be coupled with a commensurate increase in accessible green or wooded landscapes.[18] And if we consider that may cities around the world retain their "rustbelt" remnants of an earlier industrial age, biophilia suggests both the opportunity and a strategy to rebuild and reforest them in more humane ways.

In the last few years the idea of biophilic design has also come to architecture, with a greater emphasis on such features as water, fresh air, sunlight, plants, views of nature – more literally a green architecture. The design of health facilities, schools, and workplaces are obvious areas where such strategies can be applied, but these principles, as architecture throughout its history repeatedly demonstrates, are not really new and can be applied to all areas of design. What is also becoming evident is the expansion of the idea of biophilic design to consider such things as architectural scale, proportions, materials, ornamentation, or more generally the human response to the built environment.[19] But here biophilic design crosses over with still another new field that is also in the early stages of formation.

Neuroaesthetics

If in recent years we have made enormous strides in the molecular understanding and sequencing of the human genome, these advances have been matched in many ways by our neurological understanding of the human brain. With the new scanning technologies – such as fMRIs, PETs, EEGs, MEGs – we now have (also becoming ever more refined) real-time images of the working brain, and our knowledge of how the brain functions has probably grown more since the 1980s than over the entire course of human history. One of the things that has become apparent, in addition to our appreciation of the tremendous neural complexity that has evolved, are the processes by which the brain actively engages or perceives the world. We are not only beginning to understand such formerly elusive phenomena as memory-formation and consciousness, but also the means by which people think creatively and evaluate the world artistically.[20]

The latter field has been termed "neuroaesthetics," which can be defined as the neurological study of "the neural processes involved in human art behavior."[21] It is made enormously complicated by the fact that there are a host of variables affecting aesthetic judgments, such as the visual training we receive, our gender, the meaning of objects, emotional variables, and of course such things as culture and changing fashions. Thus, although still a young area of research, it is one that has already sprouted several distinct branches. Some researchers are attempting to define the neurological stages of the aesthetic experience – that is, how we perceive, implicate, and integrate memories, classify, cognitively master, and evaluate artistic works and buildings.[22] Others are attempting to define the locations or pathways in the brain where this activity takes place as we make judgments of beauty.[23] Still another school, working from an ethological perspective, sees artistic production not specifically as an aesthetic activity but as an instinct grounded in genetic structures not necessarily focused on beauty; one that arises in our emotional responses and is therefore connected to such communal activities as bonding and ritualization.[24]

The question of where all of this activity will lead is of course a difficult one to answer at the moment. Some neurobiolgists, such as Semir Zeki, have argued that "there can be no satisfactory theory of aesthetics that is not neurobiologically based," and by this he means that if the brain has the Darwinian task of acquiring knowledge about the world to insure our survival, art must support this task.[25] And if the role of the brain has evolved to seek out those permanent and characteristic properties of objects and surfaces, art must be an extension of these neural processes – that is, art exploits, in his words, "the characteristics of the parallel-processing perceptual system of the brain."[26] From such a perspective, art thrives on such things as thematic complexity and ambiguity, the latter defined as the certainty of several possible interpretations, all of which are equally appealing.

Wherever these directions will lead, one thing is now becoming clear through these models. Architecture – far from being a highly conceptualized exercise as theory has often made it out to be – is also, and perhaps preeminently, an emotive and multisensorially based experience, the response of an embodied organism to a world that provides it with necessary stimulation. As does music, a building has the capacity to elicit immediate emotive responses, and the better the architect can understand this process the more successful (life-sustaining) a design will be. Whether neuroscientists can also shed light on such traditional architectural issues as visual complexity, order, scale, rhythm, ornamentation, or even the seemingly timeless issue of whether there are neurologically preferred architectural proportions remains uncertain at this time.[27] Nevertheless, it is becoming very apparent that as we advance our knowledge in these areas, the basis for design 10 or 20 years into the future will very likely look quite different to how it does today. We are, arguably, entering an entirely new phase of architectural theory.

Notes

Prelude: 1960s

1 Lewis Mumford's remarks on "Bay Region Style" were made in his regular column "Status Quo," *The New Yorker*, 11 (October 1947), pp. 108–109. The Museum of Modern Art responded with a symposium consisting mainly of opponents to a regional style. See "What is Happening to Modern Architecture?" *Museum of Modern Art Bulletin*, 15 (Spring 1948).

2 See Aldo van Eyck's response to the Bridgewater questionnaire in Sigfried Giedion (ed.), *A Decade of New Architecture* (Zurich: Editions Girsberger, 1951), p. 37. Van Eyck concluded his remarks with a series of stirring questions, among them, "Does CIAM intend to 'guide' a rational and mechanistic conception of progress towards an improvement of human environment?"

3 For an overview of the Moroccan and Algerian presentations, as well as the British presentation in Aix-en-Provence, see Eric Mumford, *The CIAM Discourses on Urbanism, 1928–1960* (Cambridge, MA: MIT Press, 2000).

4 For the criticisms of the Torre Velasca at the CIAM '59 conference, see Oscar Newman, *New Frontiers in Architecture: CIAM '59 in Otterlo* (New York: Universe Books, 1961), pp. 92–101. See Banham's essay "Neoliberty: The Italian Retreat from Modern Architecture," *Architectural Review*, 125 (April 1959), p. 235.

5 Reyner Banham, *Theory and Design in the First Machine Age* (New York: Praeger Publishers, 1967), p. 10.

6 Banham, *Theory and Design* (note 5), pp. 329–330.

7 Banham conducted this "trial" in six installments of *Architectural Review* between February and September 1962. For a good summary of the fascination of this period with megastructures, see his later book *Megastructures: Urban Futures of the Recent Past* (New York: Harper and Row, 1976).

An Introduction to Architectural Theory: 1968 to the Present, First Edition.
Harry Francis Mallgrave and David Goodman.
© 2011 Harry Francis Mallgrave and David Goodman. Published 2011 by Blackwell Publishing Ltd.

8   Yona Friedman, *L'Architecture mobile: Vers une cité conçue par ses habitants* (Paris: Casterman, 1970; published privately in 1959).

9   See Noboru Kawazeo (ed.), *Metabolism 1960: Proposals for a New Urbanism* (Tokyo: Bijutsu shuppansha, 1960) and Kisho Noriaki Kurokawa, *Metabolism in Architecture* (Boulder: Westview, 1977).

10 See Peter Cook (ed.), *Archigram* (Basel: Birkhäuser, 1972) and Simon Sadler, *Archigram: Architecture without Architecture* (Cambridge, MA: MIT Press, 2005).

11 Banham, *Theory and Design* (note 5), pp. 325–326.

12 John McHale, *R. Buckminster Fuller* (New York, George Braziller, 1962); R. Buckminster Fuller and John McHale, *Inventory of World Resources: Human Trends and Needs* (Carbondale, Southern Illinois University Press, 1963).

13 R. Buckminster Fuller, *Ideas and Integrities: A Spontaneous Autobiographical Disclosure*, ed. Robert W. Marks (New York: Collier Books, 1963), p. 270.

14 Ekistics, the study of human settlements, was also the title of a journal that Doxiadis launched in 1955, under the editorial control of Jacqueline Tyrwhitt. The latter had long ties with CIAM, and it was she, for instance, who invited Sigfried Giedion to attend the Delos ceremony, the first of 12 such events bringing together technology experts and thinkers from around the world.

15 See, for instance, Barbara Ward, *Spaceship Earth* (New York: Columbia University Press, 1966). The book was based on a series of lectures given in 1965.

16 Kenneth Boulding, "Earth as a Spaceship," May 10, 1965, Washington State University, Committee on Spaces Sciences, in Kenneth E. Boulding Papers, Archives (Box 38), University of Colorado at Boulder Libraries.

17 Boulding, "Earth as a Spaceship" (note 16). See also, Kenneth Boulding, "The Economics of the Coming Spaceship Earth," in Henry Jarrett (ed.), *Environmental Quality in a Growing Economy* (Baltimore: Johns Hopkins University Press, 1966), pp. 3–14.

18 See the opening chapter, "Why a 'Modern' Architecture?" in J. M. Richards, *An Introduction to Modern Architecture* (Harmondsworth: Penguin Books Limited, 1940).

19 Serge Chermayeff and Christopher Alexander, *Community and Privacy: Toward a New Architecture of Humanism* (Garden City, NJ: Doubleday Anchor, 1965), p. 20.

20 Christopher Alexander, "The Synthesis of Form; Some Notes on a Theory," (PhD dissertation, Harvard University, 1962), p. 3. See also, *Notes on the Synthesis of Form* (Cambridge, MA: Harvard University Press, 1964).

21 For some remarks on the debate, see Alison Smithson (ed.), *Team 10 Meetings 1953–1984* (New York: Rizzoli, 1991), pp. 68–69, 78, and Francis Strauven, *Aldo van Eyck: The Shape of Reality* (Amsterdam: Architectura & Naturi, 1998), pp. 397–398.

22 Christoper Alexander, "A City is Not a Tree," part one in *Architectural Forum* (April 1965), pp. 58–62, part two in *Architectural Forum* (May 1965), pp. 58–61.

23   I thank Peter Land for showing me many of his documents related to the PREVI project.

24   Marshall McLuhan and Quentin Fiore, *The Medium Is the Message: An Inventory of Effects* (New York: Bantam, 1967), p. 16.

1   *Pars Destruens:* 1968–1973

1   See, for instance, Robert Venturi, *Complexity and Contradiction in Architecture* (New York: Museum of Modern Art, 1966), pp. 48–53.

2   Venturi, *Complexity and Contradiction* (note 1), p. 102.

3   Venturi, *Complexity and Contradiction* (note 1), p. 103.

4   See Melvin Webber, "The Urban Place and the Nonplace Urban Realm," in M. Webber *et al.* (eds), *Explorations into Urban Structure* (Philadelphia: University of Pennsylvania Press, 1964), p. 147.

5   Denise Scott Brown, "The Meaningful City," *Journal of the American Institute of Architects* (January 1965), pp. 27–32. Cited from the reprint in *Connection* (Spring 1967), p. 50.

6   Robert Venturi and Denise Scott Brown, "A Significance for A&P Parking Lots, or Learning from Las Vegas," *Architectural Forum*, March 1968, pp. 39–40.

7   Denise Scott Brown and Robert Venturi, "On Ducks and Decoration," *Architecture Canada*, October 1968, p. 48.

8   Robert Venturi, Denise Scott Brown, and Steven Izenour, *Learning from Las Vegas: The Forgotten Symbolism of Architectural Form* (Cambridge, MA: MIT Press, 1972/1977), pp. 137, 163.

9   Tomás Maldonado, *Design, Nature & Revolution: Toward a Critical Ecology*, trans. Mario Domandi (New York: Harper & Row, 1972), p. 64. The book originally appeared in Italian as *La speranza progettuale. Ambiente e società* (Turin: Einaudi, 1970), and, from remarks made in 1971, it is clear that Scott Brown, at least, was familiar with it.

10 Denise Scott Brown, "Learning from Pop," *Casabella*, 359–60 (December 1971), p. 15.

11 Scott Brown, "Learning from Pop" (note 10), p. 17.

12 Kenneth Frampton, "America 1960–1970: Notes on Urban Images and Theory," *Casabella* (note 10), p. 31.

13 Giuseppe Samonà, *L'urbanistica e l'avvenire della città* (1959), Leonardo Benevolo, *Le origini dell'urbanistica moderna* (1963), and Carlo Aymonino, *La città territorio* (1964), *La formazione del concetto di tipologia edilizia* (1965), and *Origini e sviluppo della città moderna* (1965).

14 Aldo Rossi, *A Scientific Autobiography*, trans. Lawrence Venuti (Cambridge, MA: MIT Press, 1981), p. 15.

15 Aldo Rossi, *L'architettura della città* (Padua: Marsilio Editori, 1966); *The Architecture of the City*, trans. Diane Ghirado and Joan Ockman

(Cambridge, MA: MIT Press, 1982), p. 41. Rossi cites the definition from Quatremère de Quincy's *Dictionnaire historique d'architecture* (1832).

16 Giorgio Grassi, *La costruzione logica dell'architettura* (Padua: Marsilio Editori, 1967), pp. 11, 104.

17 On Tafuri's early published writings, see Giorgio Ciucci, "The Formative Years," in *Casabella*, 619–620 (January/February 1995), pp. 13–25. See also his book *Ludovico Quaroni e lo sviluppo dell'architettura moderna in Italia* (Milan: Edizioni di Comunità, 1964).

18 Negri, a professor of political philosophy at the University of Padua, preached an aggressive line of violence and revolutionary confrontation, while Tronti had joined the PCI with the intention of weaning it of its bureaucratic inclinations. The split became manifest in 1968 when Negri rejected an essay by Tronti for the second issue of *Contropiano* – "Il partito come problema" (The party as a problem). It was then accepted by the other editors and published, forcing Negri to resign his editorial position. For one take on the dispute, see Alberto Asor Rosa, "Critique of Ideology and Historical Practice," in *Casabella*, 619–620 (January/February 1995), p. 29.

19 Manfredo Tafuri, *Teorie e storia dell'architettura* (Rome: Laterza, 1968); *Theories and History of Architecture*, trans. Giorgio Verrecchia (New York: Harper and Row, 1980), pp. 232–233.

20 Manfredo Tafuri, see Luisa Passerini, "History as Project: An Interview with Manfredo Tafuri," Rome, February/March 1992, trans. Denise L. Bratton, in *Any*, 25/26 (2000), pp. 40–41. See also, Walter Benjamin, "The Destructive Character," trans. Rodney Livingstone *et al.*, in *Walter Benjamin: Selected Writings*, Vol. 2, 1927–1934 (Cambridge, MA: Harvard Belknap Press, 1999), pp. 541–542.

21 Manfredo Tafuri, "Toward a Critique of Architectural Ideology," trans. Stephen Sartarelli, in K. Michael Hays (ed.), *Architecture Theory since 1968* (Cambridge, MA: MIT Press, 2002), p. 14. "Per una critica dell'ideologia architettonica" originally appeared in *Contropiano*, 1 (January–April 1969).

22 Tafuri, "Toward a Critique," (note 21), pp. 19, 28.

23 Kurt W. Forster, "No Escape from History, No Reprieve from Utopia, No Nothing: An *Addio* to the Anxious Historian Manfredo Tafuri," *Any*, 25/26 (2000), p. 62. For other readings of Tafuri's historiography, see Tomas Llorens, "Manfredo Tafuri: Neo-Avant-Garde and History," *On the Methodology of Architectural History, Architectural Design Profile*, 51 (6/7) (1981), pp. 82–95; Fredric Jameson, "Architecture and the Critique of Ideology," in Joan Ockman *et al.* (eds), *Architecture, Criticism, Ideology* (Princeton: Princeton Architectural Press, 1985); Joan Ockman (ed.), "Postscript: Critical History and the Labors of Sisyphus," in *Architecture, Criticism, Ideology* (Princeton: Princeton Architectural Press, 1985), pp. 51–87, 182–189; and Panayotis Tournikiotis, *The Historiography of Modern Architecture* (Cambridge, MA: MIT Press, 1999). See also Patrizia Lombardo's excellent portrait of the intellectual climate of Venice during this period in her introduction to Massimo Cacciari,

Architecture and Nihilism: On the Philosophy of Modern Architecture, trans. Stephen Sartarelli (New Haven: Yale University Press, 1993).

24 Manfredo Tafuri, *Progetto e utopia* (Bari: Laterza & Figli, 1973); *Architecture and Utopia: Design and Capitalist Development*, trans. Luigia La Pena (Cambridge, MA: MIT Press, 1976), p. 56.

25 Tafuri, *Progetto e utopia* (note 24), p. 182.

26 Manfredo Tafuri, *History of Italian Architecture, 1944–1985*, trans. Jessica Levine (Cambridge: Cambridge University Press, 1989), p. 136; "*L'Architecture dans le Boudoir*: The Language of Criticism and the Criticism of Language," trans. Victor Caliandro, *Oppositions* 3, in *Oppositions Reader* (New York: Princeton Architectural Press, 1998), p. 299.

27 Rafael Moneo, "Aldo Rossi: The Idea of Architecture and the Modena Cemetery," *Oppositions* 5, in *Oppositions Reader* (New York: Princeton Architectural Press, 1998), p. 119.

28 Aldo Rossi, Introduction to *Architettura Razionale: XV Triennale di Milano Sezione Internazionale di Architettura* (Milan: Franco Angeli, 1973), p. 17.

29 Massimo Scolari, "Avanguardia e nuova architettura," pp. 153–187. Trans. Stephen Sartarelli as "The New Architecture and the Avant-Garde," in K. Michael Hays, *Architecture Theory since 1968* (Cambridge, MA: MIT Press, 2000), pp. 133–134.

30 Scolari, "Avanguardia," (note 29), pp. 136–137.

31 In support of these parameters, Scolari cites Gregotti's *Orientamenti nuovi nell'architettura italiana* (*New Directions in Italian Architecture*), which appeared in 1969.

32 Joseph Rykwert, "15a Triennale," in *Domus*, 530 (January 1974), p. 4.

33 Colin Rowe, "The Mathematics of the Ideal Villa," in *Architectural Review*, 101 (March 1947), pp. 101–104. Reprinted in *The Mathematics of the Idea Villa, and Other Essays* (Cambridge, MA: MIT Press, 1976). On the life and ideas of Rowe, see Joan Ockman, "Form without Utopia: Contextualizing Colin Rowe" (review essay), *Journal of the Society of Architectural Historians*, 57 (December 1998), pp. 448–456, and the special issue of *Architecture New York* (*ANY*) devoted to Rowe, 7–8 (1994).

34 On Harris's role within the program see Lisa Germany, *Harwell Hamilton Harris* (Berkeley: University of California Press, 2000), pp. 139–156.

35 On the Texas Rangers, see Alexander Caragonne, *The Texas Rangers: Notes from the Architectural Underground* (Cambridge, MA: MIT Press, 1995).

36 Peter Eisenman, "The Formal Basis of Modern Architecture" (PhD dissertation, Cambridge University, 1963). On Eisenman and his writings during these years, see chapter eight of the dissertation of Louis Martin, "The Search for a Theory in Architecture: Anglo-American Debates, 1957–1976" (Ph.D. diss., Princeton University, 2002).

37 See Colin Rowe and Robert Slutzky, "Transparency: Literal and Phenomenal," part one in *Perspecta*, 8 (1963), and part two in *Perspecta*, 13–14 (1971).

38 Various documents related to the founding of CASE and the IAUS are found at the Canadian Centre for Architecture, Montreal.

39 House I, commissioned by Professor and Mrs Paul Benacerraf, was built as an addition to a house in Princeton and served as a toy museum.

40 See Frank Lloyd Wright, "The Cardboard House," lecture delivered at Princeton University, reprinted in *Frank Lloyd Wright: Collected Writings, Volume 2, 1930–32* (New York: Rizzoli, 1992).

41 Peter Eisenman (ed.), "House I," in *Five Architects: Eisenman, Graves Gwathmey, Hejduk, Meier* (New York: Oxford University Press, 1975), p. 15.

42 Rosalind Krauss, "Death of a Hermeneutic Phantom: Materialization of the Sign in the Work of Peter Eisenman," in Peter Eisenman, *House of Cards* (New York: Oxford University Press, 1987), p. 173.

43 Louis Martin speculates that Eisenman first came across Chomsky's *Syntactic Structures* (1957) early in 1969, at the instigation of Richard Falk, who commissioned House II. See Louis Martin, "Search for a Theory" (note 36), p. 549.

44 Peter Eisenman, "From Object to Relationship: The Casa del Fascio by Terragni," in *Casabella*, 344 (January 1970), p. 38.

45 The first essay of this title, which were footnotes below a blank (conceptual) text, appeared in *Design Quarterly* in 1970. The full article appeared in *Casabella*, 359–360 (November–December 1971), pp. 49–57.

46 The first (limited) edition was *Five Architects: Eisenman, Graves Gwathmey, Hejduk, Meier* (New York: George Wittenborn & Co., 1972); citations are from the 1975 reprint (New York: Oxford University Press).

47 Ken Frampton, interview with Stan Allen and Hal Foster, in *October*, 106 (Fall 2003), p. 42.

48 Kenneth Frampton, "Frontality vs. Rotation," *Five Architects* (note 46), p. 12.

49 Colin Rowe, Introduction, *Five Architects* (note 46), p. 4.

50 Rowe, Introduction (note 46), pp. 5–7.

51 For a history of the publication, see Joan Ockman, "Resurrecting the Avant-Garde: The History and Program of *Oppositions*," in Beatriz Colomina, *Architecture Reproduction* (New York: Princeton Architectural Press, 1998), pp. 180–199.

52 "Editorial Statement," *Oppositions*, 1 (1973), n.p.

53 See Manfredo Tafuri, "*L'Architecture dans le boudoir*: The Language of Criticism and the Criticism of Language," trans. Victor Caliandro, *Oppositions*, 3 (May 1974). This essay was based on a lecture he gave at Princeton University in the spring of 1974.

2   The Crisis of Meaning

1 Charles W. Morris, "Foundations of the Theory of Signs," in *International Encyclopedia of Unified Science*, vol. 1, no. 2 (Chicago: University of Chicago Press, 1939), pp. 91, 99, 108; see also C. Hartshorne and P. Weiss (eds),

The Collected Papers of Charles Sanders Peirce, 8 vols. (Cambridge, MA: Harvard University Press, 1974).

2 Charles Morris, "Intellectual Integration," typewritten manuscript in the archives of the Institute of Design, University of Illinois at Chicago, Box 3, folder 64. On the program of the New Bauhaus and its successor, the Institute of Design, see Alain Findeli, "Moholy-Nagy's Design Pedagogy in Chicago (1937–46)," in *Design Issues*, 7 (1) (Autumn 1990), pp. 4–19.

3 On the history of this institution (which closed its doors in 1968), see Herbert Lindinger (ed.), *Ulm Design: The Morality of Objects, Hochschule für Gestaltung Ulm 1953–68*, trans. David Britt (Cambridge, MA: MIT Press, 1991), and René Spitz, *hfg ulm: The View Behind the Foreground* (Stuttgart: Axel Menges, 2002).

4 Tomás Maldonado, "Notes on Communication," *Uppercase*, 5 (1962), p. 5.

5 The five articles by Maldonado and Giu Bonsiepe appeared in *Uppercase*, 5, edited by Theo Crosby. Maldonado had earlier published his essay "Communication and Semiotics in the trilingual publication *Ulm* 5 (1959).

6 Joseph Rykwert, "Meaning and Building," *Zodiac 6: International Magazine of Contemporary Architecture* (1960), pp. 193–196. In a reprint of the essay in *The Necessity of Artifice* (1982), Rykwert pointed out that what he meant by "semantic study" was "Charles Saunders Peirce's restatement of Locke's postulated science of signs."

7 Christian Norberg-Schulz, *Intentions in Architecture* (London: Allen & Unwin, 1963). Cited from the paperback edition (Cambridge, MA: MIT Press, 1968), pp. 99, 188, 104n.87.

8 See Sergio Bettini, "Semantic Criticism; and the Historical Continuity of European Architecture," *Zodiac 2: International Magazine of Contemporary Architecture* (1958); Giovanni Klaus Koenig, *Analisi del linguaggio architettonico* (Florence: Liberia editrice Fiorentina, 1964); Renato De Fusco, *Architettura come mass medium: Note per una semiologia architettonica* (Bari: Dedalo, 1967); Umberto Eco, *La struttura assente: Introduzione alla ricerca semiologica* (Milan: Bompiani, 1968).

9 George Baird, "'La Dimension Amoureuse' in Architecture," in Charles Jencks & George Baird (eds.), *Meaning in Architecture* (London: Design Yearbook Limited, 1969), pp. 78–99.

10 Charles Jencks, "Semiology and Architecture," in Charles Jencks and George Baird (eds), *Meaning in Architecture* (London: Design Yearbook Limited, 1969), pp. 10–25.

11 The papers were published by Tomás Llorens in Spanish in *Arquitectura, historia y teoria de los signos: El symposium de Castelldefels* (Barcelona: La Gay Ceincia, 1974). For an extended discussion of the conference, see Louis Martin, "The Search for a Theory in Architecture: Anglo-American Debates, 1957–1976" (PhD dissertation Princeton University, 2002), pp. 671–690.

12 Geoffrey Broadbent, "The Deep Structures of Architecture," in G. Broadbent, R. Bunt, and C. Jencks (eds), *Signs, Symbols, and Architecture* (Chichester: John Wiley & Sons, Ltd, 1980), pp. 119–168.

13   Juan Pablo Bonta, "Notes for a Theory of Meaning in Design," in Broadbent, Bunt, and Jencks, *Signs* (note 12), pp. 274–310; *Architecture and Its Interpretation: A Study of Expressive Systems in Architecture* (New York: Rizzoli, 1979). Bonta does not yet use the term "pseudo signals" in his earlier paper.

14   Charles Jencks, "Rhetoric in Architecture," *AAQ: Architectural Association Quarterly*, 4 (3) (Summer 1972), pp. 4–17. Reprinted in Broadbent, Bunt, and Jencks, *Signs* (note 12), p. 17.

15   Alan Colquhoun, "Historicism and the Limits of Semiology," in *Essays in Architectural Criticism: Modern Architecture and Historical Change* (Cambridge, MA: MIT Press, 1985), pp. 129–138. The essay first appeared in *Op. Cit.* (September 1972).

16   Mario Gandelsonas, "Semiotics as a Tool for Theoretical Development," in Wolfgang F. E. Preiser (ed.), *Environmental Design Research: Symposia and Workshops*, Vol. 2 (Stroudsburg, PA: Dowden, Hutchinson & Ross, 1973), pp. 324–329.

17   D. Agrest and M. Gandelsonas, "Semiotics and Architecture: Ideological Consumption or Theoretical Work," *Oppositions*, 1 (1973), pp. 93–100.

18   Umberto Eco, "Function and Sign: The Semiotics of Architecture," in Broadbent, Bunt, and Jencks, *Signs* (note 12), pp. 11–69. The chapters first appeared in English in *VIA: The Student Publication of the Graduate School of Fine Arts* (University of Pennsylvania) 2 (1973), pp. 130–150.

19   Robert A. M. Stern and Architectural League of New York, *40 under 40: An Exhibition of Young Talent in Architecture* (New York: Architectural League of New York, 1966).

20   Robert A. M. Stern, *New Directions in American Architecture* (New York: George Braziller, 1969).

21   "Five on Five," *Architectural Forum*, 138 (4) (May 1973), pp. 46–57. The titles of the individual essays were Robert Stern, "Stompin' at the Savoye"; Jaquelin Robertson, "Machines in the Garden"; Charles Moore, "In Similar States of Undress"; Allan Greenberg, "The Lurking American Legacy"; and Romaldo Giurgola, "The Discreet Charm of the Bourgeoisie."

22   Stern, "Stompin' at the Savoye" (note 21), pp. 46–48.

23   Greenberg, "The Lurking American Legacy" (note 21), p. 55; Giurgola, "The Discreet charm of the Bourgeoisie" (note 21), p. 57.

24   Charles Moore, "In Similar States of Undress" (note 21), p. 53.

25   Robertson, "Machines in the Garden" (note 21), p. 53.

26   Editorial preface to "Five on Five" (note 21) p. 46.

27   Paul Goldberger, "Should Anyone Care About the 'New York Five'? … Or About Their Critics, The 'Five on Five'?" *Architectural Record* (February 1974), p. 113–114.

28   "White, Gray, Silver, Crimson," News Report in *Progressive Architecture* (July 1974), p. 30.

29   "White and Gray," *a + u: Architecture and Urbanism*, 4 (52) (1975), pp. 25–80.

30 Colin Rowe, "Collage City," *Architectural Review*, 158 (942) (August 1975), p. 81. A portion of this text also appeared in the *A + U: Architecture and Urbanism* cited in note 29. Although many of the images were the same, the text was rewritten in Rowe and Fred Koetter's book, *Collage City* (Cambridge, MA: MIT Press, 1978).

31 Arthur Drexler, Preface to (exhibition catalog) *The Architecture of the Ecole des Beaux-Arts* (New York: Museum of Modern Art, 1975), pp. 3–4.

32 Arthur Drexler (ed.), *The Architecture of the Ecole des Beaux-Arts* (New York: Museum of Modern Art, 1977), pp. 50–51.

33 Robert Middleton, "Vive l'Ecole," *Architectural Design*, 48, (11/12) (1978), p. 38.

34 Ada Louise Huxtable, "The Gospel According to Giedion and Gropius is under Attack," *New York Times*, June 27, 1976.

35 George Baird, in William Ellis (ed.), "Forum: The Beaux-Arts Exhibition," *Oppositions*, 8 (Spring 1977), p. 160.

36 Ellis, "Forum" (note 35), pp. 162 & 164.

37 Ellis, "Forum" (note 35), pp. 165–166.

38 Mario Gandelsonas, Editorial, "Post-Functionalism," *Oppositions*, 5 (Summer 1976), n.p.

39 Peter Eisenman, Editorial, "Post-Functionalism," *Oppositions*, 6 (Fall 1976), n.p.

40 Eisenman, Editorial, (note 39), n.p.

41 Charles Jencks, "The Los Angeles Silvers," *a + u: Architecture and Urbanism*, 5 (70) (October 1976), p. 14.

42 The term is a political reference to the trial of the "Chicago Seven," which stemmed from the disruption of the Democratic Party Convention in Chicago in 1968.

43 Oswald W. Grube, Peter C. Pran, and Franz Schulze, *100 Years of Architecture in Chicago: Continuity of Structure and Form*, trans. David Norris (Chicago: Follett Publications Co., 1976). The exhibition took place at the Museum of Contemporary Art, Chicago.

44 Stuart Cohen and Stanley Tigerman, *Chicago Architects* (Chicago: Swallow Press, 1976).

45 See the exhibition catalogue, *Seven Chicago Architects: Beeby, Booth, Cohen, Freed, Nagle, Tigerman, Weese* (Chicago: Richard Grey Gallery, 1977). On the exhibition "Exquisite Corpse," see *A + U: Architecture and Urbanism*, 7 (93) (June 1978), pp. 96–104. The colloquium took place October 25–26, 1977, at the Graham Foundation and at IIT's Crown Hall. Audio tapes of the event, from which Toshio Nakamura hoped to produce published transcripts of the proceedings, were unfortunately lost. On the "Chicago Seven," see the Vance bibliography prepared by Lamia Doumato, "Chicago Seven," National Gallery of Art, Bibliography, A 792 (1982).

46 The two volumes devoted to the Chicago Tribune competition documented the original *Tribune Tower Competition*, appended with a series of *Late Entries*

(New York: Rizzoli, 1980). The exhibition was organized by Stanley Tigerman, Stuart E. Cohen, and Rhona Hoffman.

47   Robert A. M. Stern, "Gray Architecture as Post-Modernism, or, Up and Down from Orthodoxy," *L'Architecture d'aujourd'hui*, 186 (August–September 1976); the original English version of the article was lost but was reconstructed for K. Michael Hays (ed.), *Architecture Theory since 1968* (Cambridge, MA: MIT Press, 2000), pp. 242–243.

48   Stern, "Gray Architecture" (note 47), p. 245.

49   Robert A. M. Stern, "New Directions in Modern American Architecture; Postscript at the Edge of Modernism," *AAQ*, 9, (2–3) (1977), pp. 66–71.

3   Early Postmodernism

1   Joseph Hudnut, "The Post-Modern House," *Architectural Record*, 97 (May 1945), pp. 70–75.

2   Nikolaus Pevsner, "Architecture in Our Time: The Anti-Pioneers," *The Listener*, 29 (12) (1966).

3   Charles Jencks, "A Genealogy of Post-Modern Architecture," *A.D. Profile*, 4 (1977), p. 269.

4   See Joseph Rykwert, "Ornament is no Crime," in *Studio International*, 190 (October 1975), pp. 91–97, republished in *The Necessity of Artifice* (New York: Rizzoli, 1982), p. 97. In remarks prefacing the reprint of the essay in 1982, Rykwert apologized for the "unfortunate and precocious use of the term," which in fact was intended in the opposite sense to the later meaning of the word.

5   See Charles Jencks, "The Rise of Post Modern Architecture," *AQ: Architectural Association Quarterly*, 7 (4) (October/December 1975), pp. 3–14. See also his prefatory comments to "Post-Modern History," *A. D. Profiles*, 1 (1978), p. 14.

6   Charles Jencks, *Modern Movements in Architecture* (Garden City, NY: Anchor Books, 1973).

7   Charles Jencks and Nathan Silver, *Adhocism: The Case for Improvisation* (New York: Doubleday, 1972).

8   Charles Jencks, "Ersatz in LA," *Architectural Design*, 43 (September 1973), pp. 596–601.

9   Jencks, "Post Modern Architecture" (note 5), p. 3.

10 Jencks, "Post Modern Architecture," (note 5) p. 10. On the similarity to Donaldson, see "Preliminary Discourse before the University College of London" (1842), in Harry Francis Mallgrave (ed.), *Architectural Theory: An Anthology from Vitruvius to 1870* (Oxford: Blackwell Publishing, 2006), I: 478.

11 Charles A. Jencks, *The Language of Post-Modern Architecture* (New York: Rizzoli Interrnational, 1977), p. 9.

12 Giedion used this term to counsel the reader in a "Preliminary Remark" to *Bauen in Frankreich, Bauen in Eisen, Bauen in Eisenbeton* (Leipzig: Klinkhardt & Biermann, 1928).

13 Jencks, *Language* (note 11), p. 43.

14 Jencks, *Language* (note 11), p. 83.

15 Jencks, *Language* (note 11), p. 97.

16 Jencks, *Language* (note 11), p. 101.

17 Charles Moore, "On Post-Modernism," *A.D. Profile*, 4 (1977), p. 255.

18 Paul Goldberger, "Post-Modernism: An Introduction," *A.D. Profile*, 4 (1977), p. 260.

19 Geoffrey Broadbent, "The Language of Post-Modern Architecture: A Review," *A.D. Profile*, 4 (1977), p. 272.

20 Charles Jencks, "The 'Tradition' of Post-Modern Architecture," *Inland Architect* (November 1977), pp. 14–23, (December 1977), pp. 6–15.

21 Jencks, " 'Tradition' " (note 20), pp. 19–22.

22 Jencks, " 'Tradition' " (note 20), p. 19. For critical reviews of Jencks's term or alternatives, see C. Ray Smith, *Supermannerism: New Attitudes in Post-Modern Architecture* (New York: E. P. Dutton, 1977); Michael McMordie, review of *The Language of Post-Modern Architecture*, *Journal of the Society of Architectural Historians*, 38 (4) (December 1979), p. 404; and *CRIT 4: The Architectural Student Journal* (Fall 1978), which contain the three articles of Christian K. Laine, "The Freeze of Architectural Thought"; Jeffrey M. Chusid, "The Failures of Postmodernism: Escaping into Style"; and Shelly Kappe, "Postmodernism, An Historicism Hype: A New Elitism Masquerading as Popularism." See also, Conrad Jameson, "Modern Architecture as an Ideology: Being the Sociological Analysis of a Radical Traditionalist," *AAQ: Architectural Association Quarterly*, 7 (4) (October/December 1975), pp. 15–21.

23 Paolo Portoghesi, "The End of Prohibitionism," in Gabriella Borsano (ed.), *Architecture 1980: The Presence of the Past, Venice Biennale* (New York: Rizzoli, 1980), p. 9.

24 Vincent Scully, "How Things Got To Be the Way They Are Now," in Borsano, *Architecture 1980*, pp. 15–20.

25 Charles Jencks, "Toward Radical Eclecticism," in Borsano, *Architecture 1980*, pp. 30–37.

26 Tom Wolfe, *From Bauhaus to Our House* (New York: Farrar Straus Giroux, 1981).

27 Manfredo Tafuri, *History of Italian Architecture, 1944–1985*, trans. Jessica Levine (Cambridge, MA: MIT Press, 1989); originally published as *Storia dell'architettura italiana, 1944–1985* (Turin: Giulio Einaudi, 1986).

28 Tafuri, *Italian Architecture* (note 27), pp. 190–192.

29 Rob Krier, *Urban Space* (New York: Rizzoli, 1979). See also his follow-up study, *On Architecture* (London: Academy Editions/St. Martin's Press, 1982).

30   Robert L. Delevoy, "Diagonal: Towards an Architecture," in *Rational Architecture: The Reconstruction of the European City* (Brussels: Archives d'Architecture Moderne, 1978), p. 15.

31   Anthony Vidler, "The Third Typology," in *Rational Architecture* (note 30), pp. 31–32. The essay also appeared in *Oppositions 7* (Winter 1976).

32   Léon Krier, "The Reconstruction of the City," in *Rational Architecture* (note 30), pp. 40–41.

33   Léon Krier, "The Blind Spot," *AD Profiles* 12, *"Urban Transformations,"* 48 (4) (1978), pp. 219–221.

34   See, "The Brussels Declaration: Reconstruction of the European City," trans. Karl Kropf, in Charles Jencks and Karl Kropf, *Theories and Manifestoes of Contemporary Architecture* (Chichester: Wiley-Academy, 2006), pp. 176–177.

35   Maurice Culot and Léon Krier, "The Only Path for Architecture," trans. Christian Hubert, *Oppositions*, 14 (Fall 1978), pp. 40–43.

36   Maurice Culot, "Reconstructing the City in Stone," trans. S. Day, in Charles Jencks and Karl Kropf, *Theories and Manifestoes* (note 34), p. 178.

4   Modernism Abides

1   On the life and work of Khan, see Yasmin Sabina Khan, *Engineering Architecture: The Vision of Fazlur R. Khan* (New York: W. W. Norton & Company, 2004). See also the remarks of Bruce Graham, in Betty J. Blum (Interviewer), *Oral History of Bruce John Graham*, The Art Institute of Chicago (May 25–28, 1997) p. 125.

2   For a biographical account of Myron Goldsmith, see his oral history in Betty J. Blum (Interviewer), *Oral History of Myron Goldsmith*, The Art Institute of Chicago (July 25–26, September 7, October 5, 1986). See also, Edward Windhorst, *High-Rise and Long-Span Research at Illinois Institute of Technology: The Legacy of Myron Goldsmith and David C. Sharpe* (Chicago: Illinois Institute of Technology, 2010).

3   For a discussion of the "tube" concept, see Inaki Abalos and Juan Herreros, *Tower and Office: From Modernist Theory to Contemporary Practice* (Cambridge, MA: MIT Press, 2003), pp. 54–70. See also, Myron Goldsmith, David C. Sharpe, and Mahjoub Elnimeiri, "Architectural-Structural Integration," in Paul J. Armstrong (ed.), *Architecture of Tall Buildings: Council of Tall Buildings and Urban Habitat* (New York: McGraw-Hill, 1995), pp. 102–106.

4   Myron Goldsmith, "The Tall Building: The Effects of Scale" (Thesis Project, Illinois Institute of Technology, 1953). The essay, "The Effects of Scale," was later reprinted in an expanded version in Myron Goldsmith, *Buildings and Concepts*, ed. Werner Blaser (New York: Rizzoli, 1987), pp. 8–22. Goldsmith, in his oral history, later noted that "at the time I considered the diagonally braced steel building more important" than his main concrete design. See Blum, *Oral History of Myron Goldsmith* (note 3), p. 59.

5 See Edward Windhorst and Kevin Harrington, *Lake Point Tower: A Design History* (Chicago: Chicago Architecture Foundation, 2009).

6 Sasaki's design is published in Windhorst, *High-Rise and Long-Span Research* (note 2), pp. 20–21.

7 One experiment, in fact, involved Phyllis Lambert's top-floor unit at the nearby Mies tower. Ms Lambert, the current director of the Canadian Centre for Architecture, was a student at IIT at the time.

8 A. G. Krishna Menon, "A Ninety Story Apartment Building Using an Optimized Concrete Structure" (thesis project, Illinois Institute of Technology, 1966). The project was also published in Windhorst, *High-Rise and Long-Span Research* (note 2), pp. 26–27.

9 See Yasmin Sabina Khan, *Engineering Architecture* (note 1), p. 225.

10 Khan, *Engineering Architecture* (note 1), pp. 222–225.

11 The most comprehensive discussion of Otto and his work is found in Winfried Nerdinger (ed.), *Frei Otto Complete Works: Lightweight Construction Natural Design* (Basel: Birkhäuser, 2005).

12 Frei Otto, *Das hängende Dach: Gestalt und Struktur* (Berlin: Bauwelt-Verlag, 1954).

13 Frei Otto, *Zugbeanspruchte Konstruktionen: Gestalt, Struktur und Berechnung von Bauten aus Seilen, Netzen und Membranen* (Frankfurt/M: Verlag Ullstein, 1962). The second volume appeared in 1966.

14 Dietmar M. Steiner, "New German Architecture in the International Context," in Ullrich Schwarz (ed.), *New German Architecture: A Reflexive Modernism* (Ostfildern-Ruit: Hatje Cantz Verlag, 2002), p. 343.

15 For a comprehensive discussion of Otto's contribution to this project, see Mick Eekhout, "Frei Otto and the Munich Olympic Games: From the Measuring Experimental Models to the Computer Determination of the Pattern," in *Zodiac 21* (1974), pp. 12–73.

16 See especially Christian Brensing, "Frei Otto and Ove Arup: A Case of Mutual Inspiration" and Michael Dickson, "Frei Otto and Ted Happold: 1967–1996 and Beyond," in Nerdinger, *Frei Otto Complete Works* (note 11), pp. 102–123. See also "Lennart Grut, Ted Happold and Peter Rice Discuss Frei Otto and His Work," in *Architectural Design* (March 1971), pp. 144–155. See also Peter Rice's comments on Otto in *Peter Rice: An Engineer Imagines* (London: Artemis, 1994), pp. 25, 66, 95; and Michael Dickson, "The Lightweight Structures Laboratory," *The Arup Journal* (March 1975), pp. 11ff.

17 Frei Otto, "Biology and Building," *IL 3* (October 15, 1971), p. 7.

18 Frei Otto and Bodo Rasch, *Finding Form: Towards an Architecture of the Minimal* (Munich: Edition Axel Menges, 1995), trans. Michael Robinson, p. 15.

19 Otto and Rasch, *Finding Form* (note 18), p. 17.

20 Frei Otto, "Pneus in Nature and Technics," *IL 9* (September 28, 1977), p. 22.

21 Otto, "Pneus in Nature" (note 20), p. 13.

22 *IL 14*, "Adaptable Architecture" (December 29, 1975), p. 166.

23   For a history of Arup and the office, see Peter Jones, *Ove Arup: Masterbuilder of the Twentieth Century* (New Haven: Yale University Press, 2006). The attribution of the idea to Arup is made by Peter Jones, although it was earlier countered by Yuzo Mikami, in *Utzon's Sphere* (Tokyo: Shoku Kusha, 2001).

24   For details of Rogers's life and work, see Bryan Appleyard, *Richard Rogers: A Biography* (London: Faber and Faber, 1986).

25   For details of his life and work, see Martin Pawley, *Norman Foster: A Global Architecture* (London: Universe Publishing, 1999), and Malcolm Quantrill, *The Norman Foster Studio: Consistency through Diversity* (London: E & FN Spon, 1999).

26   Reyner Banham, *Megastructure: Urban Futures of the Recent Past* (New York: Harper & Rowe, 1976), p. 212. See also Peter Rice, *An Engineer Imagines* (London: Artemis, 1994), pp. 25–46. Rice refers to the building as an "information machine."

27   Alan Colquhoun, "Plateau Beaubourg," in Alan Colquhoun, *Essays in Architectural Criticism: Modern Architecture and Historical Change* (Cambridge, MA: MIT Press, 1985), pp. 112, 114.

28   Kenneth Powell, *Lloyd's Building: Richard Rogers Partnership* (London: Phaidon Press, 1994), pp. 6, 29. Rogers also discusses its energy efficiency in *Cities for a Small Planet* (Boulder: Westview Press, 1998), pp. 96–97.

29   Norman Foster, "Design for Living," *BP Shield* (March 1969); cited from *Foster Associates: Recent Works* (London: Academy Editions/ St. Martin's Press, 1992), p. 25.

30   See Ian Lambot, *Norman Foster, Foster Associates: Buildings and Projects*, Vol. 2, 1971–1978 (Hong Kong: Watermark, 1989), pp. 58–59.

31   Kisho Kurokawa, *Metabolism in Architecture* (London: Studio Vista, 1977), p. 25.

32   Kiyonori Kikutake *et al.*, Preface, *Metabolism: Proposals for New Urbanism* (Tokyo: Bijutu Syuppan Sha, 1960).

33   Kurokawa, *Metabolism in Architecture* (note 31), pp. 92–94.

34   Kurokawa, *Metabolism in Architecture* (note 31), p. 87.

35   Kurokawa, *Metabolism in Architecture* (note 31), pp. 67–74.

36   Kurokawa, *Metabolism in Architecture* (note 31), pp. 75–85.

37   See Kisho Kurokawa, "Media Space, or En-Space, in *Metabolism in Architecture* (note 33), pp. 171–179; "The Philosophy of Coexistence," *Japan Architect*, 247 (October–November 1977), pp. 30–31; "The Philosophy of Symbiosis: From Internationalism to Interculturalism," *Process: Architecture*, 66 (March 1986), pp. 48–55; "Le Poétique in Architecture: Beyond Semiotics," *Process: Architecture*, 66 (March 1986), pp. 153–159; "The Architecture of Symbiosis," in *Kisho Kurokawa: The Architecture of Symbiosis* (New York: Rizzoli, 1988), pp. 11–19.

38   Kisho Kurokawa, "The Philosophy of Symbiosis: From Internationalism to Interculturalism," in *Process* (note 37), p. 52. The "Desiring-Machines" is the first chapter of Gilles Deleuze and Félix Guattari's *Anti-Oedipus: Capitalism and Schizophrenia*.

39   Kisho Kurakawa, "The Architecture of Symbiosis" (note 37), p. 97.

40 The "New Wave in Japanese Architecture" seems to have been a term first invoked by Kazuhiro Ishii and Hiroyuki Suzuki in *Japan Architect*, 247 (October–November, 1977), pp. 8–11. It was also employed by Kenneth Frampton for the exhibition *New Wave of Japanese Architecture*, Catalogue 10 (New York: Institute for Architecture and Urban Studies, 1978).

41 Botond Bognar, *Contemporary Japanese Architecture: Its Development and Challenge* (New York: Van Nostrand Reinhold, 1985), p. 183.

42 Charles Jencks, "Isozaki's Paradoxical Cube," in *Japan Architect*, 229 (March 1976), p. 49.

43 Arata Isozaki, "From Manner, to Rhetoric, to ...," in *Japan Architect*, 230 (April 1976), p. 64. See also "About My Method," in *Japan Architect*, 188 August 1972), pp. 22–28.

44 See David B. Stewart's discussion of Isozaki's seven operations in *The Making of a Modern Japanese Architecture: 1868 to the Present* (Tokyo: Kodansha International, 1987), pp. 240–241.

45 Isozaki, "From Manner, to Rhetoric, to ..." (note 43), p. 65.

46 Fumihiko Maki, "Movement Systems in the City, *Connection* (Winter 1966), pp. 6–13.

47 Fuhihiko Maki, "An Environmental Approach to Architecture," in *Japan Architect* (March 1973), pp. 19–22.

48 Fumihiko Maki, "At the Beginning of the Last Quarter of the Century: Reflections of a Japanese Architect," *Japan Architect*, 219 (April 1975), pp. 19–22.

49 Fumihiko Maki, "On the Possibilities of Twilight," in *Japan Architect*, 249 (January 1978), p. 5.

50 Fumihiko Maki, "Reflections on the Design," in *Japan Architect*, 219 (April 1975), p. 30.

51 Fumihiko Maki, *An Aesthetics of Fragmentation* (New York: Rizzoli, 1988), p. 51.

52 Fumihiko Maki, "City, Image, Materiality" (1986), in *An Aesthetics* (note 51), pp. 12.

53 Maki, "City, Image, Materiality" (1986), in *An Aesthetics* (note 51), p. 11, 15.

54 Christopher Alexander, Murray Silverstein, Shlomo Angel, Sara Ishikawa, and Denny Abrams, *The Oregon Experiment* (New York: Oxford University Press, 1975); Christopher Alexander, Sara Ishikawa, Murray Silverstein with Max Jacobson, Ingrid Fiksdahl-King, and Shlomo Angel, *A Pattern Language: Towns, Buildings, Construction* (New York: Oxford University Press, 1977); Christopher Alexander, *The Timeless Way of Building* (New York: Oxford University Press, 1979).

55 Alexander, *The Timeless Way* (note 54), p. 229.

56 Herman Hertzberger, "Homework for More Hospitable Form," *Forum*, XXIV (33) (1973).

57 The first edition, *Gourna: A Tale of Two Villages* (Cairo: Ministry of Culture, 1969), was not widely circulated. See *Architecture for the Poor* (Chicago: University of Chicago Press, 1973).

5   Postmodernism and Critical Regionalism

1   See Emilio Ambasz (ed.), *Precursors of Post-Modernism: Milan 1920s–30s* (New York: The Architectural League, 1982).

2   Editorial, *The Harvard Architecture Review*, 1 (Spring, 1980), p. 6.

3   Robert A. M. Stern, "The Doubles of Post-Modern," *The Harvard Architecture Review*, 1 (Spring 1980), pp. 84–86.

4   Michael Graves, "A Case for Figurative Architecture," in *Michael Graves, Buildings and Projects: 1966–1981* (New York: Rizzoli, 1982), p. 13.

5   Charles Jencks, *What is Postmodernism?* (London: Academy Editions, 1986), cited from 1987 revised 2nd edition, p. 14.

6   Jencks, *What is Postmodernism?* (note 5), p. 28.

7   Jencks, *What is Postmodernism?* (note 5), pp. 20–22.

8   Jencks, *What is Postmodernism?* (note 5), p. 32.

9   Charles Jencks, *What is Postmodernism?* (London, Academy Editions, revised 3rd edition, 1989), p. 58.

10   Heinrich Klotz, *The History of Postmodern Architecture*, trans. Radka Donnel (Cambridge, MA: MIT Press, 1988), p. 425.

11   Klotz, *Postmodern Architecture* (note 10), p. 434.

12   Aldo van Eyck, "Rats Posts and Pests," *RIBA Journal*, vol. 88, #4 (April 1981), p. 47.

13   Van Eyck cites from a letter that he says he received from the editors of a book in preparation, *Why is British Architecture so Lousy?* The project seems to have been diverted or abandoned. The accuracy of Krier's statement cannot be verified.

14   Van Eyck, "Rats Posts and Pests" (note 12), p. 48.

15   Geoffrey Broadbent, "The Pests Strike Back!" *RIBA Journal*, 88 (11) (November 1981), pp. 34.

16   Vittorio Gregotti, editorial "The Obsession with History," *Casabella*, 478 (March 1982), p. 41.

17   Josef-Paul Kleihues, "1984: The Berlin Exhibition, Architectural Dream of Reality?" *Architectural Association Quarterly*, 13 (23) (January–June 1982), p. 38. For a critical analysis of the IBA program, see Diane Ghirardo, *Architecture after Modernism* (London: Thames and Hudson, 1996), pp. 108–130.

18   Richard Streiter, "Aus München" (1896), in Richard Streiter, *Ausgewählte Schriften zu Aesthetik und Kunst-Geschichte* (Munich: Delphin, 1913). For a discussion of Streiter, see Harry Francis Mallgrave, *Modern Architectural Theory: A Historical Survey 1673–1968* (New York: Cambridge University Press, 2005), pp. 208–211.

19   James Ford and Katherine Morrow Ford, *The Modern House in America* (New York: Architectural Book Publishing Co., 1940).

20   Katherine Morrow Ford, "Modern is Regional," *House and Garden* (March 1941), pp. 35–37.

21   See Lewis Mumford, Sky Line, "Status Quo," *The New Yorker* (October 11, 1947), pp. 108–109. See also "What is Happening to Modern Architecture?" *Museum of Modern Art Bulletin* 15 (Spring 1948). Both have been reprinted in Vincent B. Canizaro's anthology, *Architectural Regionalism: Collected Writings on Place, Identity, Modernity, and Tradition* (New York: Princeton University Press, 2007). See also, Mallgrave, *Modern Architectural Theory* (note 18), pp. 336–340.

22   The articles are numerous, but see especially Elizabeth Gordon, "The Threat to Next America" *House Beautiful* (April 1953), 126–127; and Joseph Barry, "Report on the American Battle between Good and Bad Modern Houses," *House Beautiful* (May 1953), pp. 172–73, 266–73

23   Harwell Hamilton Harris, "Regionalism and Nationalism," in *Harwell Hamilton Harris: A Collection of His Writings and Buildings*, 14 (5) (School of Design, North Carolina State University, 1965); also reprinted in Canizaro, *Architectural Regionalism* (note 21), pp. 56–65.

24   J. M. Richards, "The New Empiricism: Sweden's Latest Style," *Architectural Review* (101) (June 1947), pp. 199–204.

25   See Bruno Zevi, "A Message to the International Congress of Modern Architecture," in Andrea Oppenheimer Dean's *Bruno Zevi on Modern Architecture* (New York: Rizzoli, 1958), pp. 127–132.

26   Sigfried Giedion, "The State of Contemporary Architecture I: The Regional Approach" in Canizaro, *Architectural Regionalism* (note 21), pp. 311–319.

27   Alexander Tzonis, Liane Lefaivre, Anthony Alofsin, "Das Frage des Regionalismus," in M. Andritzky, L. Burchardt, and O. Hoffmann (eds), *Für eine andere Architektur*, Vol. 1 (Frankfurt: Fischer, 1981), pp. 121–134.

28   Alexander Tzonis and Liane Lefaivre, "The Grid and the Pathway: An Introduction to the Work of Dimitris and Susana Antonakakis. With Prolegomena to a History of the Culture of Modern Greek Architecture," *Architecture in Greece*, Vol. 15 (1981), p. 176.

29   Tzonis and Lefaivre, "The Grid and the Pathway" (note 28), p. 178.

30   Kenneth Frampton, "On Reading Heidegger," *Oppositions*, 4 (October 1974), n.p.

31   Martin Heidegger, "Building Dwelling Thinking," trans. Albert Hofstadter, in *Poetry, Language, Thought* (New York: Harper & Rowe, 1971), pp. 145–161; slightly revised in Martin Heidegger, *Basic Writings* (New York: Harper & Rowe, 1977), pp. 323–339.

32   This was a point made earlier by Heidegger in his essay "The Origin of the Work of Art," *Basic Writings* (note 31), pp. 153–154.

33   Frampton, "On Reading Heidegger" (note 30), n.p.

34   Frampton, "On Reading Heidegger" (note 30), n.p.

35   Christian Norberg-Schulz, *Existence, Space & Architecture* (New York: Praeger Publishers, 1971), p. 7. On his review of Venturi's book, see Mallgrave, *Modern Architectural Theory* (note 18), p. 403.

36   Norberg-Schulz, *Existence, Space & Architecture*, pp. 39–69.

37   Norberg-Schulz, *Existence, Space & Architecture*, p. 114.
38   Christian Norberg Schulz, *Meaning in Western Architecture* (New York: Praeger Publishers, 1975); *Genius Loci: Towards a Phenomenology of Architecture* (New York: Rizzoli, 1980).
39   Kenneth Frampton, "Towards a Critical Regionalism: Six Points for an Architecture of Resistance," in Hal Foster (ed.), *The Anti-Aesthetic: Essays on Postmodern Culture* (Seattle: Bay Press, 1983), p. 19.
40   Frampton, "Towards a Critical Regionalism" (note 39), p. 28.
41   A point Frampton makes in "Ten Points on an Architecture of Regionalism: A Provisional Polemic," in *Center 3: New Regionalism* (Austin: Center for American Architecture and Design, 1987), pp. 20–27. See also Kenneth Frampton, "*Rappel à l'ordre*: The Case for the Tectonic," in *Architectural Design*, 60, (1990), pp. 19–21.
42   Juhani Pallasmaa, "Tradition & Modernity: The Feasibility of Regional Architecture in Post-Modern Society," *Architectural Review*, 188, (1095) (May 1988), pp. 27.
43   Juhani Pallasmaa, "The Geometry of Feeling," *Encounters: Architectural Essays* (Helsinki: Rakennusieto Oy, 2005), pp. 90, 96.
44   Pallasmaa, "Tradition & Modernity" (note 42), p. 34.
45   Rafael Moneo, "Aldo Rossi: the Idea of Architecture and the Modena Cemetery," trans. Angela Giral, *Oppositions*, 5 (1976), cited from K. Michael Hays (ed.), *Oppositions Reader* (New York: Princeton University Press, 1998), p. 122; "Aldo Rossi," *Theoretical Anxiety and Design Strategies in the Work of Eight Architects* (Barcelona: ACTAR, 2004), p. 142.
46   Rafael Moneo, "The Idea of Lasting: A Conversation with Rafael Monel, *Perspecta*, 24 (1988), pp. 148–149.
47   Moneo, "The Idea of Lasting" (note 46), p. 155.
48   Francesco Dal Co and Giuseppe Mazzariol, *Carlo Scarpa: Opera completa* (Milan: Electa, 1984); *Carlo Scarpa: The Complete Works* (New York: Rizzoli, 1984).
49   "Azure block" was a phrase used by Scarpa in referring to the sky. See Carlo Bertelli, "Light and Design," in Dal Co and Mazzariol, *Carlo Scarpa* (note 48), p. 191.
50   Francesco Dal Co, "The Architecture of Carlo Scarpa," in Dal Co and Mazzariol, *Carlo Scarpa* (note 48), p. 42.
51   Marco Frascari, "The Tell-the-Tale Detail," *VIA 7* (Cambridge, MA: MIT Press, 1984), p. 30.

6   Traditionalism and New Urbanism

1   Charles Knevitt first reported this unsuccessful intervention in "Architects Challenge Prince to Think Modern," *The Times* (June 1,1984). See also the story of the fateful day as relayed by Michael Manser, "The Prince and Architects," in *Architectural Design*, 59, (5/6) (1989), p. 17.

2   See the official website for the Prince of Wales, "Speeches and Articles," May 30, 1984, "A Speech by HRH The Prince of Wales at the 150th anniversary of the Royal Institute of British Architects (RIBA), Royal Gala Evening at Hampton Court Palace." An abridged version of this speech, and several others, is conveniently presented by Charles Jencks, in *The Prince, the Architects and the New Wave Monarchy* (London: Academy Editions, 1988), pp. 43–50. Many of the details noted here were earlier reported by Jencks. See also Andreas C. Papadakis, "Prince Charles and the Architectural Debate," *Architectural Design*, 59, (5/6) (1989).

3   "Prince among Architects," *The Times* (June 1, 1984).

4   Quoted in Charles Knevitt, "Architects Challenge Prince to Think Modern," *The Times* (June 1, 1984).

5   Simon Jenkins, *The Sunday Times* (June 3, 1984). Cited from Jencks, *The Prince, the Architects* (note 2), p. 55.

6   Jencks, *The Prince, the Architects* (note 2), p. 56.

7   Michael Manser, "The Art of Building the Perfect Marriage," *The Sunday Times* (June 10, 1984). Cited from Jencks, *The Prince, the Architects* (note 2), p. 52.

8   Richard Rogers, Letter to *The Times* (June 9, 1984).

9   Speech to the Institute of Directors, February 26, 1985. Cited from Charles Jencks, *The Prince, the Architects* (note 2), p. 44.

10 Speech on the occasion of The Times/RIBA awards for Community Architecture, June 13, 1986. Cited from Charles Jencks, *The Prince, the Architects* (note 2), p. 45.

11 Speech given to the Building Communities Conference, November 27, 1986. Cited from Charles Jencks, *The Prince, the Architects* (note 2), p. 46.

12 On the history of this site and the early debate, see the various articles in Andreas C. Papadakis, "Paternoster Square and the New Classical Tradition," *Architectural Design*, 62 (5/6), May–June 1992.

13 The author of the master plan (1956) was the architect and planner Lord Holford.

14 The six unsuccessful schemes were presented by Francis Duffy, "Power to the City: Paternoster," in *The Architectural Review*, 183 (1091) (January 1988).

15 See the official website for the Prince of Wales, "Speeches and Articles," May 30, 1984, "A speech by HRH The Prince of Wales at the Corporation of London Planning and Communication Committee's Annual Dinner, Mansion House, London, 1 December 1987." See also Jencks, *The Prince, the Architects* (note 2), pp. 47–49.

16 Jencks, *The Prince, the Architects* (note 2), pp. 47–49.

17 See Charles Jencks, "Ethics and Prince Charles," in Papadakis, "Prince Charles and the Architectural Debate" (note 2), p. 26.

18 Of the several presentations of this scheme, see "Public Design," *Architects' Journal*, 187 (27) (July 6, 1988), pp. 24–26.

19 "Public Design," (note 18), p. 24.

20   The Simpson scheme was then advanced to another variation, see "Paternoster Square and the New Classical Tradition," *Architectural Design* (May–June 1992). In 1996 this revised scheme was supplanted by another master plan by William Whitfield, which became the basis for the realized project.

21   On the first presentation of this project, see Léon Krier, "Master Plan for Poundbury Development in Dorchester," in Papadakis, "Prince Charles and the Architectural Debate," (note 2), pp. 46–55.

22   Compare Charles Jencks's account of Prince Charles's position in Jencks, *The Prince, The Architects* (note 2) with his "Ethics and Prince Charles," in Papadakis, "Prince Charles and the Architectural Debate" (note 2), pp. 24–29.

23   Richard Rogers, "Pulling down the Prince," *The Times* (July 3, 1989). Cited from Papadakis, "Prince Charles and the Architectural Debate" (note 2), p. 67.

24   Norman Foster, "The Force for Good but the Wrong Target," *The Sunday Times* (December 6, 1987). Cited from Jencks, *The Prince, The Architects* (note 2), p. 54.

25   See Cantacuzino's letter to the Editor, *The Times* (June 6, 1984).

26   Introduction to Charles, Prince of Wales, *A Vision of Britain: A Personal View of Architecture* (London: Doubleday, 1989), p. 9.

27   Charles, Prince of Wales, *A Vision of Britain* (note 26), pp. 10–11.

28   Charles, Prince of Wales, *A Vision of Britain* (note 26), p. 77.

29   Prince Charles's love for the history and the traditions of Britain compose a strong mantra throughout the book.

30   Charles, Prince of Wales, *A Vision of Britain* (note 26), p. 143.

31   Roger K. Lewis, "Florida Developer Tries a Variation on Old Concept of a New Town," *The Washington Post*, (December 6, 1986), p. E14.

32   Steve Garbarino, "Cracker: Rustic Native Style Makes a Comeback because, in this Climate, It Makes Sense," *St. Petersburg Times* (July 12, 1987), p. H1.

33   Joseph Giovannini, "The Nation: Today's Planners Want to Go Home Again; In the suburbs: Bringing Back Front Porches, Town Squares," *The New York Times* (December 13, 1987), sect. 4, p. 6.

34   Philip Langdon, "A Good Place to Live, *The Atlantic Monthly*, 261 (3) (March 1988), pp. 39–60.

35   Langdon, "A Good Place to Live (note 34), p. 39.

36   Langdon, "A Good Place to Live (note 34), p. 46.

37   Langdon, "A Good Place to Live (note 34), p. 46. On the work of Nolen, see his *New Towns for Old: Achievements in Civic Improvements in some American Small Towns and Neighborhoods*, reprint (Boston: University of Massachusetts Press, 2005); and Millard F. Rogers Jr, *John Nolen and Mariemont: Building a New Town in Ohio* (Baltimore: Johns Hopkins University Press, 2001).

38   John Nolan, "What is Needed in American City Planning?" (1909), address to the first National City Planning Conference, Washington, DC. Cited from Bruce Stephenson's interesting essay, "The Roots of the New Urbanism: John Nolen's Garden City Ethic," *Journal of Planning History*, 1 (2) (2002), p. 104.

39 Sim Van der Ryn and Peter Calthorpe (eds), *Sustainable Communities: A New Design Synthesis for Cities, Suburbs, and Towns* (San Francisco: Sierra Club Books, 1986).

40 See Peter Calthorpe, "Pedestrian Pockets: New Strategies for Suburban Growth," in Doug Kelbaugh (ed.), *The Pedestrian Pocket Book: A New Suburban Design Strategy* (New York: Princeton Architectural Press, 1989), p. 11.

41 Doug Kelbaugh, Preface, in *The Pedestrian Pocket Book* (note 40), p. vii.

42 Kurt Andersen, "Oldfangled New Towns," *Time Magazine* (May 20, 1991).

43 Peter Calthorpe, *The Next American Metropolis: Ecology, Community, and the American Dream* (New York: Princeton Architectural Press, 1993).

44 For the debate and its postscripts, see Cynthia C. Davidson (ed.), *Architecture New York*, 1 (July/August, 1993), pp. 28–38.

45 The founding moments in the creation of New Urbanism are discussed in two introductory essays by Stefanos Polyzoides and Elizabeth Moule in Todd W. Bressi (ed.), *The Seaside Debates: A Critique of New Urbanism* (New York: Rizzoli, 2002).

46 The Ahwahnee Principles appear as essays by Peter Calthorpe, Andrés Duany, and Elizabeth Plater-Zyberk, and Elizabeth Moule and Stefanos Polyzoides, in Peter Katz, *The New Urbanism: Toward an Architecture of Community* (New York: McGraw-Hill, 1994), pp. xi–xxiv.

47 Elizabeth Moule, "The Charter of the New Urbanism," in Bressi, *The Seaside Debates* (note 45), p. 21.

48 Congress for the New Urbanism, *Charter of the New Urbanism* (New York: McGraw-Hill, 2000), p. v–vi.

49 Randall Arendt (Principle Two), Ken Greenberg (Principle Twenty-Seven), Myron Orfield (Principle Nine), in "Charter of the New Urbanism" (note 47), pp. 29–34, 173–175, and 64–69.

50 Douglas Kelbaugh (Principle Twenty-Four) and Mark M. Schimmenti (Principle Twenty-Seven), in "Charter of the New Urbanism" (note 47), pp. 155–159, 169–171.

51 Vincent Scully, Afterword, "The Architecture of Community," in Peter Katz, *The New Urbanism* (note 51), p. 230.

7 Gilded Age of Theory

1 On the Frankfurt School, see Rolf Wiggershaus, *The Frankfurt School: Its History, Theories, and Political Significance*, trans. Michael Robertson (Cambridge, MA: MIT Press, 1995).

2 See Hanah Arendt (ed.), Walter Benjamin, *Illuminations* (New York: Schocken Books, 1969).

3 Herbert Marcuse, *Eros and Civilization: A Philosophical Inquiry into Freud* (Boston: The Beacon Press, 1955).

4   Herbert Marcuse, *One-Dimensional Man: Studies in the Ideology of Advanced Industrial Society* (Boston: Beacon Press, 1964).

5   Max Horkheimer and Theodor W. Adorno, *Dialectic of Enlightenment* (New York: Continuum, 1989). The German first edition of the book was published by Querido of Amsterdam in 1947, and reprinted by S. Fischer Verlag in 1969. The first English translation by Herder and Herder appeared in 1972.

6   T. W. Adorno, *Aesthetic Theory*, trans. C. Lenhardt, ed. Gretel Adorna and Rolf Tiedemann (London: Routledge & Kegan Paul, 1984), p. 321. First published in Germany in 1970.

7   See "Death of the Author," in Roland Barthes, *Image, Music, Text*, trans. Stephen Heath (New York: Noonday Press, 1998), pp. 142–148. See also, Barthes's *The Pleasure of the Text*, trans. Richard Miller (New York: Hill and Wang, 1975).

8   Michel Foucault, *The Order of Things: An Archaeology of the Human Sciences*, trans. Alan Sheridan (New York: Pantheon, 1970; orig. *Les Mots et les choses: un archéologie des sciences humaines*,1966)

9   *The Archaeology of Knowledge*, trans. A. M. Sheridan Smith (New York: Pantheon, 1972; orig. *L'Archéologie du Savoir* (1969)).

10 Jean Baudrillard, *The System of Objects* (London: Verso, 1996), from *Le Systeme des objets* (Paris: Denoel-Gonthier, 1968); *The Consumer Society* (*La Societe de consommation* (Paris: Gallimard, 1970).

11 See Jean Baudrillard, *Symbolic Exchange and Death*, trans. Iain Hamilton Grant (London: Sage Publications, 1993), p. 74. French edition, *L'Echange symbolique et la mort* (Paris: Editions Gallimard, 1976).

12 Jean-François Lyotard, *The Postmodern Condition: A Report on Knowledge*, trans. Geoff Bennington and Brian Massumi (Minneapolis: University of Minnesota Press, 1979), p. xxiv.

13 A few of the more classic texts on Derrida and deconstruction are Jonathan D. Culler, *On Deconstruction: Theory and Criticism after Structuralism* (London: Routledge and Kegan Paul, 1983), Rudolphe Gasché, *The Tain of the Mirror: Derrida and the Philosophy of Reflection* (Harvard: Cambridge University Press, 1986), Christopher Norris, *Derrida* (Cambridge, MA: Harvard University Press, 1987).

14 *Of Grammatology*, trans. Gayatri Chakravorty Spivak (Baltimore: Johns Hopkins, 1976), *De la Grammatologie* (Paris: Les Editions de Minuit, 1967). See also, *Writing and Difference*, trans. Alan Bass (Chicago: University of Chicago Press, 1978), *L'Ecriture et la différence* (Paris: Editions du Seuil, 1967); *"Speech and Phenomena" and Other Essays on Husserl's Theory of Signs*, trans. David B. Allison (Evanston: Northwestern University Press, 1973), *Le Voix et le phénomène, introduction au problème du signe dans la phénomenologie de Husserl* (Paris: Presses universitaires de France, 1967).

15 Jürgen Habermas, "Modernity—An Incomplete Project," in Hal Foster (ed.), *The Anti-Aesthetic: Essays on Postmodern Culture* (Seattle: Bay Press, 1983), p. 3.

16 Habermas, "Modernity" (note 15), p. 13–14.

17 Andreas Huyssen, "Mapping the Postmodern" (1984), in *After the Great Divide: Modernism, Mass Culture, Postmodernism* (Bloomington: Indiana University Press, 1986), p. 209, 220.

18 Foster, Preface, *The Anti-Aesthetic* (note 15), p. xii.

19 Frederic Jameson, "Postmodernism and Consumer Society," in *The Anti-Aesthetic* (note 15), p. 125, 113.

20 Jameson, "Postmodernism" (note 19), p. 124–125. See his remarks on Venturi and Scott Brown in "The Cultural Logic of Late Capitalism," in *Postmodernism, or, The Cultural Logic of Late Capitalism* (Durham: Duke University Press, 1991), p. 2. The essay first appeared in *New Left Review* in 1984.

21 K. Michael Hays, "Critical Architecture: Between Culture and Form," in *Perspecta*, 21 (1985), p. 528–530.

22 Gianni Vattimo and Pier Aldo Rovatti (eds), *Il pensiero debole* (Milan: Garzanti, 1983).

23 First published as "Arquitectura Dédil/Weak Architecture," *Quaderns d'Arquitecturi I Urbanisme*, 175 (October–December 1987); cited from Ignasi de Solà-Morales, *Differences: Topographies of Contemporary Architecture*, trans. Graham Thompson, ed. Sarah Whiting (Cambridge, MIT Press, 1997), pp. 56–70.

24 Diana Agrest, "Design versus Non-Design," paper presented at the First International Congress of Semiotic Studies in Milan in July 1974; first published in *Oppositions* 6 (Fall 1976). Cited from K. Michael Hays, *Architectural Theory since 1968* (Cambridge, MA: MIT Press, 2002), pp. 209–212.

25 Peter Eisenman, "Post-Functionalism," in *Oppositions*, 6 (Fall 1976), n.p.

26 Peter Eisenman, in Cynthia Davidson (ed.), *Tracing Eisenman: Complete Works* (New York: Rizzoli, 2006), p. 73. See also "Conversation with Peter Eisenman," in Jean-François Bédard (ed.), *Cities of Artificial Excavation: The Work of Peter Eisenman, 1978–1988* (Montreal: Centre Canadien d'Architecture, 1994), p. 121. Eisenman developed his ideas in three lectures in 1975 and 1976, and in a special issue of the Japanese journal *Architecture and Urbanism*, 1, January 1980.

27 Peter Eisenman, *House X* (New York: Rizzoli, 1982), p. 34–36.

28 The texts were initially published in *Harvard Architectural Review*, 3 (Winter 1984), p. 146. They are cited here from Bédard, *Cities of Artificial Excavation* (note 26). On Rossi's influence, see "Interview: Peter Eisenman," *Transition*, 3 (3–4) (April/July 1984), p. 39.

29 In Bédard, *Cities of Artificial Excavation* (note 26), p. 47.

30 In Bédard, *Cities of Artificial Excavation* (note 26), p. 78.

31 In Bédard, *Cities of Artificial Excavation* (note 26), p. 73.

32 "Conversation with Peter Eisenman," in Bédard, *Cities of Artificial Excavation* (note 26), p. 119.

33 Peter Eisenman, "The Beginning, the End and the Beginning Again," *Casabella*, 520/521 (January/February, 1986), p. 44.

34   Peter Eisenman, "The End of the Classical: The End of the Beginning, the End of the End," *Perspecta*, 21 (1985); cited from Robert A. M. Stern, Alan Plattus, Peggy Deamer (eds), *[Re] Perspecta: The First Fifty Years of the Yale Architectural Journal* (Cambridge, MA: MIT Press, 2004), pp. 547–548.

35   See Lynne Breslin, "An Interview with Peter Eisenman," *The Pratt Journal of Architecture*, Vol. 2 (1988), p. 109.

36   Tschumi's early career is covered especially well by three shorter texts: Louis Martin, "Transpositions: On the Intellectual Origins of Tschumi's Architectural Theory," *Assemblage*, 11 (1990), pp. 23–35; Giovanni Damiani (ed.), *Bernard Tschumi* (New York: Rizzoli, 2003); Bernard Tschumi and Enrique Walker, *Tschumi on Architecture: Conversations with Enrique Walker* (New York: Monacelli Press, 2006).

37   Tschumi and Walker, *Bernard Tschumi on Architecture* (note 36), p. 19; and Bernard Tschumi, "The Environmental Trigger," in James Gowan (ed.), *A Continuing Experiment : Learning and Teaching at the Architectural Association* (London: Architectural Press, 1975), p. 93.

38   Tschumi and Walker *Bernard Tschumi on Architecture* (note 36), p. 19.

39   See Dennis Hollier, *Against Architecture: The Writings of Georges Bataille* (Cambridge, MA: MIT Press, 1989), pp. 57–73. The French edition appeared in 1974.

40   Bernard Tschumi, "Question of Space: The Pyramid and the Labyrinth (or the Architectural Paradox)," in *Studio International*, 190 (977) (September/October 1975), p. 142.

41   See Bernard Tschumi, " Le Jardin de Don Juan ou la ville masquée," *L'Architecture d'aujour'hui*, 187 (October/November 1975), pp. 82–83; "The Pleasure of Architecture," *Architectural Design*, 47 (March 1977), pp. 214–218; "Architecture and its Double," *Architectural Design*, 50 (11–12) (1978); *Architectural Manifestoes*, exhibition catalogue published by Artists' Space (New York 1978); "Joyce's Garden in London: A Polemic on the Written Word and the City," *Architectural Design*, 50 (11–12) (1980), p. 22; "Architecture and Limits I," *Artforum*, 19 (4) (December 1980), p. 36; "Architecture and Limits II," *Artforum*, 19 (7) (March 1981), p. 45; "Architecture and Limits III," *Artforum*, 20 (1) (September 1981), p. 40; "Episodes in Geometry and Lust," *Architectural Design*, 51, (1/2) (1981), pp. 26–28.

42   Bernard Tschumi, "Architecture and Transgression," in *Oppositions*, 7 (Winter 1976), cited from K. Michael Hays (ed.), *Oppositions Reader* (New York: Princeton Architectural Press, 1998), pp. 356, 363.

43   Bernard Tschumi, "Violence in Architecture," *Artforum*, 20 (1) (September 1981), p. 44.

44   Bernard Tschumi, *The Manhattan Transcripts: Theoretical Projects* (New York: St. Martin's Press, 1981).

45   Damiani, "Continuity," in *Bernard Tschumi* (note 36), p. 169n.29.

46   Bernard Tschumi, in Tschumi and Walker, *Tschumi on Architecture* (note 36), p. 40.

47   For Tschumi's discussion, see his *Cinegramme Folie: Le Parc de la Villette* (New York: Princeton Architectural Press, 1987).

48   See Manfredo Tschumi, "The Ashes of Jefferson," in *The Sphere and the Labyrinth* (Cambridge, MA: MIT Press, 1987), p. 300.

49   Tschumi, *Cinegramme Folie* (note 47), p. vi.

50   Tschumi, *Cinegramme Folie* (note 47), p. vii.

51   Upon winning the competition, Tschumi was asked by a French official to change the name to *fabrique*, which the architect rejected because of the loss of this association. See "Interview between Alvan Boyarsky and Bernard Tschumi," in *La Case vide: La Villette, 1985* (London: Architectural Association, 1986), p. 25.

52   On their collaboration, see Jean-Louis Cohen, "The Architect in the Philosopher's Garden: Eisenman at La Villette," in Bédard, *Cities of Artificial Excavation* (note 26), pp. 219–226.

53   Bédard (ed.), *Cities of Artificial Excavation* (note 26), fig. 68. On Derrida's choice of the term *chora*, see Geoffrey Broadbent and Jorge Glusberg (eds), *Deconstruction: A Student Guide* (London: Academy Editions, 1991), pp. 77–79.

54   Jacques Derrida, "Point de folie – maintenant l'architecture," in *La Case vide* (London: Architectural Association: 1986), p. 11.

8   Deconstruction

1   Friedrich Achleitner, "Viennese Positions," in *Lotus*, 29 (1981). Cited in Kenneth Frampton's, "Meditations on an Aircraft Carrier: Hollein's Mönchengladbach," in *Hans Hollein*, a + u, (Tokyo: Yoshio Yoshida, 1985), p. 143. See also Joseph Rykwert's insightful essay in the same volume, "*Irony, Hollein's General Approach.*"

2   Hans Hollein, "Alles ist Architektur" (1967), online at www.hollein.com (accessed October 2, 2010).

3   Hans Hollein, "Zurück zur Architektur" (1962), online at www.hollein.com (accessed October 2, 2010).

4   Hans Hollein, "Post Office Savings Bank and Church of St. Leopold," in Yukio Futagawa (ed.), *Global Architecture* (1978). He applies this quoted epithet to Fischer von Erlach.

5   See James Stirling, "The Monumentally Informally," in Robert Maxwell (ed.), *James Stirling: Writings on Architecture* (Milan: Skira, 1998), pp. 151–159.

6   James Stirling, "James Stirling: Architectural Aims and Influences," in Maxwell, *James Stirling* (note 5), p. 137.

7   Rafael Moneo, *Theoretical Anxiety and Design Strategies in the Work of Eight Contemporary Architects* (Cambridge, MA: MIT Press, 2004), p. 41.

8   Francesco Dal Co, "The World Turned Upside-Down: The Tortoise Flies and the Hare Threatens the Lion," In *Frank O. Gehry: The Complete Works* (New York: Monacelli Press, 1998), p. 48.

9　Gottfried Semper, *Ueber die bleiernen Schleudergeschosse der Alten und zweck-mässige Gestaltung der Wurfkörpher im Allgemeinen: Ein Versch die dyna-mische Entstehung gewisser Formen in der Natur and in der Kunst nachzuweisen* (Frankfurt: Verlag für Kunst und Wissenschaft, 1859), subtitle, p. 8ff., 60. See also Gottfried Semper, *Style in the Technical and Tectonic Arts, or Practical Aesthetics*, trans. H. F. Mallgrave and Michael Robinson (Los Angeles, Getty Publication Programs, 2004), pp. 94–95.

10　Frank Gehry, "The Lecture," in Germano Celant, *Il Corso del Coltello, The Course of the Knife: Claes Oldenburg, Coosje van Bruggen, Frank O. Gehry* (New York: Rizzoli, 1987), pp. 212–213.

11　On the theme of Koolhaas and Berlin, see Fritz Neumeyer, "OMA's Berlin: The Polemic Island in the City," in *Assemblage*, 11 (April 1990, pp. 36–53).

12　The project won a competition sponsored by *Casabella* and first appeared in that journal in June 1973, pp. 42–46; it was reprinted in part in *Architectural Design* 5 (47) (1977), p. 328. See Koolhaas's description in "Sixteen Years of OMA," in Jacques Lucan (ed.), *OMA – Rem Koolhaas: Architecture 1970–1990* (New York: Princeton Architectural Press, 1991), p. 162.

13　"Rem Koolhaas and Elia Zenghelis, "Exodus or The Voluntary Prisoners of Architecture," *Casabella*, 378 (June 1973), p. 44.

14　On the important of Natalini for Koolhaas, see "La Deuxième chance de l'architecture moderne … entretien avec Rem Koolhaas," *Architecture d'Aujourd'hui*, 238 (April 1985), p. 2.

15　Rem Koolhaas and Gerrit Oorthuys, "Ivan Leonidov's Dom Narkomtjazjprom, Moscow," *Oppositions* 2 (January 1974), pp. 95–103. The essay also resulted in an exhibition, Vieri Quilici, *Ivan Leonidov: Catalogue 8* (New York: Institute for Architecture and Urban Studies, 1981).

16　Rem Koolhaas, "The City of the Captive Globe, 1972," in *Delirious New York* (New York: Monticello Press, 1994), p. 294.

17　See Jean-Louis Cohen, "The Rational Rebel, or the Urban Agenda of OMA," in Lucan, *OMA – Rem Koolhaas* (note 12).

18　Koolhaas, *Delirious New York* (note 16), pp. 9–10.

19　Koolhaas, *Delirious New York* (note 16), p. 148.

20　Koolhaas, *Delirious New York* (note 16), p. 251.

21　Rem Koolhaas, *Rem Koolhaas: Conversations with Students*, ed. Sanford Kwinter (Houston: Rice School of Architecture, 1996), p. 14.

22　Zaha Hadid, "The Peak, Hong Kong," in *AA Files*, 4 (July 1983), p. 84.

23　Zaha Hadid, *Planetary Architecture Two* (London: Architectural Association, 1983), n.p.

24　See Jeffrey Kipnis, Preface in Daniel Libeskind, *The Space of Encounter* (New York: Universe, 2000), p. 10.

25　See Libeskind, "Endspace," in *Micomegas*, republished in Daniel Libeskind, *Countersign*, Architectural Monograph No. 16 (London: Academy Editions, 1991), p. 15.

26 Daniel Libeskind, "Three Lessens in Architecture," in *Countersign* (note 25), p. 47.

27 Daniel Libeskind, "The Maledicta of Style," *Precis*, 5 (Fall 1984), p. 25.

28 See the author's own description of the work in his two texts, "Between the Lines," in Daniel Libeskind, *The Space of Encounter* (New York: Universe, 2000), pp. 23–29.

29 "About Assemblage," *Assemblage* 1 (1986), p. 5.

30 Two brief reports of the Tate symposium exist: "Deconstruction at the Tate Gallery," in *Deconstruction in Architecture: An Architectural Design Profile* (London: Academy Editions, 1988), p. 7, and David Lodge, "Deconstruction: A Review of the Tate Gallery Symposium," in Andreas Papadakis, Catherine Cooke, and Andrew Benjamin (eds), *Deconstruction: Omnibus Volume* (New York: Rizzoli, 1989), pp. 88–90.

31 The full text of the Derrida interview is in *Deconstruction: Omnibus Volume* (note 29), pp. 71–75.

32 *Architectural Design*, Design profile *Deconstruction in Architecture*, 58 (3/4) (London: Academy Group, 1988), p. 17.

33 Cited from Lodge, "Deconstruction" (note 30), p. 89.

34 Andreas Papadakis, "Deconstruction at the Tate Gallery," in *Deconstruction in Architecture* (note 30), p. 7. See also the comments of David Lodge, in "Deconstruction" (note 30), pp. 88–90.

35 Wigley's dissertation was revised and published as *The Architecture of Deconstruction: Derrida's Haunt* (Cambridge, MA: MIT Press, 1993).

36 A point made in conversations with the author.

37 Philip Johnson, Preface, *Deconstructivist Architecture* (New York: the Museum of Modern Art, 1988), p. 7.

38 Mark Wigley, Introduction, *Deconstructivist Architecture* (note 37), p. 16.

39 Wigley, Introduction *Deconstructivist Architecture* (note 37), p. 20.

40 Joseph Giovannini, "Breaking All the Rules," *The New York Times* (June 12, 1988), Section 6, p. 40.

41 Catherine Ingraham, "Milking Deconstruction, or Cow Was the Show?" in *Inland Architect*, 32 (5) (September/October 1988), pp. 62–63.

9 The Wake of the Storm

1 Jeffrey Kipnis, "*Nolo Contendere*," in *Assemblage* 11 (April 1990), pp. 54.

2 Kipnis, "*Nolo Contendere*" (note 1), p. 57.

3 In the final issue of *Assemblage* in 2000 (*Assemblage*, 41 (April 2000), p. 27), Rodolphe El-Khoury would parody the journal's penchant for identity politics with a mock title page for a forthcoming issue entitled: *The Winking Eye: Contested Occularcentrism in Postcolonial Queer Space*.

4 Jeffrey Kipnis, "Towards a New Architecture," *Architectural Design*, 102 (March/April 1993) p. 42.

5   Kipnis, "Towards a New Architecture," (note 4), p. 42.

6   Kipnis, "Towards a New Architecture," (note 4), pp. 42–45.

7   Kipnis, "Towards a New Architecture," (note 4), p. 45.

8   Gilles Deleuze, *The Fold: Leibniz and the Baroque*, trans. Tom Conley (Minneapolis: University of Minnesota Press, 1993), pp. 81–82.

9   Deleuze, *The Fold* (note 8), pp. 34–35, 121.

10   Greg Lynn, "Probable Geometries: The Architecture of Writing in Bodies", *ANY*, 0/0 (May/June 1993).

11   Greg Lynn, "Architectural Curvilnearity: The Folded, the Pliant, and the Supple," in *Architectural Design*, 102 (March/April 1993) pp. 8–12.

12   Kenneth Powell, "Unfolding Folding," *Architectural Design*, 102 (March/April 1993).

13   Greg Lynn, "Multipicitous and Inorganic Bodies," *Assemblage*, 19 (December 1992) p. 42.

14   Peter Eisenman, cited in Rodolfo Machado and Rodolph El-Khoury (eds), *Monolithic Architecture* (Munich: Prestel, 1995), p. 80.

15   Jeffrey Kipnis, "Towards a New Architecture," *Architectural Design*, 102 (March/April 1993) pp. 45–46.

16   See Preston Scott Cohen, "Two Houses," *Assemblage*, 13 (December 1990), pp. 72–87; Jesse Reiser and Nanako Umemoto, "Aktion Polophile: Hypnerotomachia → Ero/machia/hypniahouse," pp. 88–105. Citation from Ben Nicholson, "The Kleptoman Cell, Appliance House," p. 106.

17   See his discussion of these issues in Preston Scott Cohen, *Contested Symmetries and Other Predicaments in Architecture*. (New York: Princeton Architectural Press. 2001), pp. 12–15.

18   See Cecil Balmond, *Informal* (Munich: Prestel, 2002).

19   Cecil Balmond "New Structure and the Informal," in *Assemblage*, 33 (August 1997), p. 55.

20   For a discussion of developments in "Parametric" and "Algorithmic" design, see Kostas Terzidis, *Algorithmic Architecture* (Oxford: Architectural Press, 2006), Michael Meredith, *From Control to Design: Parametric/Algorithmic Architecture* (Barcelona: Actar, 2008).

21   Manuel Gausa, "Land Arch: Landscape and Architecture, Fresh Shoots," in *Quaderns d'arquitectura i urbanisme*, 217 (1997), p. 52.

22   Rem Koolhaas and Bruce Mau, *S,M,L,XL* (Monacelli, 1995) p. 1223.

23   See Farshid Moussavi and Alejandro Zaera-Polo, "Operative Topographies" and "Graftings: Peripheral Thought," in *Quaderns d'arquitectura i urbanisme*, 220 (1998), pp. 34–41.

24   Zaha Hadid, "Vitra" in *El Croquis*, 52 (January 1992) p. 110.

25   William J. R. Curtis has suggested that the flowing, continuous, and overlapping social spaces produced by Miralles and Pinós were implicit rejections of absolutes, and of the neo-rationalist classicism associated with the Franco dictatorship, but Miralles and Pinós do not make this claim directly. See William J. R. Curtis, "Mental Maps and Social Landscapes," *El Croquis*, 49–50 (September 1991), pp. 6–20.

26 Enric Miralles, "Eyebrows," in *El Croquis* 49–50 (Sept. 1991) p. 110.
27 Enric Miralles and Carme Pinós, "Archery Ranges," in *El Croquis*, 49–50 (September 1991) p. 32.

10 Pragmatism and Post-Criticality

1 Robert Somol and Sarah Whiting, "Notes Around the Doppler Effect and Other Moods of Modernism," in *Perspecta*, 33 (2002), p. 75.
2 Jeffrey Kipnis, "Recent Koolhaas," *El Croquis*, 79 (1996), p. 26. In the text, Kipnis writes that "One frustrated critic, retreating to mythic platitudes, writes, 'There is no other way to put it; Koolhaas is the Le Corbusier of our times.'" In the associated footnote Kipnis refers back to the very same article in which it appears – a circular reference.
3 A reference to Alan Greenspan's oft-cited remarks of 1996 on the overvaluation of the stock market.
4 Michael Speaks, "It's out there ... the Formal Limits of the American Avant-Garde," in *Architectural Design*, 68 (5/6) (May–June 1998) p. 30.
5 See the notes of the ArchiLab International Conference proceedings at http://www.archilab.org/public/2000/catalog/ftca01en.htm (accessed October 2, 2010). The name "ArchiLab" was typical of the movement to align architecture with the technical innovations of the information-technology sector and to cast the discipline as an objective, research-based field of investigation.
6 For work produced by the "Harvard Project on the City," see Stefano Boeri, Harvard Project on the City, Muliplicity, and Jean Attali, *Mutations* (Barcelona: ACTAR, 2001); Chuihua Judy Chung, Jeffrey Inaba, Rem Koolhaas, and Sze Tsung Leong, *Great Leap Forward* (Cologne: Taschen, 2002); Chuihua Judy Chung, Jeffrey Inaba, Rem Koolhaas, and Sze Tsung Leong, *The Harvard Design School Guide to Shopping* (Cologne: Taschen, 2002).
7 Interview, Alejandro Zaera-Polo and Rem Koolhaas, "The Day After," *El Croquis*, 79 (1996), p. 12.
8 Interview, Alejandro Zaera-Polo and Rem Koolhaas, "Finding Freedoms," *El Croquis*, 53 (1993), p. 31.
9 Stanley Tigerman (ed.), *The Chicago Tapes* (New York: Rizzoli, 1987), pp. 168–173.
10 Rem Koolhaas, *Delirious New York* (New York: Monacelli, 1994), pp. 152–158.
11 Interview, Alejandro Zaera-Polo and Rem Koolhaas, "Finding Freedoms," *El Croquis*, 53 (1993), p. 8.
12 Robert Somol would later distinguish between form (read Eisenman) and "shape," arguing that "shape" projects like Zeebrugge were, in part, immediate and graphic, rather than difficult and textual. See Robert Somol, "12 Reasons to Get Back into Shape," in Rem Koolhaas, *Content* (Cologne: Taschen, 2004), pp. 86–87.

13   Interview, Alejandro Zaera-Polo and Rem Koolhaas, "Finding Freedoms," *El Croquis*, 53 (1993), pp. 29–30.

14   Rem Koolhaas, *El Croquis*, 79 (1996), p. 74.

15   O.M.A., Rem Koolhhaas, and Bruce Mau, *S,M,L,XL* (New York: Monacelli, 1995), pp. 502–515.

16   Michael Speaks, *Big Soft Orange* (New York City: Storefront for Art and Architecture, 1999).

17   Winy Maas and Jacob van Rijs with Richard Koek (eds), *FARMAX: Excursions on Density* (Rotterdam: 010 Publishers, 1998). pp. 100–103.

18   Ben van Berkel and Caroline Bos, *Move: Imagination* (Amsterdam: UN Studio and Goose Press, 1999), vol. 1, p. 15.

19   Van Berkel and Bos, *Move* (note 18), vol. 1, p. 27.

20   Rem Koolhaas, *Content* (Cologne: Taschen, 2004), p. 20.

21   Sanford Kwinter, "FFE: Le Trahison des Clercs (and other Travesties of the Modern)," *ANY*, 24 (1999), p. 62.

22   Dave Hickey, "On Not Being Governed," in *The New Architectural Pragmatism: A Harvard Design Magazine Reader* (Minneapolis: University of Minnesota Press, 2007), p. 100.

23   Somol and Whiting, "Notes Around the Doppler Effect" (note 1), pp. 73–77.

11   Minimalisms

1   Rosalind Krauss, "The Grid, the /Cloud/, and the Detail," in Detlef Mertins (ed.), *The Presence of Mies* (New York: Princeton Architectural Press, 1994), p. 133.

2   Kenneth Frampton, "*Rappel à l'ordre:* The Case for the Tectonic," in *Architectural Design*, 60 (1990), p. 19.

3   Kenneth Framption, *Studies in Tectonic Culture: Poetics of Construction in Nineteenth and Twentieth Century Architecture* (Cambridge, MA: MIT Press, 1995).

4   See Terrence Riley, *Light Architecture* (New York: Museum of Modern Art, 1995), p. 9

5   Jefffrey Kipnis and Jacques Herzog, "A Conversation." Special issue, *El Croquis*, 60+84 (2000) p. 35.

6   Alejandro Zaera-Polo and Jacques Herzog, "Continuities." Special issue, *El Croquis*, 60+84 (2000), p. 16.

7   Zaera-Polo and Herzog, "Continuities" (note 6), p. 18.

8   Kipnis and Herzog, "A Conversation," *El Croquis* (note 5), p. 33.

9   See, for example, K. Michael Hays, "Critical Architecture: Between Culture and Form," in *Perspecta*, 21 (1984), pp. 14–29; Josep Quetglas, *Fear of*

Glass (Basel: Birkhaüser, 2001); or Ignasi de Solà-Morales, "Mies van der Rohe and Minimalism," in Mertins, *The Presence of Mies* (note 1), pp. 149–155.

10   Jean Nouvel, project description from Ateliers Jean Nouvel, www.jeannouvel. com (accessed October 5, 2010).

11   Toyo Ito, "Vortex and Current: On Architecture as Phenomenalism," in *Architectural Design*, 62 (9/10) (September/October 1992), p. 22–23.

12   See Toyo Ito, *Sendai Mediatheque* (Barcelona: Actar, 2003), pp. 15, 25. See also the informative essays in Ron Witte (ed.), *Toyo Ito: Sendai Mediatheque* (Munich: Prestel Verlag, 2002).

13   Rafael Moneo, *Rafael Moneo 1967–2004.* "El Escorial," *El Croquis* editorial (2004) p. 350.

14   Rodolfo Machado and Rodolphe el-Khoury, for instance, describe the work in terms of its monolithic character. See their *Monolithic Architecture* (Munich: Prestel, 1995).

15   See, Luigi Snozzi, *Costruzione e progetti 1958–1993* (Lugano: ADV Publishing House, 1995).

16   Ulrike Jehle-Schulte Strathaus, "Modernism of a Most Intelligent Kind: A Commentary on the Work of Diener & Diener," in *Assemblage*, 3 (July 1987) pp. 72–75.

17   John Pawson, *Minimum* (London: Phaidon Press, 1996), p. 7, and John Pawson, "La Expresion Sencilla del Pensamiento Complejo," *El Croquis*, 127 (2005) p. 6.

18   Álvaro Siza, "On my work," in Kenneth Frampton (ed.), *Álvaro Siza: Complete Works* (London: Phaidon Press, 2000), p. 72.

19   Steven Holl, *Anchoring: Selected Projects 1975–1988* (New York: Princeton Architectural Press, 1989).

20   Steven Holl, *Intertwining* (New York: Princeton Architectural Press, 1996), p. 11.

21   Steven Holl, Juhani Pallasmaa, and Alberto Pérez-Gómez (eds), "Questions of Perception: Phenomenology of Architecture." Special issue, *a + u* (July 1994); republished under the same title (San Francisco: William Stout, 2006).

22   Juhani Pallasmaa, "An Architecture of the Seven Sense." Special issue, *a + u* (note 21), p. 30. See also his expansion of these themes in *The Eyes of the Skin: Architecture and the Senses* (Chichester: Wiley-Academy, 1996/2005).

23   See Richard Neutra, *Survival through Design* (London: Oxford University Press, 1954); Steen Eiler Rasmussen, *Experiencing Architecture* (Cambridge, MA: MIT Press, 1959).

24   Peter Zumthor, *Thinking Architecture* (Basel: Birkhaüser, 2006), p. 26.

25   Zumthor, *Thinking Architecture* (note 24), p. 17.

26   Zumthor, *Thinking Architecture* (note 24), pp. 31–32.

12   Sustainability and Beyond

1   For the purposes of this discussion, we will use the term "sustainability" to encompass an array of words often used to define this shift in priorities: green, eco-friendly, eco-designed, biophilic design, evidence-based design, and high performance.

2   See United Nations Document A//42/427, "Our Common Future: Report of the World Commission on Environment and Development," http://www.un-documents.net/ocf-02.htm (accessed October 2, 2010).

3   Victor Papanek, *The Green Imperative: Natural Design for the Real World* (New York: Thames & Hudson, 1995), p. 236. His earlier and classic book on this theme was *Design for the Real World: Human Ecology and Social Change* (New York: Pantheon Books, 1971).

4   See "The Hannover Principles: Design for Sustainability," William McDonough Architects, 1992. http://www.mcdonough.com/principles.pdf (accessed October 2, 2010).

5   See William McDonough, "Declaration of Interdependence," in Andrew Scott (ed.), *Dimensions of Sustainability* (London: E & FN Spon, 1998), pp. 61–75.

6   William McDonough and Michael Braungart, *Cradle to Cradle: Remaking the Way We Make Things* (New York: North Point Press, 2002) p. 156.

7   Leon van Schaik, "The Aesthetics of Sustainability" in Kristin Feiress and Lukas Feiress (eds), *Architecture of Change: Sustainability and Humanity in the Built Environment* (Berlin: Gestalten, 2008), p. 133.

8   Ken Yeang, "A Theoretical Framework for the Ecological Design and Planning of the Built Environment," PhD dissertation, University of Cambridge, 1975.

9   Ken Yeang, *Eco Skyscrapers* (Victoria, Australia: Images Publishing Group, 2007), p. 20.

10   Ken Yeang, *Ecodesign: A Manual for Ecological Design* (London: Wiley-Academy, 2006) p. 23.

11   Ken Yeang, "Green Design," *Architecture of Change* (note 7), p. 229.

12   Documents of the cities' policies are also available online. See Timothy Beatley's discussion of both of these plans in *Green Urbanism: Learning from European Cities* (Washington: Island Press, 2000). See also, Stephen M. Wheeler and Timothy Beatley, *Sustainable Urban Development Reader* (New York: Routledge, 2008).

13   The two principal texts that have created new fields are Edward O. Wilson, *Sociobiology: The New Synthesis* (Cambridge, MA: Harvard University Press, 1975) and Jerome H. Barkow, Leda Cosmides, and John Tooby (eds), *The Adapted Mind: Evolutionary Psychology and the Generation of Culture* (New York: Oxford University Press, 1992).

14   The two seminal studies in this regard are Jay Appleton, *The Experience of Landscape* (London: New York, 1975), and Gordon H. Orians, "Habitat

Selection: General Theory and Theory and Applications to Human Behavior," in Joan S. Lockard (ed.), *The Evolution of Human Social Behavior* (New York: Elsevier, 1980), pp. 49–66.

15 This literature on both habitat selection and the benefits of contact with nature is vast. See, for example, Gordon H. Orians, "An Ecological and Evolutionary Approach to Landscape Aesthetics," in Edmund C. Penning-Rowsell and David Lowenthal (eds), *Landscape Meanings and Values* (London: Allen and Unwin, 1986); Stephen Kaplan and Rachel Kaplan, *Cognition and Environment: Functioning in an Uncertain World* (New York: Praeger, 1982); Stephen R. Kellert and Edward O. Wilson, *The Biophilia Hypothesis* (Washington, DC: Island Press, 1993); Gordon H. Orians and Judith H. Heerwagen, "Evolved Responses to Landscapes," in Barkow, Cosmides, and Tooby *The Adapted Mind* (note 13); Roger S. Ulrich, "Biophilia, Biophobia, and Natural Landscapes," in Kellert and Wilson, *The Biophilia Hypothesis*; Stephen Kaplan, "The Restorative Benefits of Nature: Toward an Integrative Framework," *Journal of Environmental Psychology*, 15 (1995), pp. 169–182; Rachel Kaplan, Stephen Kaplan, and Robert Ryan, *With People in Mind: Design and Management of Everyday Nature* (Washington: Island Press, 1998); Rachel Kaplan, "The Nature of the View from Home: Psychological Benefits," *Environment and Behavior*, 33, (507) (2001), pp. 507–542; Agnes E. van den Berg, Terry Hartig, and Henk Staats, "Preference for Nature in Urbanized Societies: Stress, Restoration, and the Pursuit of Sustainability," *Journal of Social Issues*, 63 (1) (2007), p. 91.

16 See Edward O. Wilson, *Biophilia: The Human Bond with Other Species* (Cambridge, MA: Harvard University Press, 1984).

17 Roger S. Ulrich, "View through a Window May Influence Recovery from Surgery," *Science*, New Series, 224 (4647) (April 27, 1984), pp. 420–421. See also Terry Hartig, "Healing Gardens – Places for Nature in Health Care," *Medicine and Creativity*, 368 (December 2006), pp. 536–537; Tina Bringslimark, Terry Hartig, and Grete Grindal Patil, "Psychological Benefits of Indoor Plants in Workplaces: Putting Experimental Results in Context," *HortScience*, 42 (3) (June 2007), pp. 581–587.

18 See in particular Timothy Beatley, "Toward Biophilic Cities: Strategies for Integrating Nature into Urban Design," in Stephen R. Keller, Judith H. Heerwagen, and Martin L. Mador, *Biophilic Design: The Theory, Science, and Practice of Bringing Buildings to Life* (New York: John Wiley & Sons, 2008), pp. 277–296.

19 See Stephen S. Kellert, *Building for Life: Designing and Understanding the Human–Nature Connection* (Washington, DC: Island Press, 2005), and various essays in Keller, Heerwagen, and Mador, *Biophilic Design* (note 17).

20 For two general studies on the application of neuroscience to architecture see John P. Eberhard, *Brain Landscape: The Coexistence of Neuroscience and Architecture* (Oxford: Oxford University Press, 2008) and Harry Francis

Mallgrave, *The Architect's Brain: Neuroscience, Creativity, and Architecture* (New York: Wiley-Blackwell, 2010).

21   Martin Skov and Oshin Vartanian, *Neuroaesthetics* (Amityville, NY: Baywood Publishing, 2009), p. 11.

22   See especially the work of Helmut Leder, especially Leder *et al.*, "A Model of Aesthetic Appreciation and Aesthetic Judgments," *British Journal of Psychology*, 95 (2004), pp. 489–508.

23   Perhaps the majority of neuroaesthetics is pursuing this direction. For an attempt to coordinate the findings of three such studies, see Marcos Nadal *et al.*, "Towards a Framework for the Study of the Neural Correlates of Aesthetic Preference, *Spatial Vision*, 21 (3–5) (2008), pp. 379–396.

24   A leader of this school is Ellen Dissanayake, see her *Art and Intimacy: How the Arts Began* (Seattle: University of Washington Press, 2000), and Steven Brown and Ellen Dissanayake, "The Arts Are More than Aesthetics: Neuroaesthetics as Narrow Aesthetics," in Skov and Vartanian, *Neuroaesthetics* (note 21), pp. 43–58.

25   See Semir Zeki, "Artistic Creativity and the Brain," *Science*, 293 (5527) (July 6, 2001), p. 52, and *Inner Vision: An Exploration of Art and the Brain* (Oxford: Oxford University Press, 1999). Zeki was also the first scientist to employ the term "neuroaesthetics."

26   Semir Zeki, "Art and the Brain," *Journal of Consciousness Studies: Controversies in Science and the Humanities* (June/July 1999), 6 (6–7), p. 77.

27   For an interesting study on proportions, see Cinzia Di Dio, Emiliano Macaluso, and Giacomo Rizzolatti, "The Golden Beauty: Brain Response to Classical and Renaissance Sculptures," *PLoS ONE*, 2 (11). For a more general view of the artistic and architectural experience, see David Freedberg and Vittorio Gallese, "Motion, Emotion and Empathy in Esthetic Experience," *Trends in Cognitive Sciences*, 11 (5) (May 2005), pp. 197–203.

Acknowledgments

We would like to thank the many people who have contributed in some way to the book, either by reading portions of the text or by consenting to share their participation in the events portrayed. They include Francesco Dal Co, Kenneth Frampton, Julia Bloomfield, Stanley Tigerman, Mark Wigley, George Schipporeit, Donna Robertson, Preston Scott Cohen, and K. Michael Hays. Architects and offices who have been so kind as to supply us with images and permissions for publication are Christopher Alexander's Center for Environmental Structure, Eisenman Architects, Tigerman McCurry Architects, Léon Krier, Edward Windhorst, Kisho Kurokawa Architect and Associates, the office of Prince Charles, the Prince of Wales, Duany Plater-Zyberk & Company, Calthorpe Associates, Bernard Tschumi Architects, Atelier Hollein, Tim Brown, Preston Scott Cohen, Office for Metropolitan Architecture, Herman Miller, Inc., and Foster + Partners. Felicity Marsh has shouldered the difficult task of editing the manuscript with her usual sage talent and thoughtful sensitivity. Jayne Fargnoli, at the Malden office of Wiley-Blackwell, has strongly supported the project from its inception, and she has been assisted in this regard by the able Margot Morse and Matthew Baskin. We thank Lisa Eaton in the Oxford office for her sensitivity in overviewing the cover design. At the Graham Resource Center we had the assistance of the always efficient Matt Cook, Kim Soss, Rich Harkin, Stuart MacRae, as well as the staff of the Galvin Library. Special thanks to Susan Mallgrave and Romina Canna. Finally, a first historical study of a living period is impossible to write without a few omissions or factual errors. We have attempted to write a fair and even history of the events portrayed, and we apologize to all who may feel neglected or who believe that their views or acts have been wrongly portrayed.

An Introduction to Architectural Theory: 1968 to the Present, First Edition.
Harry Francis Mallgrave and David Goodman.
© 2011 Harry Francis Mallgrave and David Goodman. Published 2011 by Blackwell Publishing Ltd.

Index

An Introduction to Architectural Theory: 1968 to the Present, First Edition.
Harry Francis Mallgrave and David Goodman.
© 2011 Harry Francis Mallgrave and David Goodman. Published 2011 by Blackwell Publishing Ltd.